Out of the Blue

Also by Mark Victor Hansen (with Jack Canfield)

Chicken Soup for the Soul

A 2nd Helping of Chicken Soup for the Soul

A 3rd Serving of Chicken Soup for the Soul

The Aladdin Factor

Dare to Win

Out

of the

Blue

Delight Comes
Into Our Lives

Mark Victor Hansen
& Barbara Nichols

with Patty Hansen

Cliff Street Books

An Imprint of HarperPerennial
A Division of HarperCollinsPublishers

A hardcover edition of this book was published in 1996 by HarperCollins Publishers.

HarperCollins books may be purchased for educational, business, or sales pro-motional use. For information please write: Special Markets Department, HarperCollins Publishers, Inc., 10 East 53rd Street, New York, NY 10022.

First Cliff Street Books/HarperPerennial edition published 1997.

Designed by Nancy Singer

The Library of Congress has catalogued the hardcover edition as follows:

Out of the blue : delight comes into our lives / [compiled by] Mark
Victor Hansen and Barbara Nichols.
    p. cm.
ISBN 0-06-017376-9
    1. Spiritual life—Anecdotes. 2. Joy—Religious aspects. I. Hansen, Mark
Victor. II. Nichols, Barbara.
BL624.088 1996
158'.12—dc20   96-14838

ISBN 0-06-092838-7 (pbk.)

97 98 99 00 01 ❖/RRD 10 9 8 7 6 5 4 3 2 1

Barbara wishes to dedicate *Out of the Blue:*
To Mary and Nick, who made sure there was always delight.

Patty and Mark dedicate *Out of the Blue:*
To Shirley Day Shaw, who has graced our lives with humor, devotion,
passion, and unconditional love. We love you, Mom!
Also to the memory of Peggy Bassett, who embodied divine delight
while on this planet . . . and Fred Bassett, the angel who took care of her
during her last years with us.

The Path of Delight

Taking delight in who you are, what you do, and what you
 have is the secret of personal power, satisfaction, and
 high-energy living.

Delight connects you with the beauty and power of the universe,
 with your Higher Power, with Divinity.

Delight means feeling and expressing the joy of life, rejoicing in
 the beauty and richness of being.

Delight is a powerful liberating force that frees your creativity,
 talents, abilities, and capacities.

Delight anchors you in the eternal now and lets you see the best
 of it.

Delight inspires hope.

Delight feeds the heart and nurtures the soul.

Delight brings zest into your life.

Delight makes you receptive and confident.

Delight is contagious; it is the greatest gift you can give to
 yourself and others.

The path of delight is there; it has always been there, waiting for
 you. . . .

Contents

❧

4 The Sky's the Limit

5 The Delight Between Us All

Acknowledgments

❦

*W*hen a reader curls up with a book, he or she has very little idea how much work went into producing that book—especially a book like this, which has contributions from so many people. It takes much more effort to do such a book than to sit down and write one oneself from beginning to end. No one person could possibly have put together *Out of the Blue*. The people who helped deserve a round of applause.

Barbara wishes to thank Sri Chinmoy, whose ideas on Delight sparked this entire project. And Agraha Levine, M.D., Ph.D., who supplied such fine research material. I am forever grateful.

My deepest gratitude goes to Katy Kidwell at Kathryn Kidwell Editorial Service, who handled the million and one details of gathering, sorting, reading, editing, phoning, faxing, nudging, and chasing permissions that the reader never sees, but without which there would be no book. Thanks, Katy, for shouldering so much responsibility and for bringing great delight to me, to the writers who loved working with you, and to the readers of this book.

Thank you, too, to Mary-Pat Hoffman for bringing many talented writers from the heartland to our attention and for friendship and moral support that goes well beyond the bonds of sisterhood.

I am enormously grateful to Homer Pyle, one of the most gifted (and fastest) editors in the business, who can smooth out a rough spot and add just the right word effortlessly—and with great good humor.

Thanks to Bill Dortch of hIdaho Designs, who forged the computer connections that made this all work and designed my "way cool" Delight Site on the Web (http://www.webomat.com/bluehorizon). I am delighted with your presence and support.

Thanks to Roy and Nympha Cole for their endless fountain of laughter that restores creativity. A dab of Nympha's Flowers of Mendocino always stirs my heart and renews my delight.

My love and gratitude to Bob Pittman for being the angel of this book. May the highest Delight shine on your path.

Great appreciation to David S. Lampel for his knowledge of the Bible and for his online inspirations, which you can see at http://www.iclnet.org/pub/resources/text/aspects/aspects-home.html.

Mark and Patty extend their gratitude: To our staff, without all of you we could never function—especially to Michelle Adams, who helped long hours past quitting time with great love. Also to Chris Russell, Alan Garner, and Patti Rose for help, ideas, and inspiration. Thank you also, Eva, Melanie, and Elisabeth, for holding our home together while we were both working and away from you.

Patty wishes to thank JoAnne Finkelor, wherever you are. And to our contributors who were timely and cooperative, you are awesome!

From all of us, our endless thanks to Lois de la Haba, our agent and friend, who was always there, and to her able assistants, David Goldsmith and Laura de la Haba, who added great grace to this project.

Our boundless respect and gratitude to the staff at Harper-Collins. To Diane Reverand, our marvelous editor, for your continual patience and creative soul. You are a true delight! To Meaghan Dowling, for her enthusiasm and editorial moxie; to Joseph

Montebello, for an irresistible cover; to David Flora, for making the wheels turn with ease. Also to Paul Olsewski, Mary Kurtz, and Nancy Singer. You've all been a delight to work with.

Our lifelong appreciation to booksellers and librarians everywhere, who are keepers of the eternal flame of literacy and knowledge. Thanks to you, many delightful hours of our lives have been spent curled up with a good book, sharing dreams and wisdom with fine writers, expanding the horizons of our minds, hearts, and spirits.

Mark Victor Hansen
Barbara Nichols
Patty Hansen

Out of the Blue

Introduction

∞

When Mark and I first met, long before we decided to collaborate on this book, we discovered that each of us had had extraordinary experiences that came out of the blue and brought delight into our lives. In this book, we present some of our personal epiphanies and magical moments of delight and a great many stories from other people who have had such glimmerings.

Mark's favorite personal experience occurred when he met his wife, Patty, at a church when he was presenting a workshop.

It was a hot summer afternoon, and I was standing outside the church after my presentation greeting the people who had attended. A gorgeous woman came up and we started a conversation. One thing led to another, and we decided to go for a bike ride together at the beach. As we pedaled along, I felt an opening in my chest in the region of my heart. I had heard we have energy centers in certain parts of our physical and emotional bodies, but this was the first time I had ever actually felt so much focused energy.

"What an incredible woman," I said to myself, though it was too soon to say it to her. I'd just met her and my heart was opening.

Soon our relationship began to blossom. The first day I visited Patty's home I walked into the kitchen, and was delighted to find painted on the ceiling a beautiful blue sky with billowy white clouds. I had that head-to-toe tingle you get when destiny is at work. Out of the blue, I *knew* that Patty was the woman with whom I would share my life.

Since I travel all the time in my work, I knew I would have to find a wife who was complete in and of herself, who could function happily on her own and create a home for the two of us. When I saw the lovely clouds on her ceiling, all of my bells and whistles went off. I knew I had found her at last—a woman who was not only beautiful and intelligent, but who lived with joy, flair, and independence. All of this on top of opening my heart on our first date! There has never been a greater delight in my life.

Heaven Can Hardly Wait

We can create heaven right here on earth when we are in delight. We're here to do just that—it's our sacred mission. And heaven can hardly wait! It slips through the ordinary fabric of our lives as flashes of intuition and instants of blessings. Plato, Confucius, Buddha, the wisdom books of Vedanta and the Old Testament, the teachings of Jesus, and the mystical schools of Islam all tell the great truth: We can live in a state of joy, bliss, and ecstasy if we choose. We're meant to live a spirited, spiritual life. Those flashes of energy that come out of the blue are reminders and guiding lights to our own personal path.

Some mystical traditions, particularly those of the East, use the term *Supreme Delight* to denote heaven. Westerners find use of the word *delight* to describe Supreme Reality, or God, both illuminating and inspiring.

Delight Comes into Our Lives

Love, joy, and *bliss* are also terms used for describing that highest of all powers, but *delight* has the advantage of being used in our everyday language to express the smallest and simplest of pleasures. In English, we use the word *delight* to describe the information our five senses bring us—delightful scents, sights, sounds, flavors, and tactile experiences. The beauty and pleasure of everyday life can remind us of the delights of heaven, and perhaps are intended to do so. The experiences we call "everyday epiphanies" are fascinating glimpses of delight. They seem to be occurring with great frequency today.

In the great harmony of the world, all spiritual and religious delights come into alignment and form a path to God. The same life force lives in us all—the burst of energy that opens flower petals is the same energy that creates the stars. It is the same energy that comes out of the blue to inspire, excite, and delight us with the gifts of understanding, compassion, and reassurance.

The idea that delight can be a path between heaven and earth strikes a familiar chord. It is an idea as old as written language, with deep roots in the cultures and traditions of many lands. In major religions and philosophies there are stories of human beings who find God by searching for the true essence of earthly delights. Since the beginning of time, saints, poets, scholars, and mystics of every persuasion have suggested that we take the *via positiva,* or way of joy, affirmation, and delight. We can sing and dance our way to heaven. We can create heaven on earth.

A Brief History of Delight

Centuries before Christ, in ancient Greece, Plato spoke of a ladder to the sky—a ladder we could climb from our everyday experience to the highest province of the soul. From the delights of the senses, he told us, we can learn to delight in God, the soul of the world. Anything that is in essence good, true, and beautiful may become a path to the spirit most high as we progressively experience those qualities. A perfect flower can become a vehicle of enlightenment if we reach beyond our ordinary understanding of its exquisite fragrance, color, and form and see it as a reflection of God.

All of the world's great spiritual systems tell us to live in peace, love, and joy, in harmony with infinite delight. Though the details and specifics may differ along these paths, the central ideas are universal. On every path, delight can be traced like a golden thread from its source in divinity through the fabric of everyday life.

The five major religions, Hinduism, Buddhism, Judaism, Christianity, and Islam, are sometimes described as five fingers on the same hand. Each finger is separate and distinct, but when you go deeper, you find that they all have the same source in the palm of the hand. When you discover their depth, you find the inner wisdom we all share. On the surface there are contradictions, but experiences of infinite delight are quite similar.

Existence Is Delight

In India, thousands of years before the Christian era, Hindu philosophers put forth theories about the universe. The concept of *satchitananda*, which translates to existence-consciousness-bliss, is basic to Hindu belief. Bliss, or delight, is inseparable from existence and consciousness, and together they form the essence of all that is. The essence of the air around us is existence-consciousness-bliss, the essence of water, of animals, plants, the whole cosmos is *satchitananda*, and so are we. Existence, consciousness, and bliss together are an all-pervasive atmosphere that exists, awarely and delightfully, within us and all around us. Even today in India, a common expression is "Life is very beautiful, you know," accompanied by dazzling smiles, even in the midst of grinding poverty.

Delight comes in both an uppercase and lowercase version. There's delight, and then there's Delight. In the spiritual practices of yoga and meditation, we learn to attain moments of pure bliss and delight; as we become established in our practice, these moments may expand and become a "state." With devotion and dedication, we can establish ourselves in a state of bliss, a state of boundless joy and energy, which brings us closer to the reality of Supreme Delight.

The ancient Sanskrit text the *Vijnanabhairava* tells us:

> When one identifies with the incomparable delight of song or other things, this concentrated person becomes one with that delight. Wherever the mind finds its satisfaction, let it be concentrated on that. In every case, the true nature of the highest Delight will shine forth.

The inner satisfaction that comes from everyday delights such as smelling a flower or eating a chocolate mousse is a blissful impulse from the highest Delight.

Does this mean that you can reach a state of cosmic bliss by contemplating dessert? Can virtually anything become a path to the highest Delight? If you are a saint or guru, the answer is probably yes. A virtuoso of the spirit can transform anything— can turn nonsense into knowledge; and can surely find enlightenment in a chocolate mousse. Those of us who are mere mortals may have a spontaneous experience of enlightenment out of the blue, but for the most part we need to choose our delights wisely, reflecting Plato's notion that the essence, or inner qualities, of the path must be good, true, and beautiful. Our souls always turn toward goodness, truth, and beauty in order to grow in stature.

Twentieth-century Indian statesman and philosopher Sri Aurobindo recommended that we develop our awareness of delight:

> In the mind it translates into a calm intense delight of perception and vision and knowledge, in the heart into a passionate delight of union, love and sympathy. In the will and vital parts it is felt as delight in action or a beatitude of the senses perceiving and meeting the One everywhere.

The Bliss of Nirvana

Siddhartha, who lived in India more than twenty-five hundred years ago, was meditating under a bodhi tree when suddenly, out of the blue, the solution to the riddle of life became clear to him. Why do we suffer? He immediately understood what to do to overcome suffering. Seeing all of life clearly, he was enlightened. Soon he was known as The Enlightened One, or Buddha. He had achieved nirvana, the ultimate detachment from the world that brings an end to suffering.

Today there are several branches of Buddhism, with more than a billion followers who surround themselves with statues of the smiling Buddha as reminders of the intrinsic all-rightness of life as it is.

Some forms of Buddhism teach a quiet path of rather withdrawn peace and contentment leading to ultimate enlightenment, the blissful state of detaching by leaving the world as much as possible. However, Mahayana Buddhism, which means The Expansive Way, regards one who lives in the world with compassion for everyone, in unity with everything around him, as having reached the highest level of enlightenment. The Dalai Lama is probably the best living example of this.

Zen scholar Alan Watts described the idea of detachment as living without "hang-ups." Mahayana Buddhism, in his view,

> opens up for us the possibility of participating in all the games of life—the patterns and gestures of the universe—without anxiety, and with compassion, realizing that every other self is, under the surface, the same self as our own. Such compassion, a "feeling/suffering with," is not mere pity in the sense that "misery loves company." It is grounded in the knowledge that existence is basically exuberance—that "energy is eternal delight," and that, improbable as it may seem, every form of being lies somewhere in the vast spectrum of ecstasy which, in Mahayana, is called the *sambhogakaya*, "The Body of Total Bliss."

Delight in Judaism

The Bible is a treasure trove of delight, especially the Old Testament, which communicates the ideas of Judaism. The Wisdom books, including Psalms and Proverbs, are not primarily religious in character, but are concerned with human solutions. They teach us how to solve problems and confer secrets of happiness and success. Wisdom teachings are attributed to sages of various tribes. The books of Wisdom and Ecclesiasticus (which were part of the Greek Bible) are attributed to sages of Israel, Solomon, and Ben Sira. They are not included in every Bible, nor are they intended to represent the prophets, priests, or the word of God. When the ancient Hebrew word signifies joy, rejoicing, great happiness, being greatly pleased, brightening up, being merry and cheerful, translations such as NIV, New Revised Standard Version, and New Jerusalem Bible, among others, may use delight as an appropriate translation.

For example, in the Book of Nehemiah, in the Chronicles, the NIV translates verse 1:11 as: "Oh Lord, let your ear be attentive to the prayer of your servant and to the prayer of your servants who delight in revering your name."

And the lovely Thirty-seventh Psalm tells us, "Delight yourself in the Lord and He will give you the desires of your heart," in the NIV; "Make Yahweh your joy and he will give you your heart's desires," in the New Jerusalem Bible. We are delighted that whatever version of the Bible you prefer, the meaning comes through.

Because we also use the words *joy, delight,* and *great happiness* interchangeably, we have quoted from Bibles that do the same. In these teachings, delight is a recurring theme. It leads us from the darkness of pettiness and conflict to the delights of openness, sharing, and the gifts of God. Wisdom is referred to in the feminine gender, and the love for her is fostered. King Solomon himself is believed to have written the Wisdom book in which he sought wisdom and showed great respect for her:

I entreated, and the spirit of Wisdom came to me.
I esteemed her more than sceptres and thrones;

. . . .
I loved her more than health or beauty,
preferred her to the light,
since her radiance never sleeps.
In her company all good things came to me,
and at her hands incalculable wealth.
All these delighted me, since Wisdom brings them. . . .
(Wisdom 7:7–12)

In these teachings, delight is frequently acknowledged as a two-way path connecting humanity with God. We learn that when we find delight on earth, it opens the way for God to find us; when God sends us delight, it is a way for us to find God. For example, in Psalm 16 we hear a joyful song sending delight to the Most High and expecting to receive more delight in return:

My heart rejoices, my soul delights,
My body too will rest secure,
For you will not abandon me. . . .
. . . .
You will teach me the path of life,
Unbounded joy in your presence,
At your right hand delight forever.

The book of Baruch, written in Babylon twenty-five hundred years ago, instructs us to "see the joy that is coming to you from God." A sense of the cosmic dimensions of delight is expressed in this verse:

. . . the stars shine joyfully at their posts,
When he calls them, they answer, "Here we are";
They shine to delight their creator.

In Hebrew, the word *Eden* means delight. Eden, the garden of delight, was the original home that God planned for us, our natural state of being. Hebrew writers taught that we can find sparks of divine delight everywhere and in everything, especially within ourselves. Jewish mystics believe that our task is to recognize and appreciate these divine sparks and liberate them from the hard shells of ego and ignorance that surround them. We do this by developing knowledge and awareness, which dissolve the dull armor that covers our sparkling higher selves. We are meant to delight our maker by uniting our inner sparks of light with the light of the heavens. It is nothing less than a holy work, and the unity with God's will shows up in the everyday things of life. A passage in Ecclesiasticus, attributed to Ben Sira, tells us:

> There are three things my soul delights in,
> and which are delightful to God and to all people:
> concord between brothers, friendship between neighbours,
> And a wife and husband who live happily together.
> (15:1–2)

Bringing delight into your life and the lives of others is the height of wisdom!

The Good News of Delight

In Christianity, the gospel, or good news, is that God is love. Jesus taught of God's love for us through miracles of healing and compassion, and his resurrection exemplifies love's powerful ability to overcome everything, even death. In probably the best-known epiphanic experience in history, Paul was "blinded by the light" on the road to Damascus. Knocked unconscious by a searing bolt of light during his journey, his sight was taken from him. Once he found the truth of his own spiritual nature within him, God restored his sight. This experience literally changed his life direction, transforming him from a persecutor of Christians into a teacher of Christ's faith, hope, and love.

In the New Testament, the story of Christ begins with joy and delight. Luke tells us that the first word the Angel Gabriel said to

Mary, the woman chosen to be the mother of Jesus, was "Rejoice!" And Matthew describes the coming of the wise men to see the newborn Jesus: "And suddenly the star they had seen rising went forward and halted over the place where the child was. The sight of the star filled them with delight." Joy was the original promise of the Christian era. Jesus' presence on the earth and his teachings were to be a source of delight to the wise and to those of good will.

We know from Paul's epistle to the Galatians that if we allow ourselves to be led by the spirit, we then are imbued with the fruits of the spirit: love, joy, peace, patience, kindness, goodness, faithfulness, gentleness, and self-control. These spiritual gifts shine in us and through us as a result of the action of the Holy Spirit. Those who live in the spirit live in love and joy, in an atmosphere of happiness. Delight, enthusiasm, and gratitude flow freely. Joy moves us to dance and sing the praises of the Lord.

The tradition of joyfully worshiping the Creator has been carried on all through the Christian era. Even when various Christian religions presented a negative view of God as a scowling, demanding taskmaster, quick to anger and slow to forgive, there were always those who knew the delights of the spirit.

Of special note are the medieval mystics who lived along the Rhine River in Germany. Their works extolling the delights of the spirit were significant in the bloody time of the Crusades and are now enjoying a renaissance as people seek a positive spirituality. One woman, Hildegard of Bingen, used her influence as abbess of a convent to write compelling letters to bishops and kings reminding them of their duty to keep the Holy Spirit alive in their souls. She had detailed visions, which were written down and rendered in visual form in paintings, and she wrote vigorous, ecstatic music to awaken everyone to the delights of creation. This inspiring, influential person brought delight to everyone in her world. "God hugs us," she told her contemporaries.

Glance at the sun. See the moon and the stars.
Gaze at the beauty of earth's greenings.
Now. Think.

What delight God gives to humankind
with all these things. . . .

Today Hildegard's books are translated into modern English and other languages and her music is recorded by major music publishers.

An eloquent spokesperson for delight in the modern world is Father John Catoir, director of the Christophers, an organization that promotes a positive view of spirituality. In his new book, *God Delights in You: An Introduction to Gospel Spirituality,* he has paraphrased the text of the Sermon on the Mount in which Jesus gave us the Beatitudes. Father Catoir's personal rendition lets us know that God delights in everyone, from the most humble to the most exalted:

You delight Me, you who are poor in spirit,
You delight Me, you who are meek and humble of heart,
You delight Me, you who long to be just and good,
You delight Me, you who are kind and merciful,
You delight Me, you who are pure of heart,
You delight Me, you who strive to be peacemakers,
You delight Me, you who are willing to suffer on my account.
Rejoice and be glad for I am preparing a great reward for you,
    and you shall see God.

Knowing that God delights in us brightens our darkest days, gives a lift to our souls, and makes our path easier to follow.

The Dance of Delight

Much delight can be found in the Muslim tradition, which includes both Arabic and non-Arabic peoples. Muhammad received the words of the Koran out of the blue from the Angel Gabriel, who visited him time and time again. The Koran, the holy book of the Muslim people, is in many ways like the Bible of the Judeo-Christian tradition, and much of the delight of the Old

Testament and New Testament is carried through. One of the great delights of Muhammad's work was felt within a few years, as feuding Arabic tribes were united under his teaching that all men are brothers, and a more peaceful nation was born.

Many Westerners tend to think of Islam in a negative sense, but some of the most spirited spiritual material written in the last thousand years has come from the Sufis, the well-known mystics of Islam, who have traditionally sought for direct personal experience of the Divine.

Perhaps the best-known of the Sufis is Jalal al-Din Rumi, a mystic who founded the order of the Whirling Dervishes in Asia Minor in the thirteenth century, and whose ecstatic poetry is quite popular today. The Dervish's "dance of delight" is intended to transport the dancer to a higher awareness of God, who is referred to as the Friend, and the Beloved.

Rumi was inflamed with delight at the appearance, out of the blue, of a great Sufi teacher, Shems, and after this inspiring meeting Rumi's work became exalted. In some circles, it is thought of as the Persian Koran, or holy book.

Throughout the Crusades and the later invasion of the Mongols, Sufis kept the positive ideas of delight before the Muslim peoples in times of chaos and cruelty. The Sufi tradition has much to offer the West, and its spiritual richness is taught by many Western teachers. In his delightful book, *The Way of Passion*, contemporary Sufi teacher Andrew Harvey urges us to transcendence, to a life

> opened up by visionary ecstasy, by dreams, by unmistakable moments of shattering insight, by immense joy. . . .
> Divine light comes up in the mind and knowledge is born of an unmistakable, irreducible identity with that Light that is bliss, peace, and awareness. This does not and cannot happen quickly. It happens in bursts. . . .

Rumi and Harvey both tell us to pay attention to those moments of delight that come out of the blue. They can change our lives forever.

Another translator of Rumi is Nevit Ergin, a California surgeon with a gift for transcendence, who teaches that love unites us with God, the Beloved, through the small delights of the everyday world.

All around is green. Flowers are everywhere.
All particles smile with reflection of Beauty.
Everything sparkles like jewels.
Love and Beloved are united everywhere.

Our moments of bliss, our inspirations, our hopes and dreams are an important part of our spiritual path. Rumi reminds us, again in the words of Ergin:

I am the One who wrote all this
On your imagination.
How can I not know the secret of your Heart?
I am inside of your Soul.

The Ongoing Delight of Life

We live at a very rich time. In spite of terrible dangers, we have wonderful knowledge to share among the world's peoples. The message of delight is one of the greatest hope and happiness for all.

For most of us, the trick is to keep from getting sidetracked in small pleasures. Savor small delights, for they are part of the whole—but don't settle for them. There's more in store at a higher octave of consciousness.

Out of the Blue

This is not just a "good news" book; when taken to heart, it can set your spirit free. We follow the steps of great teachers who brought forth and continue to put forth ideas of a positive, joyful life—such teachers as William James, Buckminster Fuller, Alan Watts, and Matthew Fox, and such great motivators as Norman Vincent Peale and Robert Schuller. We let people tell their stories—stories that will entertain and inspire belief in ourselves and in a harmonious universe. These anecdotes exemplify depth and wisdom, kindness and joy, positive energy, a sense of humor, great love and respect for others, and a deep connection with the Creator of us all.

Many of the people we spoke with had a turning point or epiphany, when their souls took a giant step forward and their lives shifted into high gear. They became aware of something strong and powerful that helped them make their lives worthwhile—something that they discovered "out there" or within their own hearts.

James Michener, one of the greatest American writers of all time, did not start writing books until an epiphanic experience turned him around, changed his life, and set him upon a new course.

South Pacific

On a stormy night in the South Pacific our plane was trying in vain to land on the Tontouta airstrip but could not do so. We had to rev the engines and make another pass. Another failure. Another big circle in the night sky, knuckles white with fear. This time we made it and gave thanks. Later, at midnight, I went out and walked the length of the airstrip, looking at the dim outlines of the mountains we had so narrowly missed.

And as I stood there in the darkness I caught a glimpse of the remaining years of my life and I swore an oath that when peace came, if I survived, I would live the rest of my years 'as if I were a great man.' I did not presume to think that I would *be* a great man. I have never thought in those terms, but by damn I could conduct myself as if I were. I would adhere to my basic principles. I would bear public testimony to what I believed. I would be a better man. I would help others. I would truly believe and act as if all men were my brothers. And I would strive to make whatever world in which I found myself a better place. In the darkness a magnificent peace settled over me, for I saw that I could actually attain each of those objectives, and I never looked back.

Two immediate consequences: I started the next day to draft the book *Tales of the South Pacific.* And shortly thereafter my entire staff, flying back to Tontouta, hit one of those shadowy mountains and all were killed. I'd had cause to be white knuckled.

James A. Michener

In preparing this book, we interviewed a potpourri of people from nine to ninety-nine and from all walks of life. We found many who have an active connection with their own inherent spiritual nature. We call this the delight connection. Those on a path of positive spirituality find happiness, joy, and bliss shining through all areas of their lives, including their personal and business relationships. Every one of these people glows with delight, no matter what trials life may have handed them.

We are pleased to share with you the delight that enlivens the ordinary and extraordinary moments of our lives and the lives of people whose stories you will find in this book.

We hope you find enough inspiration to warm your heart and open your mind to the possibility that when we choose to live in delight, we can create a glorious world. The last section of the book brings you 52 Delight Igniters, things you may wish to try in order to make a positive change in your life. As your daily thoughts and actions become imbued with delight, you may become an inspiration to others, and the delight revolution will grow.

We hope that *Out of the Blue* brings you at least one "Aha!" experience that stimulates your mind and opens your heart to the great outpouring of delight that is waiting for you.

With love and delight,
Mark Victor Hansen
Barbara Nichols
Patty Hansen

1

The Delight of Life

I have always been delighted at the prospect
of a new day, a fresh try, one more start, with
perhaps a bit of magic waiting somewhere
behind the morning. . . .

J. B. PRIESTLEY

If we told you that you could create a world of peace, harmony, and joy, where would you start? How would you find the wherewithal to pull off such a magnificent undertaking? Some of us would consult scientists, and others would turn to spiritual advisors to help us find the path and the power to create this miracle. But what if we told you that the solution was as simple—and profound—as seeking delight?

Delight is high-level, high-quality happiness. It is that head-to-toe tingle we feel when something goes exceedingly well, that surge in the region of the heart when love and joy are flowing. It is a solid feeling of being permanently connected to our own good. Delight is the fire of enthusiasm that turns work into play and challenges into pleasurable learning experiences. It is having natural zest for life, loving one another without fear, laughing out loud. Delight is passion and enjoyment, singing in the shower, dancing in the street.

Delight is that sudden brilliance that jolts you with renewed energy after driving for hours over boring freeways and suddenly coming upon a beach with sunlight dancing over miles of glittering waves. It is that burst of pride you feel when a loved one regards you as a hero of cosmic proportions.

The word *delight* is used to describe our most positive feelings and experiences. A quiet moment contemplating the stars in the sky can bring us delight; so can holding a child's hand, taking a nap in a hammock, catching a whiff of sea air, enjoying our work, or having a great laugh with a friend. In the grand scheme of things, the range of delight makes enormously good sense—our everyday pleasures remind us of heaven and can bring us closer to its gates.

Human beings are meant to communicate with the Creator. We get a flash of wisdom out of the blue, and suddenly the klieg lights of our inner theater come on. We are illuminated and inspired with ideas and energy, or we are filled with grace and love. When we are aware of the creative energy of the universe, we can accomplish incredible things.

∞

Barbara Van Diest is a counselor in Tucson, Arizona, who teaches about gifts of the spirit. A few years ago, she was working as an actress when this minor miracle helped change her course.

Roses Happen

It had been a frenetic afternoon of meetings and arguments. Everyone in the cast had frayed nerves—and the heat of the day made it even worse. The only one to keep her head was Maria. She had been wonderful to all of us. Ever since rehearsals began, she had been like a mother hen, with soothing words and kind pats on our shoulders.

The cast broke for dinner, and I decided to drive home to change into more comfortable clothes before the evening session started. As I pulled out of the parking lot in Beverly Hills, I suddenly thought, Maria deserves a rose. I wished I had time to get one for her. But I barely had time to zip out to my home at the beach, change, and then race back to town for the continuation of our meeting.

I was stopped at a light near our building, when out of the blue a young man in the car next to mine rolled down his window and handed me a beautiful long-stemmed rose. The light changed and he was gone before I could mutter my thanks.

I thanked God instead and thought, if He can send me a rose on Sunset Boulevard, we can certainly trust. If we open our hearts and let it be, it will come.

Barbara Van Diest

Heaven and earth meet in humanity; the contact point is delight. Delight is that part of us that is our Higher Power, our little portion of God. Delight is the magic spark of divinity in everyone, waiting to ignite. At the electrifying moment when delight enters, we are fueled with enough power and energy to light up the skies. We can live in this state of bliss all the time, no matter what our circumstances.

Psychology refers to peak experiences, and religions use terms like being born again, having a *satori*, reaching nirvana, or having a manifestation of grace or a visit from the Holy Spirit. Spiritual teachers say that we can expand these moments into ongoing "states" if we establish a relationship with God through prayer and meditation.

Finding Delight

The path to delight is a journey without distance. Beyond the dark alleys, secret passages and ghost-lined attic of your mind is a place of bliss, the place from which we all started. Bliss is the essential state. It is having joy with or without a reason. Watch any baby and you'll see that she bubbles with delight for no reason at all.

If you want to reach a state of bliss, then go beyond your ego and the internal dialogue. Make a decision to relinquish the need to control, the need to be approved, and the need to judge. Those are the three things the ego is doing all the time. It's very important to be aware of them every time they come up.

In meditation, you put your ego aside and experience the self in stillness and silence. When you slip into the silent space between your thoughts, God is revealed. You come to a state in which you are connected with everything that exists. This is bliss.

If you could put your attention on the timeless, get your ego out of the way, and be totally natural, you would have a bliss experience all the time.

Deepak Chopra

There is no end to delight, for the universe is made of it.

When you become aware of this extraordinary truth, a color, a sound, a sigh, the smallest and the largest thing can provide a transformative experience. Who can forget the thrill of discovering a bird's nest and watching tiny chicks emerge from their shells? Who can deny the passion and power of the sky? Such are the opportunities to expand your awareness of delight.

When you understand the range and power of delight and allow it to work in your life, you will be amazed at how much energy you have, how readily you attract what you need and want. Delight makes you positively irresistible. You will find that whatever you want, wants you too—even if it is to be found on the other side of the world. You couldn't go to greater lengths, in any sense of the word, than Rick and Diana Stafford did to find the delight of their lives.

Vladimir's Song

The orphanage near Moscow was a dark place, with never enough fuel to keep it warm, not enough food or love to nurture the little ones. But it was the only home Vladimir had ever known. Afflicted with clubbed hands and feet, he could barely walk at seven, and had no hope of keeping up with the other children in the games that were their only source of fun. The desperately overworked doctors and nurses at the orphanage had made a special effort to keep Vladimir with them for an extra two years. They worried what might happen to this special little boy with the big smile and twisted hands and feet if he were sent to the "asylum" for children over five years old.

Vladimir was particularly sweet-natured. The grim orphanage had not darkened his spirit, though his frail little body appeared to be curling in on itself from lack of attention. The one thing Vladimir excelled in was singing. He loved music with a passion and gave it his all.

When an American radio producer taped a report on the sad condition of Russian orphanages, Vladimir was chosen to sing a folk song. His sweet voice rose over the stone walls as a testament to the unquenchable spirit of the children who lived there.

Half a world away, Rick Stafford was negotiating rush-hour traffic near Cincinnati, on his way to work as a corporate trainer, when he heard the report on Russian orphanages. The tiny voice touched Rick's heart with so much power that he was electrified, and knew immediately, beyond any doubt, that he would adopt this boy.

Rick and Diana both had degrees in music—it was their greatest delight. Music was a second language, a joyful medium for them, a means of communication that they understood well. Little Vladimir's song spoke the language of their hearts. The couple had been childless for twelve years and had tried twice to adopt, but without success. They had almost given up. With Diana finishing her graduate degree, they didn't have the resources to try again. Still, they wanted a child and had been praying, trying to "inspire God."

There were miles of red tape to cut through, but things started falling into place in a series of events that amazed everyone. The path to Moscow was smoothed by people who contributed money when they read the story in the paper, and Cradle of Hope, the international adoption agency, agreed to take care of expenses for surgery to straighten Vladimir's hands and feet.

The timing of events was crucial. The week the Staffords' representative went to get his picture and medical reports, Vladimir was scheduled to be moved to the dreaded asylum. The day the adoption papers were signed was the day a law went into effect in Russia suspending all adoptions until new laws could be written. Most of the time Rick and Diana didn't know how close they were cutting it.

Six months after the radio broadcast, Rick and Diana flew to Moscow to pick up their son. The moment Diana saw Vladimir coming down the hall at the orphanage, her heart almost burst with joy. It was delight at first sight.

Back in Ohio, the Staffords' son is learning English and making friends at a great rate. Even before his surgery, his shoulders have opened out and his range of motion has greatly improved. Rick and Diana think it's because now he can get a hug whenever he needs one. The Stafford family is singing together every night. Their favorite song is the delightful old Russian melody that brought them together—Vladimir's song.

Barbara Nichols

Daily Delight

We tend to forget about delight in the rush of daily life. When asked what delights us, many of us are hard-pressed for an answer. We might know what makes us happy or pleases us, but delight seems too much to hope for. Dinner was "fine, dear"; that's a "nice" picture on the wall. We're pleased, but a little burdened, with a new job. How we cling to that safe middle zone! Delight is reserved for special times like holidays and honeymoons, but if we feel delight on an ordinary day, we probably try to suppress it. How embarrassing it would be to be caught jumping for joy! So we slog through our time on this beautiful planet overlooking our enormous potential for high-level happiness.

Sometimes, try as you may, you can't avoid having an encounter with delight. No matter what you do, it persists until it gets through.

Celestial Delight

We had stayed in San Francisco for Christmas, my friend Patrick and I, though all of our classmates had gone home. We had what we considered very important papers to do and didn't want to get derailed by our families' holiday hullabaloo.

The first few days of self-imposed Christmas exile went well enough—we stiff-upper-lipped it, kept our noses to the grindstone, and ignored the holiday spirit in the air. By the time Christmas Eve arrived, we were irritable and snapping at each other.

"Patrick," I sniffed, by now on the verge of tears, "maybe trying to put Christmas out of our minds wasn't such a good idea."

Patrick muttered something like "poor baby" and suggested taking a break and going to Chinatown. There would be lights and colors of a different kind, and we would be surrounded by Buddhists who celebrated other holidays. It was business as usual there; we'd be safe from Christmas. Besides, wonton soup was just what the doctor ordered.

The cable car clanked and shuddered down to Chinatown

through a dense and silent fog and deposited us on Grant Avenue just as night fell. It was as deserted as we'd ever seen it, a bleak street when we had expected hustle and bustle. As we headed toward our favorite restaurant, we saw lights approaching, smudgy and indistinct in the fog. Then we heard silvery little voices that sounded like a choir of angels, singing "Silent Night."

Stunned, we stood in our tracks as a troop of Chinese children emerged from the gloom caroling with all their might, their beatific faces wreathed in the glow of candles they were carrying. They couldn't have been more than six years old, this band of black-eyed cherubs, yet they carried the whole message and meaning of the holiday directly into our shut-down, hungry hearts.

They passed by, taking their pool of light with them, leaving us once again in the dismal fog lit only by signs blinking Peking Duck. We were changed irrevocably by their fleeting presence. Right there in the street, half laughing, half crying in delight, we hugged each other fiercely and shouted, "Merry Christmas!"

They may not have been real angels, but they brought with them a little glimpse of heaven, or, as the Chinese like to say, celestial delight.

Eugenie West

Childhood is a time of great enthusiasm and curiosity, which are necessary components of delight. From our first days of life, we are richly endowed with delight. To see it in action, just watch a puppy chasing its tail, or a baby gurgling away as she discovers her fingers and toes. If you're lucky enough to have a baby in the neighborhood, watch her until you remember what you knew when you arrived here but may have forgotten: Life is a treasure of discovery and excitement, a present about to be opened.

Early Childhood and the Treasure

I can remember, as if it happened last week, more than half a century ago, when I must have been about four, and, on fine summer mornings, would sit in a field adjoining the house. What gave me delight then was a mysterious notion, for which I could certainly not have found words, of a Treasure. It was waiting for me either in the earth, just below the buttercups and daisies, or in the golden air. I had formed no idea of what this Treasure would consist of, and nobody had ever talked to me about it. But morning after morning would be radiant with its promise. Somewhere, not far out of reach, it was waiting for me, and at any moment I might roll over and put a hand on it. I suspect now that the Treasure was Earth itself and the light and warmth of the sunbeams; yet sometimes I fancy that I have been searching for it ever since.

J. B. Priestley

Minute by Minute

Ninety-nine-year-old Ruth Cooke was asked what gives her delight, and she had a clear and ready answer: "Talking to you right now gives me delight. It's what is happening at this minute." Every minute of life is a great gift, no matter how old we are. Ask Evan Handler, a playwright and performer who survived terminal cancer, and he may give you the surprising answer that squirming in the dentist's chair hearing the sound of the drill gives him delight. It's not that he enjoys the pain, it's that he relishes *all* of life's experiences.

When we're fully alive, it's easy to obey the biblical directive "This is the day the Lord has made; rejoice and be glad in it."

When we live in happiness, we speak of delightful meals, of delightful events in our lives, of people who delight us, of the delight of accomplishment. Our senses are exquisitely tuned to delight—the sound of music, the glimpse of a child's face, or the touch of a loved one can bring us great joy.

We don't wait for something to come along and make us joyful; we put forth the effort ourselves and find happiness even under less-than-perfect circumstances.

One of the most delightful people we know is our friend W Mitchell. With his cosmic sense of humor and easygoing style, he soon makes you forget that his face is a patchwork of multicolored skin grafts and that the hand he extends so readily for friendship has no fingers, only stubs. Five minutes after Mark's children met him, they were singing Hawaiian songs and laughing at his gentle jokes. Although they were curious about the way he looks, his joy with life overpowers his appearance and they fell in delight with him.

The Man Who Won't Be Defeated

On the morning of June 19, 1971, I was on top of the world. I was on my way to work on my beautiful new motorcycle to a job that I loved, a San Francisco cable-car gripman. Earlier that morning I had soloed in an airplane, the fulfillment of one of my fondest dreams. I was twenty-eight, handsome, healthy and popular.

At the intersection of Twenty-sixth and South Van Ness, as I rounded the corner, my motorcycle skidded and collided with a laundry truck. The bike went down, crushing my elbow and pelvis. The gas from the motorcycle poured out and was ignited by the heat of the engine. I was burned over 65 percent of my body.

Thanks to a passing motorist, I was still alive. During the next four months I had thirteen transfusions, sixteen skin grafts, and numerous other operations. I was finally released from the hospital on a sunny San Francisco afternoon. As I walked down the street enjoying the fresh air, I passed a school playground. The children stopped and stared at my face. "Hey, everyone, come and look at the monster!" one of the kids yelled.

Although I was deeply hurt by thoughtless reactions to my appearance, I still had the love and encouragement of my friends and family—and my personal philosophy. I knew that I did not have to buy into society's notion that I had to be handsome and healthy to be happy. I was in charge of my "spaceship" and it was my up, my down. I could choose to see this situation as a setback or as a starting point. I chose to begin life again.

Within six months after the accident, I was flying planes again. I moved to Colorado and with two of my friends, I co-founded Vermont Casting, Inc. As chairman of the board, I helped build the tiny wood-stove company into Vermont's second largest employer. My net worth climbed to nearly three million dollars. I had a lovely Victorian home, my own airplane, real estate holdings, a bar—and I was not at a lack for female companionship. I was on my way to the top of the world again.

Then, on the morning of November 11, 1975, with four passengers aboard I took off in my turbocharged Cessna. About seventy-five feet up, I reduced power, and the plane dropped just like a rock back onto the runway. Pain shot up from my lower back. I smelled smoke, and I yelled to the others to get out. Almost overcome with the fear of being burned again, I started to get out—and found I could not move my legs.

In the hospital again, I was told that my twelve thoracic vertebrae were completely crushed and my spinal cord beyond repair. I was to be a paraplegic for the rest of my life. Although I had always been relentlessly optimistic, I began to have dark moments. I wondered what in the hell had happened to me. What had I done to deserve this?

But I still had the profound sense that I could create my own reality by focusing on the "can" rather than the "cannot"—and I had friends and family who believed in me. I decided to follow the advice of the German philosopher Goethe: "Whatever you can do, or dream you can, begin it. Boldness has genius, power and magic in it." Before my accidents, there were ten thousand things I could do. I could spend the rest of my life dwelling on the one thousand that I had lost, but instead I chose to focus on the nine thousand I still had left.

Since that time, I have gone on to become my town's two-term mayor, earn international recognition as an environmental activist, and run for Congress. My slogan was "Not just another pretty face!" I serve on several boards, have hosted my own public television series, and speak professionally to hundreds of groups each year sharing my message about attitude, service, and change.

I tell people that I have had two big bumps in my life. If I have chosen not to use them as an excuse to quit, maybe some of the negative experiences that they are having can be put into a new perspective. In my speeches I say, "Step back, take a wider view. Then you have a chance to realize, maybe it isn't such a big thing after all." My mission in life is to share with as many people as possible that it isn't what happens to you that is important, it is what you do about it that makes the difference.

W Mitchell

In Delight

Being in delight is much like being in love. When you are in love, colors are more vivid, trees seem to dance in the afternoon breezes—you notice the distinct blue of your loved one's eyes and compare them to summer skies. The touch of a hand to your knee sends shivers up and down your spine, and you are charged with a bolt of inner electricity. Everything you eat tastes better, everything you smell is more intense—the scent of roses, jasmine, and wild-flowers is everywhere you turn. You are in tune with the music of the spheres and the songs of angels. When you are in love, all of this and more is true.

Being in delight feels a lot like being in love. Your senses become more acute, and joy flows through your body. That head-to-toe tingle may even affect your health as physical and emo-tional well-being surge through. Your body may actually become stronger and more flexible. High blood pressure may normalize, breathing become deeper and more regular, bringing more oxygen to your cells. Vitality soars, zest increases. You'll feel great!

Along with physical liveliness comes an expanded capacity for compassion, creativity, and curiosity. You will love more easily and forgive more readily. You'll accept people, faults and all, and find yourself laughing out loud. Small things you never noticed before will take on new importance. You will notice that the curve of your child's cheek is singularly beautiful; the cloud formations in the western sky will make the drive home from work a joy. Even if your feet don't dance, your soul will, and those around you will hear your inner music.

Imagine how wonderful it would be to feel so fulfilled in your inner being without needing the reassurance of another person. When you open your heart and soul to the delight of the universe, you are filled to overflowing and delight flows out to others. Delight is an inside-out event. It comes from inside of you to bless your world, and the world around you is naturally blessed with your radiance.

You were born to live in delight. From your first giggle to your last sigh, you are here to find joy in every event. Delight is the home of your true self. The more you find in your own life, the more influence you will have on others. Ripples of delight expand, making a better world for all of us.

> Birds sing after a storm; why shouldn't people feel as free
> to delight in whatever remains to them?
> Rose Fitzgerald Kennedy

Delight comes out of the blue in the form of minor miracles and everyday epiphanies. Suddenly we have a moment of intuitive understanding, a glimmer of divinity that reaches our hearts and touches our souls, and we are filled with joy, knowledge, and peace. Our hearts and minds expand to encompass a greater reality, a larger understanding.

Here a popular author/speaker learns that when he is open to a lesson from the universe, a delightful event reminds him of his true mission in life.

Transplant in Chicago

I was on vacation in Maui, but was due in Chicago to give a speech. I grumbled about having to get on the plane and fly so long, then do interviews from morning until night, and then fly all the way back, another ten hours in a plane. I was self-absorbed, feeling sorry for myself and a little angry. I took the red-eye, flew all night long, and got in early in the morning. My New York publicist called first thing with the schedule—you speak in the afternoon, but at nine o'clock you have to do this show, and at ten o'clock you have that one, and at eleven o'clock you have an interview, and at noon there are newspaper people coming . . . There was a whole list of things I had to do all day. All I could think of were a million reasons why I shouldn't have to.

Then I got an emergency phone call from my publicist in Florida, who had just received a call from a woman in Chicago whose husband, Fred, had a liver transplant. "He's not expected to live. His last wish is to see you because your book was instrumental in his taking the risk to have the operation, and he feels you are one of the most important influences in his life."

I said, "I'd be happy to see him, but I don't have a free minute."

She said, "The only time you could see him is between eleven o'clock and noon. That's when the transplant unit is open at the University of Chicago hospital."

"I have a live interview scheduled then. Sorry."

I was about to call this man's wife with my apologies when the other phone rang. It was my New York publicist again, telling me that my eleven o'clock interview had been canceled.

So I went to the hospital after all. When I walked into Fred's room, I saw how very sick he was. His legs were sort of green and so large, even at the ankles, that they looked like tree trunks.

"I knew you'd come," he said.

There was a chinning bar suspended over his head, and he said, "Watch me, I know I can do this." He reached up and pulled himself four feet over the bed. "I'm going to make it, you see."

His wife looked at me and shook her head. "There's not much chance. The transplant isn't taking."

Fred and I had a wonderful visit. We talked for an hour, and I hugged him and told him I'd send him all my prayers. It was such a good hour. It reminded me that you have to go where you are sent.

Two years later I was back in Chicago one Friday night, speaking before about two thousand people at a church. I was talking about the oneness of life and the illusion of separateness. A man came up at intermission and said, "Wayne, remember me? It's Fred. Remember the liver transplant?" I almost fell off the stage. He didn't look at all like the man I'd met in the transplant unit. He was the healthiest, most robust person I had seen in a long time. I had him come up onstage and talk. Here's what he said:

"I thank my donor—I wouldn't be here without him. But I wouldn't have gotten to my donor without you. . . . Thank you."

In higher awareness, you are unconcerned about what's in it for you. Seeing Fred again reminded me to stop being selfish, and just to be out there doing what I know my mission is, which is to help and to serve.

Wayne Dyer

Delight is the divine spark that ignites us to become our best selves. It expands our souls and enlarges our capacities for thought, creativity, intuition, and love. Delight improves our attitude toward everyone and everything in our lives.

We come from delight. Quantum physicists tell us that the cosmos is unfolding every instant in particles and waves of energy, and we are part of that great happening. William Blake wrote centuries ago that "Energy is eternal delight." Other searchers in the realm of the soul have said that love or bliss or joy is the origin of everything. Alan Watts, the great teacher of Zen Buddhism, made the connection clear: "Existence is basically exuberance. The Universe is a celebration of love and delight that, were it otherwise, would simply not go on happening. The whole point is to be fully aware of it as it happens."

The Language of the Soul

Encounters with delight touch us at a very deep level and, if we're paying attention, can make a profound difference in our experience of life. When the powerful surge of joy and bliss radiates through your being, it amplifies your awareness of yourself. You're more than you knew. Your expanded self feels loved, protected, strengthened and capable of giving the same to others. If you are very fortunate, delight may cause you to fall in love with life or, as we choose to call it, in delight with life, on a permanent basis.

Cleve Francis is a multitalented man whose life works on many levels. Both a renowned cardiologist and a country-western singer, he is a specialist in matters of the heart. "Where the heart leads us," he says, "delight follows."

Woman Enough

She was sixteen, pregnant, and unmarried; she was a black girl in the deep south, and it was 1945, years before desegregation. The community offered her nothing but scorn and ridicule, and things got so bad that she fled in desperation to a distant uncle in Texas.

Mary worked for her room and board until a week before the baby came, with legs swollen so large she could hardly walk. When the baby was born, she was delighted with him and loved to press him to her heart and sing him lullabies. But she had no way to feed and care for both of them. A childless middle-aged couple offered to adopt the boy and give him a good education.

"No way," she replied. "I was woman enough to have that baby, and I will be woman enough to raise him." But she did ask the couple to keep her child while she worked to save money so that the two of them could get back home. The couple agreed, but were sure they'd seen the last of the young mother.

Mary left, feeling as if the bottom had fallen out of her heart. But she was true to her word. Inflamed with her love for her child, and strengthened by her desire to be with him, she did her best to survive, working as a domestic maid for about five dollars a week. Before the year was up, she went back to get her baby. They went home to Louisiana, this time for good.

Mary never gave up on anything. She married a short time

later, and over the years had five more children, who would graduate from college and go on to achieve great things in life: Faye, a
music teacher; Barbara, a mortgage banker; Lois, an intensive
care nurse; Nancy, a music therapist; and Elizabeth, a physical
therapist. Their lives were not easy but were filled with love and
delight, and gratitude for a good God who helped Mary Francis
become woman enough.

Cleve Francis, M. D. (Mary's first child)

If we are fully responsive to our soul's delight, we want to
return the favor to the universe by giving love, joy, sustenance,
and hope to other beings. When we fall in delight with life, we
can't distinguish between giving and receiving. Positive cycles of
love and happiness begin at this level of soul awareness, and serving the needs of others becomes a necessary part of the cycle. We
communicate from soul to soul by creating and sharing delight.
Our souls understand the language of delight just as our hearts
know the language of love.

Delight unites us. We become aware of this when we emerge
from a dark theater with dozens of other people after a particularly
touching movie. For an instant we see the glow of delight we're
feeling shining through strangers' eyes, and they seem like friends.
In that moment we share a deep and luminous secret: The part of
me that responds to delight is in you, too. We're all in this together.

Awakening Delight

The great secret of awakening delight is this: There isn't any
secret. You don't have to go any place, do anything, buy anything,
or improve anything about yourself to reach delight. The awakening of delight in your life is simply a choice to be in delight each
moment of your day—starting now. You can find delight within
yourself, right now in your present reality. Each of us has the
ongoing opportunity to come to that realization with every breath
we take.

Spiritual teachers and psychologists keep telling us "be here now," and "stay in the now and experience your experience," for that's where life is happening. If we can hold to the present moment, we can, at the very least, live in balance and serenity. Emotional upsets come when our minds are busy judging and comparing the present with the past and worrying about the future while the present moment is lost to eternity.

Just *being* is delightful. "Bless what there is for being," the poet W. H. Auden wrote. This simple line contains not only a great truth, but also an important clue for finding delight in the moment, which is, to bless—to praise, to be thankful for, to appreciate.

Wally Amos, of chocolate chip cookie fame, received a wonderful insight about living in the moment from a great teacher, his five-year-old daughter.

Papa, Are We Here?

Once when we were flying into Los Angeles from Honolulu and were taxiing to the terminal, Sarah woke up and very drowsily asked, "Papa, are we here yet?"

I said, "Wow! What a concept!"

People always ask, "Are we there yet." But the reality is, you are never *there*, because as soon as you get there, you're *here*. When you arrive in tomorrow, it's today. That moment helped me realize that Now is the only time there is. This moment is it.

Wally Amos

Try to find at least one gift in every situation. You can practice this every day. Be delighted with the blue sky or lovely flowers, with the music on the radio or the song in your heart. It may sound too simple or unsophisticated, like "positive thinking," but there's nothing simple about that, either. Decide to go just one day without a negative thought, and you'll see what we mean. Reining in our minds is a challenge requiring discipline and practice. Developing the will to increase delight in our lives and in the world means paying constant attention, making a thousand small choices every day. We must consistently choose to keep delight as our focus moment by moment. As good as our minds are, we can only think one thought at a time. We have billions of brain cells just waiting to go to work when we make a decision to give direction to our thoughts and ideas. Choose the positive and smile. When we give ourselves permission to revel in the positive, our world can look and feel like heaven on earth. It all depends on how you see things.

Some People See Stars

It was a night of shooting stars. I rushed home to watch the promised meteor shower. During the next few hours as I leaned back in my lawn chair, eight brilliant shooting stars streaked overhead. I felt in tune with the universe.

The next morning as I took my walk, I saw a large chunk of black pitted rock near the lake. Could it *be* one? I wondered. A meteorite that miraculously arrived intact through our earth's atmosphere? Yes, it looked similar to those I'd seen in the museum at Meteor Crater, Arizona.

I lifted the heavy rock and put it on the floor of my car and took it home. I asked the high school student next door his opinion. He'd camped out all night to watch the meteor show and counted more than thirty that blazed a trail over the lake.

He examined it carefully. "I don't know. It could be." Next I drove across town to get our newspaper editor's opinion. "There's no need for me to go out and look at it," he said. "I wouldn't know one if I saw one. Try the public library."

It was too late. I went home instead.

When my husband came in after work, I told him my story and enthusiastically showed him my prize.

"That's no meteor," he laughed. "It's just a piece of concrete somebody put around their campfire!"

My elevated spirits sank to the floor.

I called my best friend, Kay, and told her my meteor had turned to man-made stone.

"Well, you know, Janice," she said, "when some people see things in life they see concrete . . . "

"And when others see them they see stars!"

Now my "star" sits in a prominent place on our deck for all the world to see.

Janice Rose

In a world where we are bombarded with bad news and blasted with disasters every time we turn on the radio or TV, we owe it to ourselves to counter all that negativity by contributing as much positive energy as we can.

Sun Bear was a member of the Chippewa Nation and the envisioner and organizer of the well-known Medicine Wheel Gatherings that have attracted thousands of people around the world. Here, Marlise Wabun Wind describes her first meeting with him and her experience with full-blown positive thinking.

Miracle on the Subway

I had asked Sun Bear for an interview when he came to New York, and had also suggested that he and his people stay with me when they arrived. I was surprised when he took me up on the offer. As I showed him around the city, he went everywhere with an unbelievable grin on his face. It made New Yorkers wonder if he'd just been released from an institution. In the city being unhappy is normal; being happy is considered crazy. Other people's attitudes toward his delight didn't bother him at all, but it embarrassed me to be going around with this grinning Indian. That made him smile even more.

One day we got on the subway and he started beaming at everyone. One by one the passengers started smiling back. By the time we got to our destination, he had everyone on that subway car smiling. A subway full of smiling people was so incredible, it seemed a miracle.

Later, when I moved to Washington State to be part of his work, Sun Bear told me I would return to New York one day, look at what I had considered life to be about and say, "I don't believe any of this."

Several years later I was back in New York attending a conference. As I was walking down the street watching all those serious, focused people in such a hurry, I started laughing. Right there on the street I surprised myself by saying, "I don't believe this any more," and realizing I did not.

Sun Bear gave me the great gift of being able to see the world through a whole different culture. That's what a good teacher does—allows you to see through their eyes for a time. Once that happens, you'll never see the world the way you did before.

Marlise Wabun Wind

Delight Blessings

Faces will change from fear and worry to smiles, joy, and acceptance of others as more and more people learn to live in delight each and every day. Just as Sun Bear showed his friend that others can, and will, respond to a positive projection of oneself, we would like to encourage you to try it yourself. Just for one day, see delight in everyone with whom you come in contact—your friends, boss, co-workers, parents, children, even strangers in the grocery store! When you walk into a room, *see* the room filled with a soft, pink light. (The manufacturers of light bulbs have found in studies that the pink light creates a positive atmosphere, softens worry lines on people's faces, and eases tension.) We think you will have results similar to Marva Bell's when she decided to test the theory. Maybe you will like it so much you will want to see delight not just for one day, but every day!

Delight at the Bank

I was in a long, dreary line at the bank where the tellers looked harassed and the patrons looked angry and impatient. I concentrated for a moment on bringing energy to the area of my heart, and then said to myself, "*This is a delightful place. What wonderful people. I'm delighted to be here right now.*" I beamed out the words over and over. The bank manager, a serious man in a conservative suit, was walking past the line when suddenly and for no apparent reason, he began to fight a smile. One of the tellers smiled at a customer, and several people in line brightened up and began exchanging pleasantries with one another. "This is too good to be true," I thought. "It's probably just a coincidence."

I decided to test it on a hard case. My next stop was the library where I knew the librarian was depressed, pessimistic, and negative. When I asked him to help me find a book, I also silently beamed a message to him: "*You are a delight!*" He looked up, shocked, as if he'd been struck by lightning. I smiled at him, and once more thought very clearly, "*Yes, you. You are a delight.*"

He sprang into action as if a weight had been lifted from his shoulders, and went into overdrive to get materials together for me. I *knew* that the librarian had received my message. It was powerful and clear.

The important thing is that my own attitude shifted into high gear when I decided to send the highest and best message into the world, and my own day went exceedingly well. The ripple effect is incalculable. The librarian was probably happier for the rest of the day, and some of that happiness was transmitted to patrons of the library. The people in the bank may have kept the cycle going. I believe it works!

Marva Bell

Who knows how far Bell's positive thoughts traveled? There is no way to measure the effect of one person raising her level of energy, but we do know that everything in the universe is part of everything else. You can be sure that some good comes from your every high-level thought and action. When you hold the intention to be in delight and become centered and grounded in it, happiness is your everyday reality. By blessing everything, you become a blessing to yourself and others—and life can work in surprising new ways.

Life can be a grand adventure. Let your natural enthusiasm stir and lift your feet—march forward into the future boldly.

A declaration is a powerful tool to help change or strengthen your self-perception. Repeating the following declaration, both out loud and to yourself, will stabilize your intention to yourself and to the world. Declare delightful new beliefs!

Delight Declaration

Awakening Delight

I realize my life is a delight.

I look for the gift in each situation.

Renewed by my creative connection with the
universe, I boldly live my life with joy, goodness,
beauty, and ever-increasing delight.

Since I live in delight moment by moment, I
am a blessing to all I know, all I support, and
all I love.

I see my world through the eyes of delight and
I am uplifted, protected, and totally loved.

2

Light Up the Sky

Only from the heart
Can you touch the sky.

RUMI

*W*e've all seen people who have "star quality," whose smiles dazzle and whose glowing energy attracts our attention. Many people have this quality of radiance, and most of us have it when we are in delight or in love. "For angels and lovers, everything sparkles," said Marianne Williamson. The good news is you don't have to be in the movies or be in love to be a shining star.

Chinese sage Lao-tzu speaks of our "original sky-like nature." We were born with an amazingly bright inner essence. At birth, we were totally radiant, yet for most of us, our light becomes dim and our awareness of our own ability to sustain that inner glow decreases.

The difference between those of us who shine like stars and those of us who don't is that the radiant people have found their true identity and reestablished harmony with their original essence. They are aware of their spiritual connection with the universe and they create miracles around them in their everyday life. They live in delight—with intensity!

A miracle is nothing more or less than this. Anyone who has come into a knowledge of his true identity, of his oneness with the all-pervading wisdom and power, this makes it possible for laws higher than the ordinary mind knows of to be revealed to him.

Ralph Waldo Trine

When you live in delight, you don't just love life, you have a passion for life. Your life is a joy to yourself and to those around you. You are fully in touch with your own creative genius and you use your gifts to your advantage and to the advantage of the world at large. You have a sense of destiny and purpose and you are living your dreams. Your brilliance will light up a room when you walk in. The light of your soul naturally seeks union with the light beyond, and you glow.

Life is not a "brief candle." It is a splendid torch that I want to make burn as brightly as possible before handing on to future generations.

George Bernard Shaw

Some of us are afraid to commit our all to any enterprise, even to having delight in our lives some of the time. We may have heard "Don't get your heart set on it" when we were growing up, from well-meaning parents who wanted to protect us from disappointment. But putting your heart into things is as close as you'll get to a guarantee that, in the long run, you won't be disappointed. Whether it's a relationship, job, sport, creative endeavor, or community project, do everything with wholehearted delight. Make a deep personal commitment to live in delight from this point on. Enjoy to the fullest everything you do, and do that which brings you delight. Live with exuberance and enthusiasm and you will light up the sky.

Living Life with Passion

Life is either a daring adventure or nothing.
                    Helen Keller

An extraordinary high-energy life is ours if we choose to live in delight. We become stronger physically, mentally, spiritually, and emotionally. We have the means to transform our lives and influence the lives of others for the better.

You may think that happiness and delight come from things going well; but the reverse is true—things go well when you take delight in what you are doing.

Good health comes with living in delight. Health is more than physical fitness and diet. It requires buoyancy of the spirit and a positive outlook on life. Altering our attitudes has a powerful effect on our physical health. Deciding to focus on what's right with us rather than what's wrong with us can bring happiness as well as good health.

A man's health can be judged by which he takes two at a time—pills or stairs.
                    Joan Welsh

Your attitude of delight helps keep you healthy and well. The new science of psychoneuroimmunology has shown that your thinking can enhance your healing powers or it can depress and weaken them. Developing a state of delight actually bolsters your immune system.

O. Carl Simonton, founder of the Simonton Cancer Centers, is famous for showing patients how to use the power of their minds to beat disease. His integrated approach to healing includes appreciation of the body's ability to heal itself. Dr. Simonton says that excessive stress and lack of delight and fulfillment take their toll on body and soul. His clinical experiences have convinced him that healthy spiritual beliefs can improve both a patient's quality of life and the course of an illness.

"By spiritual," he says, "I don't necessarily mean belief in God or an established religion—though it can be. I mean an optimistic outlook on life—what we believe about ourselves and our place in the world. Our beliefs evolve as our understanding of and participation in life evolves. We can learn to focus on more positive beliefs about life."

The precious network of cells that makes up your body has been in preparation for billions of years. It is a place of consciousness. Some would say it is the residence of your soul. Do not think of the body as insignificant. There is light in every cell. Even the rhythm of your pulse is part of the great heartbeat of the universe.

Sensory Delights

We get information about the world through our senses. The gifts of color, taste, sound, smell, and touch give meaning and passion to life.

"Delight is built into the physiology of the senses," Sam Keen wrote in *Hymns to an Unknown God*. "If you doubt that sense and meaning are connected, try this experiment. First, subtract red . . . what kind of meaning or spiritual delight remains in a world devoid of the color red?"

Here's what happened when Barbara spent a week without red—or any other colors.

Color Dance

Winter winds sweep the North Coast, turning clouds into dancers in the sky. The year I decided to stay at the cottage after summer's end, the dancers joined forces and went wild. Rain, floods, and power outages culminated in a six-day stretch of downed lines and closed roads. I was stuck miles from nowhere alone at the end of a one-lane dirt—now mud—road. The culprit power line sagged in plain sight. Except for seventeen candles and a little firewood, I was unprepared.

The cloud dancers wore black capes, turning day into night. They danced to the incessant beat of rain pounding the roof. Depression grew despite delightful intentions. Enough had been enough for a long time.

I chopped wood and carried water, rationed my logs for cook fires, reserved my battery radio for the news, and saved my candles for an "emergency." Huddled down in quilts and Polartec jackets. Talked a lot to the dog and cats. And adjusted. What if it rained forever?

When the power company truck finally rumbled down the road, I found myself running out to greet it, fighting the urge to hug the men on the truck. All I could think was, "Now I know how they felt when Paris was liberated."

An hour later, my cottage lit up, and so did I. Color. I'd lived for almost a week with virtually no color, and now it burst through my eyes into my soul. I shouted and sang. Jumped for joy. Turned on every light, ran to the closet and grabbed bright red and blue things to toss over the brown tweed couch. Laughed and cried and stomped back at those dark cloud dancers for all I was worth. It was spontaneous, this fountain of delight, and I let it happen. I, the recipient of all this color, felt like the beloved of the universe. What a gift!

The cats and dog exchanged worried looks.

"Poor little beasties," I shouted. "You've *never* seen in color."

I wondered how they'd look in purple.

The deluge of color started a celebration that hasn't stopped.

No more beige for me. Give me color that makes me want to cheer every time.

Barbara Nichols

The senses give us great pleasure and enhance our feelings of well-being. Bringing art and music into your life is a feast for the eyes and ears that fills your soul with passion. Rich natural scents of flowers and spices can cure listlessness and bring joy. The smell of well-prepared foods cooking, freshly baked bread, salty sea air, or new-mown hay can counteract depression. Galleries and symphonies can awaken our senses. The vivid orange color of nasturtiums or the scent of lilacs in spring contribute to our sense of well-being and let us know we are part of a delightful whole.

Embracing Change

Change is the end result of all true learning. Change involves three things: First, a dissatisfaction with self—a felt void or need; second, a decision to change—to fill the void or need; and third, a conscious dedication to the process of growth and change—the wilful act of making the change, doing something.

Leo Buscaglia

If there's something you'd like to improve or change in your life, begin by taking delight in it. Be grateful, thankful, and joyful about who you are now, what you do now, and what you have now.

Even if you are overweight, unemployed, bored, or living in a tiny apartment, begin to appreciate everything—especially the parts of yourself and your life that you find upsetting. Be delighted with that paunch, or with the opportunity to find a new job or start a new enterprise, or to move to a better home. Though it may seem strange at first to love your imagined defects and difficulties, at very deep levels, a subtle shift occurs. Look at problems as gifts you were given to help transform your limited self and enlarge your soul's capacity for delight.

Sometimes you have to turn your life around to find your heart's delight. That's what happened to Paula Gentry—quite literally—when she decided to make a new start.

On the Right Track

I was always searching for something I could really integrate into my life, something that would not only be work but would be meaningful and fulfilling as well.

Living in a deteriorating relationship in Colorado was not bringing me closer to my ideal. During the Christmas holidays I decided to leave for California. I had no particular plan, but I wanted a new life.

I left Aspen the day after Christmas in my Jeep Wagoneer. Snow and freezing rain were blowing everywhere, and my mood matched the foul weather. For some reason, I was taking back roads. As I left the small town on the border between Utah and Nevada, there was a long stretch of road ahead with mountains in the background. The highway was built up with deep culverts on either side, so if you swung off the road, you'd go down into the ditch and out into the fields.

Music has always revved me up, so I had a Pointer Sisters tape on, and they were singing "I'm So Excited." I was feeling scared and excited about going off on my own when all of a sudden I saw a mound in the road up ahead and a bunch of buzzards flying around it. It must have been a dead animal. I was going too fast, and the car was in overdrive. When I tapped the brake to get it out of overdrive, I realized the road was covered with black ice. The car began spinning around and around. I started praying.

During those seconds I was spinning, a buzzard looked me straight in the eye as I zoomed past him in a swirl. I could see myself winding up in the middle of that field with buzzards flying around me or in a helicopter taking me to Aspen hospital. I prayed not to be stuck in Aspen again. "I don't want to go back, God," I prayed. "Please let me go forward in my life." That was the first time I'd really connected with God in years.

When the car finally stopped, it was pointing toward San Francisco. I was all right, the Pointer Sisters were still singing, and I knew I was doing what I was supposed to be doing.

From then on, events unfolded with near-miraculous ease. I didn't know a soul in San Francisco but I went right to Grace Cathedral on Nob Hill and asked for guidance. "Please keep me pointing in the right direction," I prayed.

Within a week, someone came into my life who suggested that I become a cosmetic consultant. I loved the product, and that person was a wonderful mentor. I never even considered anything else. Before the year was out, I had won a car and was on my way to success in a career I loved. I won two Cadillacs and three other cars, was on the National Queen's Court of Sales six times, won six diamond rings and have been a Sales Director for eight years. More than being a successful business, this career has been a vehicle through which I've evolved as a human being. I can give so much help to other women now, in their careers and personal lives—I know this is exactly where I'm supposed to be.

Paula Gentry

Making a decision to live in delight is the beginning of expansion in every way. Start sending the powerful energy of love into every part of your body and corner of your life. Remember that nothing is set in concrete—not even those problems that seem insurmountable. Every cell in your body and thought in your mind is changing every nanosecond. If you consciously choose to live in delight, you can transcend circumstance. Spiritual teacher Sri Chinmoy says, "Delight is continuous growth, fulfillment, achievement, and God-manifestation in God's own way. . . . Everything is transcending. The Supreme Being is singing the song of self-transcendence all the time."

Losing your job is a disaster. Or is it? Suzie Humphries, actress, speaker, and ex-newswoman, came through a devastating experience of change with a new sense of trust in the universe.

Life Comes Up

I used to be a television interviewer in Dallas, and was I full of myself! I decked myself out in lizard shoes, silk dresses, and eyelashes out to *there* full time. If you turned on the TV early in the morning, you'd see me talking to George Bush, John Wayne, or Clint Eastwood. I was the one with big hair. I knew I was special because I hobnobbed with all those people.

You don't get fired if you're special, do you? Well, I lost my job, and with it went my self-esteem. Not only that, I had gone through every cent I'd made buying those lizard shoes and silk dresses. I didn't have one thin dime.

I couldn't even afford my expensive apartment anymore. Luckily I had an old friend to move in with. You don't keep a high profile if you don't think you're special, so I just hid out and got depressed.

Then one day the phone rang. The local radio station needed someone to do the traffic reports while the regular traffic reporter was on vacation.

"The traffic reports? In a helicopter?" I asked, feeling my ego shrink even more. "How much does it pay?"

I showed up at six o'clock Monday morning at the heliport without even knowing where north, south, east, or west was or how to operate the radio equipment. It was the craziest traffic report in the history of Dallas, but for some reason people loved it. They called in and asked for more. Then, as fate would have it, the real traffic reporter decided not to come back to work and the job was mine. I was making more working two hours a day than I'd made working all day on the interview show. My life was coming up.

Fate had even more in store—before long, Tom came into my life and it was love at first sight. We decided to get married. As two mature adults we looked forward to a life of leisure together.

A few months later I discovered I was going to have a baby. What a shock! I was forty years old. I thought God had lost his mind. What kind of mother would I make?

What frightened me was the responsibility of another human being. If we're responsible, we're not free, I thought, and freedom had been a priority with me all my life. What I didn't know was that it is the acceptance of responsibility that makes us like ourselves.

When Josh was born, something shifted in my soul. Things I used to think were valuable, like lizard shoes and silk dresses, seemed worthless; pacifiers and applesauce took on new meaning.

And sitting in the still of the night with just a hint of moonlight shining through a half-open blind, feeling his small cheek next to mine, I knew for the first time in my whole life the delight of responsibility for another human being.

In the year that Josh was growing to one, his mother, at forty, was growing up.

I look back now and realize that if I hadn't been fired I'd still be sitting there on TV, missing the greatest gifts of my life. I think that's how it works. You get knocked down, you come back up, better and stronger than ever, with gifts you never imagined before.

Suzie Humphries

The world is changing constantly, and you are changing too. And as part of God, you are helping to create that change by the very things that change in you. Every breath you take and every beat of your heart signals life changing in you.

You can lie in bed with the covers over your head, but you're still changing. Might as well get up and go with the flow. Choose to live in delight and celebrate what is.

Unleashing Your Creative Genius

Some people find the whole idea of being creative very threatening. Being creative doesn't necessarily mean you are able to paint the Mona Lisa. It means having—and using—the ability to come up with new solutions.

> Genius, in truth, means little more than the faculty of perceiving in an unhabitual way.
> William James

A way to start your creative juices flowing and to unleash your own genius is to break up old patterns of thought and action. Practice with the small stuff. Notice which shoe you habitually tie first, and start with the other. Use your other hand to brush your teeth. Put the pepper on your eggs before the salt.

Notice your small habits, and make conscious decisions to go against them. Whenever Salvador Dali felt his creative juices start to dry up, he wore his shoes on the wrong feet all day.

Write down a problem that has you stumped and list thirty-five different ways to solve it. Don't take it too seriously—go a little crazy and be a little wild. Step outside of your current realm of possibility. Your genius is the fertile soil from which all your dreams grow.

Sometimes we need to push ourselves out of our own self-made ruts in order to see ourselves as creative beings. The easiest way to do that is to challenge either our physical or mental body by an unknown or uncomfortable position. It forces us to release our comfort zone and to look at our lives from a new perspective.

The Genius Within Us

It is interesting to note that in Webster's New World Dictionary, the first description of genius is: "According to ancient Roman belief, a guardian spirit assigned to a person at birth; a tutelary deity." We are all given creative genius as a gift when we are born. We may not know it exists, or deny its existence, but it's there within you. Your creative genius, your essential spirit, gives you natural ability in one or more areas of your life. This genius is available at all times, and when you call upon it it will be there to assist you in all that you wish to accomplish. Even if we think we cannot do something, when we call upon our own creative genius, we sometimes surprise ourselves by the ease with which we can accomplish it. Remember that the genius within you is uniquely yours, and yours alone. Ask your genius to lead you and teach you. Be proud of the genius within and use it well.

If you have never met your creative self, or experienced the results of knowing your own inner genius, it is time to give yourself permission to do so.

> The greatest trouble with most of us is that our demands upon ourselves are so feeble, the call upon the great (genius) within us is so weak and intermittent that it makes no impression upon the creative energies; it lacks the force that transmutes desires into realities.
> Orison Swett Marden

When you tap into your genius power, you'll recognize that it's God's gift to you to share with others. It is within your power to manifest your true self for the benefit of all humanity.

Mark's great mentor and teacher, R. Buckminster Fuller, had a turning point in his life when his call upon his inner genius made all the difference between life and death.

The Shore of Discovery

When Bucky was thirty-two, a combination of terrible events broke his heart and shattered his confidence. His firstborn daughter died, and he and his little family were penniless due to his business failures. He felt as if he had only brought tragedy to the lives he touched.

He left his apartment one cold and windy night with every intention of throwing himself into Lake Michigan, and relieving those he loved of the burden of his presence. He believed that if he died, his wife's family would provide for her and their newborn daughter better than he had.

He stood for many hours on the dark shore, thinking about his life and asking searching questions of his inner genius.

Bucky asked himself, "Do I believe in the possibility of a greater intelligence in Universe than man?"

And he answered his own question, "I am overwhelmed by the certainty that there is. The exquisite design of everything, from the invisible atoms, to the stars in the galaxies, functions with absolute integrity."

Talking to himself and answering his own questions from a place deep within him, he continued. "Do I know best or does God know best whether I am of any value to Universe?"

Once again, the answer came. "You do not have the right to eliminate yourself. You belong to Universe. You will fulfill your purpose in life if you dedicate yourself to serving humanity."

Bucky went home that night with a clear resolve. He would do all he could to reform the environment. He demonstrated the ultimate trust in a higher intelligence: "If the intelligence directing Universe has a use for me, it will not allow us to starve; it will see to it that I am able to carry out my resolve."

His life proved the point. Many times, when he started a new project, people would show up out of the blue at the eleventh hour to back him financially. Nature always provides for her creatures, and he knew he was part of nature. "When you set your own foot upon the right path, support is naturally there," he would tell us.

I was a research assistant to Bucky for seven years, and during that time I grew to respect him as I have no other person on this planet. He dedicated his life to demonstrating what one individual can do.

During his lifetime he created over two thousand inventions including the geodesic dome. He was awarded more than forty honorary degrees, wrote thirty books, and in his eighties still gave two hundred lectures a year.

Because he touched his inner genius one dark night, and discovered his own spiritual self, he became a visionary, humanist, author, scientist, engineer, architect, philosopher—and human treasure.

Mark Victor Hansen

Finding Delight in Your Gifts

Your creative genius is much like the soil in a garden—plant anything that you wish into the soil and it will produce fruit from the plant that you have sown. Likewise, plant your God-given gifts into the soil of your creative genius, and you will reap the rewards of your creative effort. There are people in every walk of life who have recognized and utilized their gifts—they are called masters of their trade. Your gifts are the vehicles through which your creative genius expresses itself.

Every person ever sent to earth by our Creator has great gifts and special talents. A gardener who loves to garden can make plants thrive when no one else can; a dog trainer who has a gift with animals can make even the most stubborn pooch behave.

> If a man is called to be a street sweeper, he should sweep streets even as Michelangelo painted, or Beethoven composed music, or Shakespeare wrote poetry. He should sweep streets so well that all the hosts of heaven and earth will pause to say, here lived a great street sweeper who did his job well.
>
> Martin Luther King, Jr.

Your gifts can be in any area. You may have an ability to comfort other people in times of stress, or be able to put others at ease immediately. Your gifts may be evident to other people in your life, or perhaps not known by anyone but you. Some people have excellent long-term memories or the ability to concentrate so totally that they can shut out all that is going on around them. One gift could be as simple as being able to win a spitting contest—just don't judge yourself, your gifts, and what you can accomplish with them.

Georg Vihos, a noted Detroit painter and art teacher, was once a frightened immigrant boy who was unable to speak English well enough to make friends and feel comfortable. He recounts his story of discovering some of his God-given gifts and finding his place in the world all on the same day.

The Painter

When I was just six years old, I was given the privilege of visiting my first museum and seeing great paintings. The day was glorious and ended with the awareness that my life had changed forever.

After touring the galleries with my classmates, we were given the gift of witnessing a painting come alive before our very eyes. I remember well sitting on the floor cross-legged in the front row. A tall, handsome man appeared with a beret on his head and spoke very clearly: "Good morning. I am an artist, too." I was knocked over with a soft feather. And then he began to paint the most beautiful picture I had ever seen.

The painter worked very fast with big fat brushes stroking thick scoops of color paint on the white canvas surface. Before very long the picture took shape. He was drawing me in beyond my years, into a vivid adventure far in the future. A wonderful-looking sailboat appeared. The sailcloth vessel was on the high seas, with gigantic waves all around it. The sky was yearning for more and more wind. In my imagination I was sailing the boat to a magical island of peace and pleasure. These images were frozen in time and in my active mind.

At that moment, knowing little of art and nothing of the world, I made my promise.

I was knocked over again with a second feather when we were all given tubes of watercolor paint and brushes. The artist told us it was dream paint, not available in stores, and we could paint our dreams with it. My tube contained blue paint.

Afterwards we were taken to the children's museum and were allowed to use our paints. The teacher handed me a book on birds and I was mesmerized by the picture of the bluejay. I copied the whole thing on my piece of paper. It was so good the teacher got very excited and held it up for the whole class to see. Then she put it upon the board. Everyone was praising it and saying how good it was, and my heart opened with joy.

Later I realized that I had had my first one-man show. When the going gets tough, which it always does when you choose the

life of an artist, the image of my little blue bird hanging in an
excellent museum always brings me delight.

Georg Vihos

If you aren't sure what some of your gifts are, think back to the
time when you were in school. In what areas did you excel? What
subjects did you study that seemed to be easier than others? Even
if you did not get perfect grades, were there some things that just
seemed to delight you, lift your spirit, and make your heart sing?
There are as many answers as there are people on the planet, for
all of us have at least one unique gift, or a combination of personal
assets that is ours and ours alone.

Rabbi Harold Kushner urges us to use our gifts. "The circumstances of your life have uniquely qualified you to make a contribution," he said. "And if you don't make that contribution, nobody
else can make it." We are each a thread in the tapestry of life, and
without your gifts, your weaving of your own thread, the tapestry
will be incomplete. That is what Bucky Fuller was talking about
when he said, "You do not belong to you. . . ." The world needs
you—if you don't use your unique gifts, it's like getting an incomplete in life.

Delighting in a Life of Purpose

> What an immense power over life is the power of possess-
> ing distinct aims. The voice, the dress, the look, the very
> motions of a person, define and alter when he or she
> begins to live for a reason.
>
> Elizabeth Stuart Phelps

Life's secret for experiencing true joy and delight comes from
an inner revelation that you are here on earth and in this lifetime
for a reason or a purpose. Every one of us has a unique purpose.
We can choose to become aware of it, or not—the difference to

you is a life of merely surviving—or a life full of vitality, passion, living fully awake and alive, and maybe most importantly, having a sense of your own destiny.

Inspiration

In the summer, when school was out, my mother used to take me to work with her. We'd walk the seven miles back and forth through steaming heat to her job as a maid at the "big house" in town where the family she worked for allowed me to do some yard work. Though it was a long and hot journey, I really enjoyed those walks because we got a chance to talk.

At twelve years old on the brink of my teenage years, I had begun to feel keenly the inequality of being poor and black. Though we were religious, I began to wonder whether God was punishing us for something.

"Mama, why am I black?" I stopped in the middle of the road and blurted it out, unable to keep the question inside me any longer.

My mother was infinitely wise. She looked at me as if she knew that I would eventually ask, and without hesitation she responded, "God is a good God. He made the Heavens and the Earth, He made the great mountains, rivers and oceans. He made all living creatures and He made you. He gave you a beautiful black color. God makes no mistakes, Cleve. You were put here on this Earth for a purpose and you must find it."

Her answer went straight into the deepest levels of my being and I felt the weight of the world, as I knew it then, fall from my shoulders. I was instantly filled with joy and with the knowledge that I was just what God wanted. From that day on, I never asked the question again. My mother's words were engraved on my spirit for the rest of my life. I had been put on Earth like all of God's other creations, and I was proud to be here.

I found my purpose as a physician and as an entertainer, and while it was hard, it was a challenge I knew I'd get through. When things get rough, I revisit that afternoon on that hot steamy Louisiana road and Mama's words are there to lift me up time and time again.

Cleve Francis

When you live a life of purpose you have courage. Nerve. Verve. Spirit. Spunk. The very heart of you becomes excited about life when you discover your purpose. Heartfelt delight enters your life, pushes you beyond fear, and gets you on track with your destiny.

The purpose of life is a life of purpose.

Robert Byrne

Victoria Jackson, who brought delight to millions of people with her riotous performances on *Saturday Night Live*, was faced with some difficult decisions during a turbulent time in her life a few years ago. But she dug deeply within her soul and discovered true happiness had to do with rediscovering her life purpose.

Saturday Afternoon Live

The big blue Florida skies were filled with fluffy white clouds. The flag waved, the national anthem played, and the crowd cheered. I was sitting in the school bleachers with my husband and our one-year-old, watching our daughter Scarlet cheerleading her first game. My husband, Paul, had played football, and I had cheered here long ago under the same wonderful skies. Just as my daughter was now doing, I also had worn a red uniform and shouted, "Red and white is dynamite." And in my senior year, I was homecoming queen.

Before moving back home to Miami, I had been through a time of sadness and loss. I felt that I had lost the life I valued—I missed the creative surge of Los Angeles, where I had lived for twelve years, the beauty of autumn in Connecticut, and the excitement of New York. Most of all, I missed the team effort of acting—the thrill and the joy of creating something new and making people laugh.

But here I was in Miami, and instead of wondering why I wasn't missing the career I loved, I found myself basking in the joy of motherhood and of caring for others. I was delighted in Scarlet's joy as she bounced up and down clapping. I was elated watching my one-year-old laughing with delight that she could climb so many stairs and see her big sister wave at her. My heart filled as I watched Paul glow with pride.

"It's so weird," I said to Paul. "I feel old—and young—all at the same time. How do you feel?"

He turned to me and his eyes smiled. "I feel like we are where we should be," he said.

Then I remembered a poem I had written for our yearbook when we graduated from high school years ago. It was called "A Purpose" and it began:

I started thinking to myself as graduation drew near
What should I be or do in life? What is my purpose here?
I wanted to leave my footprints on the sands of time.
I wanted to have success and be well-known.
I wanted to be rich and great and wanted much to come
From seeds through life that I, myself, had sown.

It was surprising to me how my life had started down that road of fame and fortune, just as my poem had said. But the poem ended in a much different way:

I had thought my purpose
Could be found in things on Earth.
But now I know only God can give
A life that has real worth.
I know my purpose now
And friend, I hope you find it too.
'Cause only then can you have real joy.
Let God give happiness to you.

I realized that after all the years filled with Hollywood's rewards and glamour, all the places I'd been and famous people I'd met, I still believed in the same thing. Happiness was having a *purpose*.

Sometimes my purpose had been to make A's or make Dad proud by competing in gymnastics; sometimes it was to be funny or get on TV or be in a movie, sometimes my purpose was to buy a house. Those brought temporary joy. But my main purpose, through all my life, was to praise God.

When I didn't I was miserable. And when I did, I was happy.

What a glorious Saturday afternoon!

Victoria Jackson

If you are feeling as if something may be missing in your life, you are probably being called upon to discover your purpose. You are being called by that essence of your self that yearns for expression. As you continue to think about your purpose, you may feel a little rumble of excitement. This is your destiny, your path, calling to you through your deepest desires and that which excites you.

Any path is only a path. There is no affront to yourself or others in dropping it if that is what your heart tells you to do. But your decision to keep on the path or to leave it must be free of fear and ambition. I warn you: Look at every path closely and deliberately. Try it as many times as you think necessary. Then ask yourself and yourself alone one question. It is this: Does the path have a heart?. . . Does this path have a heart is the only question. If it does, then the path is good. If it doesn't, it is of no use.

Carlos Castaneda

When you choose to set your direction toward your heart's delight, the circles you have been running around in change into spirals, and you will begin to cycle upward. You will become buoyant, in touch with the delights of your own spirit and beyond. You will meet your destiny halfway.

Peter Marshall, once chaplain of the U.S. Senate, told of an interesting chain of events that served life's purpose and helped fulfill the path of destiny for two great men.

In the Circle of Delight

Many years ago, a father, mother, and their young son journeyed from England into Scotland for a summer vacation. One day the boy found an inviting swimming hole, and like any other boy, took off his clothes and jumped in. Seized with cramps, he shouted for help.

It happened that in a nearby field a farm boy was working, and hearing the cries for help, came running, and diving in, dragged the young English boy out of the water.

The father was very grateful and the next day he called at the farmer's cottage to meet the youth who had saved his son's life.

"What do you plan to do with your life?" he asked.

"Oh, I suppose I'll be a farmer like my father," the boy answered.

"Is there something else you would rather do?"

"Oh, yes, I have always wanted to be a doctor," answered the Scottish boy. "But we are poor people, and we could never afford to pay for my education."

"Never mind that," said the English gentleman. "You shall have your heart's desire and study medicine. Make your plans and I will take care of the costs."

So the boy became a doctor.

In December 1943, Winston Churchill was dangerously ill with pneumonia somewhere in North Africa. His doctor asked Sir Alexander Fleming, the discoverer of the new wonder drug penicillin, to fly over to Africa to attend the sick statesman. Taking off in a fast bomber, Sir Alexander Fleming arrived within a few hours, administered the drug, and for the second time in Churchill's career, saved his life—for it was the young Winston Churchill whom he had pulled out of the swimming hole so many years before.

Peter Marshall

Finding Your Purpose

Ask yourself: What would I do if time and money were not a factor? What would I do with my life if I knew I only had a few (healthy) months to live?

Once you have a hint of your purpose, write it down. Even if you don't feel that your thoughts are complete, writing down your purpose helps clarify and solidify your direction. Everyone should have a written purpose—you will discover what you believe about yourself, create a compelling direction for your path, accumulate support from like-minded people who can help and assist you, feel empowered, and begin to know that you are a person of value.

This popular minister, writer, and lecturer was quite young when she first realized that her purpose in life was to become a spiritual counselor. Her moment of realization took place in a most unlikely place—a New York nightclub.

The Land and Sky Inside

When I was in my early twenties I went with a date to a nightclub in New York. Appearing there were two talented young musicians, Daryl Hall and John Oates. . . . [T]heir music had the fabulous impact of fresh beginnings and new sounds.

Something happened to me that night. I had been to many concerts before, but I had never experienced as I did then the transcendent way a musician can bring an entire room into a single heartbeat. I remember thinking, "They're priests, that's what they really are. They're priests." They weren't taking me on a magic-carpet ride to music. Music was the magic carpet on which they were taking me somewhere else, that somewhere else in the land and sky inside ourselves. It's the purpose of our lives to find that place and stay in it. . . . I became enthralled with the idea that a human being could create a space through music or anything else, where people's hearts are harmonized and lifted up. I knew that was what music did, and literature and philosophy and all art. . . . What gave a person the magician's wand, that he could wield such awesome power and transport whole groups of people to an enchanted land?

I fell in love with the thought that a human life could be a priestly conduit, a connecting link between earth and sky. . . . [A]s I grew and stumbled and, most important, as I began to love and be loved, I realized that the ultimate priest is the lover inside us, and the ultimate priesthood is the role of friend and loved one.

Marianne Williamson

When you come to the point in your life that you are using your genius to the fullest, your gifts become highly marketable when matched to the needs of humanity. If you think about the most successful people you know, you will realize that they live in harmony with their highest calling. Success means more than being number one—it means living a life of purpose, experiencing a deep sense of fulfillment, and having a wellspring of delight from following the pathway of your destiny.

Your Window to the Sky

The future belongs to those who believe in the beauty of their dreams.

Eleanor Roosevelt

At thirty-five, he had nothing but stacks of rejections and bills, a dream abandoned, and a broken family. Not a promising situation, but out of the blue the key to success came into the life of this famous writer, and he went on to have a brilliant career.

Turning Point

He could never remember a day without his dream. Ever since he was a little boy, he wanted to become a writer. His mother knew he would, too, and encouraged him every step of the way. She reminded him time and time again that some day he would be a spellbinder. They shared the delight of his dream. His gift of writing took him through journalism school at the University of Missouri, and his future looked promising.

His world changed overnight when his mother died unexpectedly and the joy went out of his work. The war was on, so he signed up for the Air Corps. When he returned, a much decorated fighter pilot, he resumed his work. He married, bought a home, established himself in all the ways a young man should, but his writing met with nothing but rejection. It wasn't supposed to be this way.

In desperation he turned to the insurance business. Though he worked very hard at sales, he barely covered his expenses. A career in sales could never engage the best of him—neither his talents nor his dreams. He was depressed, on a downward spiral that took him through alcoholism, the loss of his house, his wife, daughter, and job.

With nothing left to lose, he decided to end it all. But fate had other ideas. As this dispirited man headed for the gun dealer, he stumbled into a library instead, and found himself in front of a shelf where a book called *Success Through a Positive Mental Attitude* seemed to jump into his shaking hands. The book, by W. Clement Stone and Napoleon Hill, is one of the classics of motivational literature. He devoured the book as if it were food, and it nourished his heart and soul.

He was so impressed with the book that he applied for work with W. Clement Stone's insurance company. They gave him a chance—he received training and became manager of eight salespersons in Maine. His sales team set records, even though they had to contend with deep snows, blustering winds, and long distances between customers. His experience in Maine spurred him on to write a training manual, *How to Sell Insurance to Rural People*, and he sent it to the home office with a prayer.

His prayer was answered. The home office recognized his ability and moved him to Chicago to write sales bulletins. He was writing full-time again, and was filled with delight.

W. Clement Stone himself took notice of the talented writer

and invited him to become editor of "Success Unlimited Magazine," at the time a house organ for the company's employees. Before long, the quality of the magazine improved so much that it went beyond insurance agents to 250,000 general subscribers. The busy editor had very little time to write, but finally managed to do a piece on golfer Ben Hogan.

Several months later, and hundreds of miles away, Frederick Fell, a New York publisher, made a trip to his dentist. A copy of "Success Unlimited" just happened to be in the waiting room, and Fell picked it up. Before he could get into the dentist's chair, he decided to make an offer to the outstanding author of the article on Ben Hogan to publish any book he decided to write.

And so the career of Og Mandino finally went into high gear. Within two years' time, *The Greatest Salesman in the World* was published and reached the hearts of readers everywhere. Mandino went on to write several more books, all of which were best-sellers, and to become an enormously successful motivational speaker. His natural talents and abilities, coupled with his experience of life from its darkest depths to its most delightful heights, gave him the depth and wisdom he needed to become a spellbinder who changes people's lives.

Mark Victor Hansen

Discover Your Heart's Delight

That impossible dream you dreamed when you were young but got talked out of, the one you thought you outgrew, might be the key to awakening your genius. That special talent you never followed through on might be an important source of delight, the one you should commit to. That old dream might be the one thing that will bring the magic of meaning to your life.

Suppose you loved singing as a child, were part of the school chorus, and dreamed of being a singer when you grew up. Nothing gave you more pleasure. Now that you're an adult, you think you don't have time for such hobbies. You have your work and your family and a million other serious things that come first. You get things done, but wonder why your life lacks luster. Perhaps you should resurrect your dream.

A friend of ours tells of her father who grew up on a ranch in New Mexico a thousand miles from a city. As a boy he loved to sing and often climbed to the platform on the windmill to serenade the cattle. Years later, after he married and his business was thriving, he moved to New York to take music lessons at Juilliard Academy of the Arts. Then he became lead tenor at Manhattan's Riverside Church for two years. He went back to his business in the West after he'd satisfied his deep inner need to develop his talent. Much to the delight of the townspeople, he sang at local events for the rest of his life.

When you cease to dream you cease to live.
Malcolm S. Forbes

Are those hidden dreams always about lofty artistic and creative activities? What if you just love your business? There are elements of spiritual delight even in ordinary activities if you bring your highest intentions to them. You don't have to give up your everyday life to find your window to the sky.

Emmy Award–winning actress Doris Roberts had an event in her life that helped her realize that when you are doing what you love, you can create a connection with others that benefits everyone.

If I Can Laugh

After years of performing on Broadway, where an actor can see the audience and feel connected with them, I began to work in television. My work was challenging and enjoyable, but I never knew how it affected people.

In the series *Angie*, I played the role of Angie's mother, who raised two daughters with the proceeds of her newsstand. In one segment, I was going off to Atlantic City to gamble. It was quite a humorous situation, and I had great fun with it.

A few years later, I received a letter from a woman who had seen a rerun of the show and wanted me to know what I had done for her.

"I hope this reaches you so you know how you changed my life," the letter said. "I had decided that I didn't want to live. You see, I had been diagnosed with multiple sclerosis, and had been sitting alone in a dark room, unwilling to even eat with my family or take any part in life.

"Then one day I saw you on *Angie*—the time you were going to Atlantic City—and I heard myself laugh out loud. It was the most amazing thing. I suddenly realized that if I can laugh, maybe there is some life left in me after all."

The woman went on to tell me that she had ended her long period of isolation and had gone back to college.

Of course, I wrote to her immediately to thank her for letting me know that I had indeed touched her life.

Later a photo arrived in the mail of a smiling woman in a graduation gown. I was delighted to learn that my new friend had graduated *cum laude* from college.

I believe that when we do what we love to do, we affect other people in ways we don't know and can't understand at the time. Perhaps we never will. But it happens. I was very grateful to know I had touched someone's life in the process of having such a great time myself.

Doris Roberts

When you bring this kind of passion to your work, chances are you do it very well. But if it's not your heart's delight, you may succeed, but you may spend a lot of time running around in circles getting nowhere. The rewards may come at the end in the form of money, but how much better it would be if you were happy with what you were doing every step of the way.

Modern philosopher Sam Keen wrote in *Hymns to an Unknown God*, "You can be relatively certain that if you hate doing something, it is not your vocation. Joseph Campbell advised people who had lost their way to follow their bliss. Augustine said, 'Love and do what you want.' I know people for whom tuning an engine is a vocation, cooking a fine soup, designing an elegant house, running a day-care center, nursing the terminally sick, running a political campaign, raising organic garlic. I know of few jobs or professions that are not spiritual callings for some who practice them."

Meditate on Your Heart

Here's a meditation to help you discover your heart's delight. Sit comfortably and bring your awareness to the heart. Picture it as a symbol of love and joy. See it smiling. What brings a smile to your heart?

You might picture your heart as a valentine, or as a peach, which has the shape of a heart, or as the word *love*. Bring your hands over your heart if that helps you focus. Thank your heart for all the wonderful work it does for you, and tell it you'd like to give it its greatest desire. You might see images you consider irrelevant at first, like chocolate sundaes or bouquets of flowers. If you do, promise yourself that you'll buy flowers more often or have a chocolate sundae once in a while as a treat.

Go deeper. If you've been denying yourself your heart's delight for a long time, you may not get a response until your heart knows you're sincere. Take five minutes a day to focus on your heart and the energy of love. In that quiet place of the heart your dream lives. Eventually it will come forward. Give it value when it does. It is the most valuable part of you.

Judy, a social worker, meditated on her heart's delight and saw a huge closet filled with so many clothes that there was a revolving rack like a dry cleaner's to hold them all. They were all ballet costumes. She remembered that when she was very young she wanted to take dance lessons, but her parents said no. But there was the dream, packed away neatly in plastic bags, waiting for her. She was thirty-eight and a little overweight, but she went and found an exercise class that taught some graceful ballet movements. She got season tickets to the local ballet, joined the Friends of Ballet organization, volunteered to usher one night a month, and helped sell season subscriptions. She bought music from the great ballets, had some beautiful posters of ballerinas framed for the wall of her office—in short, she dove into ballet as an avocation. It brought her enormous delight, improved her health and her attitude, expanded her social life, brought her zest and joy every day, and contributed to the future of ballet in her city. All this happiness from a dream buried in her heart and liberated in a few five-minute meditations.

When ideas, dreams, and visions come out of the blue, some people take them very seriously indeed. Here is the story of a sickly young man whose dreams changed his life and the lives—and dreams—of everyone in the world.

One-Dream Man

One autumn day in 1900, when he was just eighteen, Robert Goddard was pruning a cherry tree when he felt the urge to lean against the trunk and close his eyes. He nodded off into that mysterious state of consciousness between waking and sleeping, and out of the blue he had a kind of epiphanic vision of an odd-looking machine that moved faster and faster and rose into the air, taking people to Mars.

When he awoke from this dream state, he knew he would design rockets and make them soar into the sky. He had read the science-fiction book *The War of the Worlds*, by H. G. Wells, the year before and was intrigued with the possibility of traveling through space. Now he knew that he would dedicate his life to making it happen.

Robert's health had been poor, but with his powerful dream leading the way, he rallied and completed his studies, knowing he must realize his vision. He earned a doctorate in physics and went to work at Princeton University as a research fellow. But in 1913, he contracted tuberculosis, and doctors told him he had only two weeks to live.

"I'm not going to die," he told the doctors. "I have too much to do."

Inspired by his dream, he refused to allow disease to conquer him. After a year of rest, Goddard was back at work and received research grants from the government to carry on his experiments. In the process of developing a high-altitude rocket, he developed, at the request of the military, a rocket weapon known to servicemen everywhere as the bazooka. But this was a sidetrack for the young man who dreamed of sending vehicles into space.

Goddard ordered a 60-foot windmill frame from Sears, Roebuck and Company, then tested rocket after rocket. In 1926 he launched a liquid-propelled rocket that went 184 feet into the air. Newspapers called him crazy, and after one of his rockets crashed and burned, a headline read: MOON ROCKET MISSES TARGET BY 238,799½ MILES. Nevertheless, Goddard's small rockets proved to be the forerunners of every rocket, missile, and space capsule we have launched.

Goddard devoted his life to advancing rocket science and even helped give birth to jet-propelled airplanes. Through decades of research, he was singlehandedly responsible for development of all the important aspects of modern rocketry. Whenever he could, he went back to that cherry tree on October 19, the anniversary of his original vision, to celebrate the magic moment of his "scientific birthday" and his emergence as a "one-dream man."

Today Robert Goddard lives in history as the father of American rocket science.

Barbara Nichols

You'll never go wrong if you meditate on the heart. As the Chinese say, "The original impulse of the heart is always good." Open your heart to your own deepest dreams. The ones you came for will always hold elements of spirit, of the goodness, truth, and beauty that Plato spoke of.

3

Reach for the Stars

A man's doubts and fears are his worst enemies.

WILLIAM WRIGLEY, JR.

Dedicate yourself to the good you deserve and
desire for yourself.
Give yourself peace of mind.
You deserve to be happy.
You deserve delight.

MARK VICTOR HANSEN

*W*hen we were children we knew the stars were there to hear our wishes and to help them come true. Somehow, in the complex process of growing up, we may have forgotten our precious heritage of the stars and stopped reaching for the highest and best. We may even think those who do are "exceeding themselves."

"We're unconsciously afraid of a reaction against us if we dare to shine fully, embrace joy, and permit ourselves to have too great a life," Marianne Williamson wrote. "The injunction against winning is subtle but strong, so we ourselves make sure no one will be able to accuse us of having broken the great unspoken rule: Do not experience heaven on earth."

When you have those fears of your own greatness and strength, your delight may diminish and your life slow to a crawl.

At some level of your consciousness, you may not believe that you have a right to happiness—at least not a lot of it. We forget that according to the Declaration of Independence of the United States every citizen has the right to "life, liberty, and the pursuit of happiness." Our founding fathers were thinking of *you* when they wrote that classic line.

"We fear our highest impulses quite as much, perhaps more, than we fear our lowest," psychologist Jean Hardy points out. "We may fear our greatness and strength—and may fail to recognize the strength and courage with which many people, in all areas of society, live their lives."

You have a right to delight. Each person was born to become fully, delightfully human, though we've learned that we are "only" human. Being fully human means becoming everything we can be. It means being lovingly aware of ourselves and others, and leading a conscious, compassionate life.

You deserve all of life's wonderful options: You deserve to be healthy, loving, loved, and beloved. Successful, prosperous, rich, and abundant. Wise, witty, and wonderful. Intelligent, strong, and self-confident. Enthusiastic, enlightened, enriched, edified, and entertained. You deserve a splendid home, terrific relationships, peace of mind, full self-expression, and the total joy of living. Life is yours to be experienced and expressed with complete delight.

Happiness . . . is not a destination: it is a manner of traveling. Happiness is not an end in itself. It is a by-product of working, playing, loving and living.

Haim Ginott

When happiness comes knocking, you may not let it in. Something keeps you from opening the door. What holds you back? What are your barriers to living that spirited, spiritual life of joy and meaning, accomplishment and satisfaction?

Self-Esteem

Our feelings of self-worth, self-esteem, and self-respect are the keys that either unlock the door of happiness or cause it to be forever rusted shut. According to Nathaniel Branden, author of *The Psychology of Self-Esteem,* "The nature of man's self-evaluation has profound effects on his thinking process, emotions, desires, values and goals." By the time we all reach adulthood, we have created a concept of who we are to ourselves based upon our childhood experiences and understanding of the world as we were growing up.

If we believe that the world is a supportive and loving reality, we are more willing to seek out new and challenging experiences that will allow us to use our inner genius and our gifts to their full extent. Contrarily, if our world seems to be a hostile and oppressive environment from which we must continually seek to escape, the promise of daily delight will seem out of reach.

Most of us have some deep-rooted feelings of low self-esteem. Once in a while, feelings of helplessness and temporary groundless fears seem to be in control of our lives; in fact, our very souls. We need to remember that these feelings of low self-worth didn't happen overnight. They are the result of years of negative programming during a time in our lives when we were most vulnerable.

The good news is that low self-esteem can be overcome regardless of our "now" experience. Since these feelings have evolved from a failure to use your mind properly, the only answer is to relearn, reprogram, and reinspire your thinking.

Your true inner beingness, your spiritual core, always has and always will resonate with the good that the universe is. You are on your own side. Once your conscious decision has been made to face the challenge of your inner growth, life will never be the same.

Sometimes it takes someone else to believe in us more than we believe in ourselves before we are willing to accept the challenge of growth.

Trouble Maker

Like a lot of the students at Jobs for Youth, Kim was a high-risk girl who came from a very precarious situation. When she was a young teenager she was kicked out of the house, and ended up living with friends. Her peers were very negative and unsupportive of her goals. In class, Kim contested everything I said. At nineteen, she was very smart, but angry and full of emotion.

With students like this, you must let them know what they can do well. Though Kim had a hard time dealing with people, she was an excellent writer. I once praised her writing and she frowned at me and didn't respond. She was very antagonistic.

As time went on, I discovered that Kim was able to see problems that other students couldn't see, and would offer solutions. It wasn't always in a positive light, but she always had relevant observations to make. I took her aside after class and told her, "You really have an ability to see what the problem is and offer a solution."

"You're just telling me that, you don't really believe it" was her answer.

"No, Kim, *you* don't really believe it" was all I could think of to say.

When she finished the class, I must admit I wasn't sorry to see her go. I was relieved that I would not have to deal with her anymore. I wasn't sure that I had gotten through to her, so before she left I met with her and told her I wanted to leave her with something she could hold on to. She told me that people tell her: "I don't know why you're going to school at Jobs for Youth, you'll never be successful. You should give up."

I said, "Kim, one day you will have to decide what you're going to believe. It's up to you." She gave me that cold look again, and I didn't feel we'd connected.

About four months later, Kim called to thank me. She had gotten a job at the phone company. She never thought she'd get this job, she told me. "To tell you the truth, in the interview they asked why they should hire me, and I couldn't think of anything except what you said. So I told them Miss McHugh thinks I'm good at solving problems. They hired me as a troubleshooter. Now I believe you."

Ann-Marie McHugh

We can control our mind's activity and growth with the assignments we give it. Looking at our fears in a rational manner, setting believable and achievable goals, using daily affirmations to control our negative self-talk, learning to forgive ourselves and others, and preserving our internal integrity will lead us forward on the path of delight. No one said it will be easy, but you are worth the effort it takes to succeed.

To preserve an unclouded capacity for the enjoyment of life is an unusual moral and psychological achievement. Contrary to popular belief, it is not the prerogative of mindlessness, but the exact opposite: It is the reward of self-esteem.

Nathaniel Branden

See Yourself in the Best Light

Most of us need to learn to truly appreciate ourselves. Self-appreciation is an art that develops your sense of perspective. Experience and accept yourself in the now, and then see yourself as the person you want to be.

Friendship with oneself is all important, because without it one cannot be friends with anyone else in the world.

Eleanor Roosevelt

We can take a hint, watching our young children. Their delight with life and themselves can teach us how to truly appreciate who we are.

Buddha on a Bike

At the age of three, I was sure that Justin had a Buddha consciousness. He was very gentle and content with life.

But a trip to the toy store brought out another facet of his being. When I bought him a bright red two-wheeled bike, Justin became a famous motorcycle racer overnight, exhibiting all the endurance and grit it takes to win.

The bike was only ten inches off the ground, so Justin was a "low rider." He put on his helmet and ran outside. First he rode around in little circles, then he stepped back, took a running start from about five feet back, jumped onto the seat—and fell off. He continued jumping on and falling off without whining or complaining. I thought, "My word, he needs airbags all around him." Finally, Justin jumped on and stayed on the seat.

I was delighted. He'd made it. But Justin had more to achieve.

"Help me start like they do at the races, Grandma," Justin shouted over his shoulder as he started making engine sounds.

"One. Two. Three," I counted.

He gave me a thumbs-up sign and took off as fast as he could.

I realized I was not watching a three-year-old on a ten-inch bike, I was watching a world-class motorcycle racer. Just as the acorn knows it is a mighty oak, this child knows he is a racer. He sees what he is becoming, not what he is.

In *Jonathan Livingston Seagull*, Jonathan was learning to fly from place to place in a split second. Chiang, his teacher, gave him great wisdom. "To fly as fast as thought to anywhere that is," he said, "you must begin by knowing that you have already arrived."

Justin was too young to have read the book, but something in him—in all of us—knows of true potential. We each have it in us to be the best of whatever we wish to be.

Mary Omwake

You can give yourself inner applause for everything in life you've ever mastered, every kind word you've uttered, generous act you've performed. Everything you've ever done deserves applause, because you've always done the best you knew how. Inner applause is a source of inner power. Know yourself at your best, even when others doubt you. Deep down in the deepest reaches of your soul, *you* know what a delight you are.

If . . . I have lost every other friend on earth, I shall at least have one friend left, and that friend shall be down inside of me.

Abraham Lincoln

Accepting Your Delightful You

If the idea that you are a delight makes you blush, you're just having a little embarrassment attack, which is a mild form of fear. To get over your embarrassment tell a selected friend, "I'm a delight," over and over until you laugh and yawn yourself free from that embarrassment. It's just a little distress pattern. All your friend has to do is look at you with full attention and complete approval, nod his or her head in agreement, and smile. Your natural discharge mechanism will get rid of your distress. Then trade places with your friend and give her equal time to do the same thing.

Creating Clarity

Once you have taken responsibility for finding your own path, you can live a spirited, spiritual life twenty-four hours a day. You will create values as well as value, and develop character along with skills.

Most importantly, you can and must set your own goals. We are beginning to understand more clearly that everything we do affects the whole of humanity. Any goals we set for ourselves are goals for everyone on the planet. Og Mandino wrote in *The Greatest Miracle in the World*, "We share the common goal of making this world a better place for all of God's creatures!" Goals empower you to do more for yourself, others, and all of humanity.

When you create time to write your goals, your mind will prioritize them for you. Your goals will awaken new ways to accomplish more in less time. Within months you will feel new peace of mind, increased personal power, a strong sense of direction, and part of a force for good in the universe.

> Far away there in the sunshine are my highest aspirations. I may not reach them, but I can look up and see their beauty, believe in them, and try to follow where they lead.
> Louisa May Alcott

There are times in everyone's life when circumstances force us to grow, learn more about ourselves, and create a new future.

Igniting My Delight

"Now what will I do?" I wondered as I heard the news. My job had vanished overnight, and so had my boss's. I would certainly miss being with Buckminster Fuller, the man I considered the modern Leonardo da Vinci. But now I had to find a new way to make a living.

"Go out and do what needs to be done that no one else is doing—something that would better everyone," Fuller told me. I had learned so much from him, I decided to build geodesic domes based on his design. I thought surely the world needed these fascinating and practical domes.

I can look back and see that I was coming from such low self-esteem I thought I was supposed to be just like Bucky. I had two master's degrees, but didn't have a real sense of myself yet. So I went into the geodesic dome business, and before long, I was totally broke. At the time it was my worst experience—yet in retrospect, it was my best.

I lost my apartment so I slept on a friend's floor in a sleeping bag. I didn't have enough money to buy food and all I could afford was bread and peanut butter. I ate peanut butter until my tongue stuck to the roof of my mouth. I was lucky enough to have a car, an ancient VW Beetle with a pitted windshield and no wipers. I bought 25 cents worth of gas at a time, which is all I could afford from the few dollars I picked up unloading railroad cars. One day I looked at the side of the boxes I was unloading. Toilet Paper, it said. What a humbling day that was.

The car radio didn't work, and my negative self-talk was really getting me. It was so bad, I decided to actually play a tape a friend had loaned me on the little tape player I kept under the seat of the car. I'd had the tape for some time, but felt I didn't need advice from anyone. Unloading toilet paper really got to me, though, so I started to listen.

The tape was by a motivational speaker named Cavett Roberts, who said things like "You are the cause or you are the effect." And, "You are the creature of circumstances or the creator of circumstances."

"What if that's true?" I wondered—and realized that Roberts was right on the money. I had created this bankruptcy. And now, I decided, I was going to uncreate it and go onward and upward. I was ready to learn.

"*Write your goals,*" Roberts said on the tape. I wrote everything I could think of that I wanted to be, have, do, and contribute. Suddenly my life seemed to unfold before me.

"Holy cow!" I said after making my list. "I really want to become a speaker." Buckminster Fuller was such a mesmerizing, enchanting speaker—it was one of the things I admired most about him. And I believed I could do it, too. I wrote my mission statement and never looked back: "I want to talk to people who care, about things that matter, to make a profound, positive difference in their lives."

Then I wrote to Cavett Roberts and volunteered to be his personal chauffeur. I would be happy to drive him around the city if he ever came to New York. Much to my delight he took me up on my offer. I picked him up in my pitted, permanently air-conditioned VW and he never batted an eye, even though he was worth millions. I barraged him with questions and he answered every one of them. We continued our acquaintance by mail, and he unfailingly answered every one of my letters. When he founded the National Speakers Association he invited me to come to the first meeting—and that was the beginning of my career.

Since then I've talked to almost two million people in person, and it's the delight of my life. I have so much fun traveling, meeting people, and helping them get their own delight ignited, it doesn't seem like work at all. If I hadn't been fired from my job as a research assistant, gone through bankruptcy, and learned to set goals, I would never have become the person I was meant to be.

Mark Victor Hansen

> Even if you're on the right track, you'll get run over if you
> just sit there.
>
> Will Rogers

Goal setting does require work—sometimes it is the hardest work there is—thinking, choosing, and rechoosing. Think thoroughly through life's most important question: *What do I really want?* Your subconscious mind wants and needs your conscious mind to tell it which direction to take. God created our minds as teleological instruments—human beings are problem-having, problem-solving animals that need objectives. Acknowledge your true desires and heart's wishes, and be unafraid to express them to yourself.

> The indispensable first step to getting the things you want
> out of life is this: Decide what you want.
>
> Ben Stein

Clarity of decision and desire backed with decisive action is personal power. Establish a fifteen-minute daily time for setting your goals. Early in the morning when your mind is fresh and clear or late at night just prior to sleep is preferable. Write your easy ideas first. Remember and remind yourself that great goals attract great energy. You have the tools to make outrageous plans and to then discover outrageous solutions.

Brian Boitano had dreamed of skating in the Olympics since he was a boy. In 1988, he accomplished that goal, winning a gold medal. He had other dreams too. When he was asked "What do you want?" he was ready with an outrageous answer.

Beyond Delight

Winning the Olympics was incredibly exciting, but skating on a glacier was an experience beyond delight. It touched my soul.

After the Olympics I was given the opportunity to do a television special, and during the preliminary meetings I was asked what I would like to do. I didn't have to stop and think.

"Go to Alaska and skate on a glacier."

In October 1988, I flew by helicopter into the Alaskan wilderness with a television crew. We landed on a remote and isolated glacier. Our headquarters were located in a tiny cabin, the only man-made shelter within hundreds of miles. First, the television crew rigged up a sound system with huge speakers, which they placed outside on the edge of the glacier so I could hear music as I skated. Then they erected a warming tent beside the glacier. It was about three feet high and six feet long, and I had to crawl inside.

In the afternoon, when the sun was directly overhead, I made the long trek down to the ice, expecting it to be uneven and covered with dirt, leaves, or gravel as outdoor ice usually is. But to my amazement the ice was smooth and so crystal clear that I could see boulders six feet down.

The temperature and wind chill factor were 30 degrees below zero. I was only allowed to skate for ten minutes at a time before going inside the warming tent. There, I was wrapped in thermal blankets between segments.

On the ice, I scarcely felt the cold, skimming along the surface without a barrier, surrounded by majestic mountains. There was no sound except the music reverberating across the ice. It was pristine and pure, and for those moments I felt a union with nature unlike anything I had experienced before or since. I was so totally immersed in the moment that I was unaware of the helicopter cameras high overhead.

Skating on the Alaskan glacier was both a high point in my life and a lesson. It showed me that winning the Olympics was to be a starting point rather than an end. I think life is a matter of constantly finding new beginnings, new challenges, different glaciers. If, through my skating, I can empower people to face their own challenges and find their own moments of pure delight, then I feel my efforts are worthwhile.

Brian Boitano

Setting Goals

Set big goals and break them down into more easily accomplished daily parts. By accomplishing big desires and plans a little at a time, you will strengthen your self-confidence. Satisfaction and fulfillment are the by-products of moving in the direction of your heart's desire. We all need a regular daily sense of accomplishment, of moving forward.

The next time you go to the store, buy a spiral-bound, lined notebook for your personal goal setting. Get started *now*.

- Mental Goals: the books I will read, audio or video tapes I will review, music I will listen to, seminars I will experience, courses I will take
- Health Goals: my desired weight and measurements, my daily exercise program, my diet and nutrition, my sleep regimen, my playtime
- Emotional Goals: accept my feelings, develop courage, offer understanding to others, speak my truth without anger, praise others
- Financial Goals: the income I desire, savings I want, the investments I would like, where I will tithe, projects and causes I will support, my net profit

- Career Goals: choose the career of my heart's desire, discover how to become more effective, list contacts I want to develop, promotions I want
- Family Goals: house chores in which I participate, leisure activities, shared time with my mate, shared time with children, scheduled time with parents, grandparents
- Social Goals: people I would like to meet, people I want to know better, friends I want to keep in touch with, entertaining I would like to do
- Spiritual Goals: schedule time for prayers and/or meditations; when and where I will attend church, temple, or synagogue; read spiritually uplifting literature; time for personal introspection

Writing your goals will banish your fear of failure—and your fear of success. The hardest part is starting; begin at once whether you are ready or not. Don't worry about punctuation and grammar—your written goals are for you and you alone. Every time you look at your goals, plan to set more; some will die a natural death, others will flourish, and still others will transcend what you have written. There are times when the universe will serve you better than you could ever have imagined.

> Once you make a decision, the universe conspires to make it happen.
>
> Ralph Waldo Emerson

Shannon Miller had been headed to the Olympics since she had started gymnastics at age five, and she won the silver medal in 1992. But on the way to the Olympics, she and her family had other goals to reach. Here is the story of how their prayers were answered.

Oklahoma OK

The thrill of finishing first at the Olympic trials and earning a place on the USA Women's Gymnastics Team was a dream I had been working for all my life. But because a dislocated elbow had prevented me from qualifying until the last minute, no reservations had been made for my family. We only had a few weeks to arrange for transportation and a place to stay—and to find money enough to take my whole family to Barcelona for the Olympic games.

The Gymnastics Federation offered room and board for two persons, but we decided that if my brother and sister couldn't go, my parents wouldn't go either. Troy and Tessa had spent too many years sharing in the trials and tribulations of my gymnastics career to miss out on the rewards. My Olympic dream had been my parents' dream and my brother's and sister's dream as well. After sharing years of work and sacrifice, I wanted them to share the thrill of the Olympic games. We had come this far as a family, and that is how it would be. The Millers were going to Barcelona! But it would take at least $25,000 to get the whole family there.

I needed floor music and choreography, many workout and competition leotards, warm-up suits, plus expenses for travel and hotels. There was little left in the savings account, and the games were barely a month away. We had only a few weeks to arrange for transportation and a place to stay—and to find the money to pay for it.

"How will we get to Barcelona?" my mother asked on the way home from the trials. We didn't have time to wonder. As we walked in the door, the phone was ringing. It was Pam, the mother of a friend of mine. A businessman in her office building had purchased airline tickets to Barcelona for the Olympics and reserved rooms in Salou, a little town about 60 miles from Barcelona. He offered them all to us for half price! And so it began, the most incredible outpouring of generosity you could ever imagine.

Out of the blue, several banks in Edmond, my home town, and in nearby Oklahoma City, called and asked how they could help. Much to our delight, the bank where my mom worked organized a fund-raising drive. They placed a large ad in the local paper letting everyone know we needed help. With the help of a local T-shirt company, which sold shirts to the bank at a large discount, the bank designed a shirt with an Olympic flame on it announcing, "I helped the Millers get to Barcelona." The shirts immediately sold out and the bank had to reorder several more times.

The local radio stations made frequent announcements about fund-raising events. The television stations got together and held a benefit softball game. A local store donated food for the concession stand, and my friends from school worked at the stand and did cheerleading routines. It seemed that the whole town had caught Olympic Fever!

A "fun park" in Edmond raised funds with a golf tournament. The father of one of my friends convinced his company, Texaco, to help, and even though they don't donate to individuals, they made an exception in our case. The list of contributors goes on and on. It seemed that everyone in Oklahoma sent in donations to make sure I had a chance to participate and bring honor to my home state.

In less than four weeks, we were able to pay for our airline tickets, hotels, and many of our expenses. American Express came in with some spending money in the form of travelers' checks. It all worked out better than we had ever imagined.

My family brought the spirit of the people of Oklahoma with them to Barcelona. And a vibrant spirit it is—people willing to give of themselves so that our family could be there to share in my dreams. I'm so proud to be part of such a generous, thoughtful, and loving community.

But the story doesn't end here. After we got home, we realized we had raised more than $35,000 and had $11,000 left. I had the wonderful experience of donating these extra funds to the Special Olympics to help disadvantaged youngsters know the joy of participating in sports events.

Shannon Miller

One last recommendation for goal setting: Tell your family and friends about your innermost desires and goals only when you believe in advance that they will support, benefit, encourage, excite, and help you move toward your dreams just as Shannon's family did. Your goals are for your eyes only unless you choose to share them. There are people, even those closest to us, who are willing to ridicule our ambitions and shoot down our dreams.

You control your future, your destiny. What you think about comes about. By recording your dreams and goals on paper, you set in motion the process of becoming the person you most want to be. Put your future in good hands— your own.

Mark Victor Hansen

Self-Talk

He who would be useful, strong, and happy must cease to be a passive receptacle for the negative, beggarly, and impure streams of thought; and as a wise householder commands his servants and invites his guests, so must he learn to command his desires and to say, with authority, what thoughts he shall admit into the mansion of his soul.

James Allen

Your mind acquires habits of thought, which play like internal tapes over and over again. Negative thoughts, known as negative self-talk, are distress patterns that circulate through your mind like dark clouds and prevent you from experiencing the shining truth of love, possibilities, and delight—all the good things that life holds for you. You may not be aware that it is even happening, but it affects your life every minute of every day.

When you begin to want to control your mind's activity, the first thing you will notice is the self-talk on your old "tapes." Really listen carefully to the words you have been saying internally to yourself over and over. "I'm not good enough." "I'll never be able to do it." "I don't deserve it." Consciously listen. It won't hurt you, they have been playing subliminally anyway. You might as well know what has been working against you below the threshold of your conscious awareness.

This inner speech, your thoughts, can cause you to be rich or poor, loved or unloved, happy or unhappy, attractive or unattractive, powerful or weak. . . .

Ralph Charell

The inner speech and self-image we create, or re-create, shape and mold the life we have or desire.

Just Be One

A score or more years ago when I was striving to become a management consultant, the magic of "just being" came home to me—literally.

At the time my family was young, which added pressures on me to succeed. I perceived my life as revolving around learning how to be a consultant and I wasn't sure I was doing well with my self-schooling. "Don't *try* to be a consultant," my wife, Louise, kept saying. "Just be one." For months her words didn't register. What did she mean? It didn't sound reasonable; my logic blocked me. "Just be one," indeed.

But the blockage wasn't total. The audaciousness of the idea appealed to me. Some of what she was trying to tell me seeped through. I finally started to listen. Hmmm, "just be one!" As that sank in, something happened to my practice. The focus on "how to become one" gradually dissolved, replaced by a clear view of what I was actually doing.

An internal shift occurred. A different spirit began to take over. My internal dialogues began to match reality: "I am now working as a consultant and doing quite well at it." Attention shifted from the work I was not *yet* doing to appreciating my *present* work.

As I grew to experience myself as a consultant, I realized the long-sought-after leap had already happened. Somewhere along the way I had bumped over from not-there-yet to there. I was already on the other side of the gap. I saw things differently, and naturally people looked at me differently.

My internal state rearranged itself to align with its "new" truth. My image, thoughts, and actions just rematerialized in the new place. Work became the delight I had hitherto hoped for. Naturally, quality improved.

Clients felt all this. As I changed my self-talk, I came to believe in myself and so did they. Suddenly I was off and running, not toward something new, but *as* something new.

Jack Hawley

Kaye Olson, who presents workshops in the Midwest on how to have more energy, suggests that you intercept negative self-talk in your mind right away. First, listen to it. Then shout STOP! Use imagery to divert your mind, by visualizing something beautiful. Or take several deep breaths. Count to ten. Play music. Go for a walk. Most importantly, replace unwanted thoughts with positive messages.

Find a motivational speaker—a minister, priest, or rabbi—who has a positive message that inspires you, and buy his or her tapes. Every time you feel that "the chattering monkey" in your mind has the better of you, listen to your tapes. Listen in your car on the way to work and listen in the bathroom while you get ready. The good thing about a tape is that the tape will encourage and uplift you from a completely nonjudgmental point of view. The information is not slanted or personalized for you—it is just healthy input for your brain that you can choose to use or not.

> The more man meditates upon good thoughts, the better will be his world and the world at large.
>
> Confucius

Write declaration statements and put them in the corner of your mirror where you do your makeup, or shave. Tape the statements to the dashboard of your car. The effect is somewhat like a subliminal message, and the positive input will plant itself into the fertile soil of your mind without much work on your part. Choose areas that you feel insecure about or that you would like to improve. For instance, if you have been feeling down, write a statement such as "Delight fills my life and overflows to everyone I meet." Keep it simple and to the point.

Keep your flame of delight lit—every time your mind challenges you with "reality" and how bad the world is out there, force yourself to listen to and see positive influences. The actress Ruth Gordon said in her autobiography, "It never does any good to face facts—the facts have never changed anyone's mind."

Delight Dampeners

There are people who bring delight wherever they go; others bring delight when they leave. If you can, stay away from these wet blankets who try to douse your delight. These delight dampeners are all lined up waiting to dissuade you from reaching the stars. They're happy to tell you, "You can't do that, you won't be able to succeed. You're silly to want to live in delight." Sometimes these people are very close to you, your best friends or your family. When they sense a change in you for the better, they become personally threatened and will fight your growth. If your newfound delight with yourself and your life makes them uncomfortable, they will be afraid they will have to change. Change is something that fills them with fear.

> Great spirits have always encountered violent opposition
> from mediocre minds.
>
> Albert Einstein

No matter how intelligent a person may be, fear of something beyond their control (like your growth) can limit and impede their thinking process. Those in opposition to you are also in a process of growth, and you need to accept where they are in their evolution and not sit in judgment of it.

Perhaps delight dampeners will accuse you of being childish or immature (as if lack of delight defines adulthood). Or . . .

Someone may come along and say "No way."

Others will say it won't work.

Still others may think you are crazy.

Someone else may rain on your parade.

Something negative could happen.

Inertia might set in and you may feel as if you can't move.

Someone would like to invalidate you because your glow is a threat to their darkness.

Remember that your glow is never a threat to their glow, just to their darkness. You may actually be able to dispel their darkness with your light. Their negativity may have become a straitjacket of the spirit, limiting their perceptions. These self-imposed limits keep them locked into patterns of thinking and behaving that do not allow for growth.

Personal blessings are a form of delight and a perfect way to spread delight to others in your life regardless of their receptivity. Hold the image of the person in your mind, and using the person's name, say, "I bless you and see the best in you." The person does not even need to know that you are sending blessings their way. When you do this at least once a day, early in the morning before rising or late at night right before you fall asleep, within a short period of time you will experience a change. If the spirit of that person is able to resonate with you and your blessing, they will become more accepting—if they are not able to, they will fall from your life as a leaf falls from a tree in autumn. You do not have to fight the negative people in your life; just remember who you are as a child of the Most High, bless them, and release them to the light.

> It is difficult to make a man miserable while he feels worthy of himself and claims kindred to the great God who made him.
>
> Abraham Lincoln

Every person in your life is there for a purpose. Each has a gift to bring: compassion, understanding, patience, and learning are examples. As a child, maybe you had an emotionally abusive parent. Now, with your adult eyes, try to see it as a gift. The gift can be that you become highly conscious that you have a choice—to imitate your parent or to choose the way of peace and fulfillment. Perhaps your parent learned his behavior from his parent and never knew there was a choice. Once you look for the gift, you can live your life in a proactive state of being, initiating your spiritual connection to those around you with love and compassion. You are not at the mercy of unconscious reactions like your parent, and you are now in a position to break the chain of emotional abuse.

If your boss treats you with lack of respect or indifference, look for the gift this person brings into your life. There will be times you may have to really try hard; however, each and every person has a gift of delight to share. If your boss is extremely organized, tell her so. There is something to admire about everyone.

Every time you feel shut down or shut out by someone, look to that person for the gift they carry, bless them, and hold fast to your own inner flame.

Facing Your Fears

Fear of failure, fear of success, fear of rejection, criticism, ill health, old age, ridicule, intimacy, humiliation, poverty—fear of being powerless, lacking control, looking stupid, feeling foolish, going crazy, losing a loved one, fear of physical harm, punishment, abandonment, obligation, commitment, judgment, responsibility—fear of falling, fear of flying, loud noises, the unknown, enclosed spaces, the dark, snakes, spiders, and lizards. Fear of fear itself. And the biggest one of all—fear of death. Have we hit yours yet?

The first thing to realize about our fears is that we all have them. Look around at your friends, family, and co-workers—everyone you know is just as afraid as you are—it is just that we are afraid of different things, and to varying degrees.

Even those whose lives seem perfect have inner doubts and fears. No one is exempt from having things go wrong.

Beautiful, talented, and successful, Cathy Lee Crosby was one of those people who seemed to have it all. With her TV show

That's Incredible in the top ten, and with starring roles in more than fifty television dramas and feature films, her career dreams were more than being fulfilled. She also enjoyed glowing good health and a loving relationship with the man of her dreams.

Then, for no apparent reason, four catastrophic events occurred that turned triumph into turmoil. Cathy Lee didn't know it at the time, but her earth-shattering experience was to become one of the greatest gifts she has ever received.

Let the Magic Begin©

∞

Cathy Lee Crosby

It was an extremely difficult time for me. Every belief and value I had embraced as the "Truth" was rocked to the core. Right at the peak of all the turmoil, an important turning point came in a conversation I had with my mother, Linda Hayes Crosby Walker.

She told me of an event that took place one afternoon when I was two years old. It was a beautiful sunny day, and my family and I were at a garden party in the back yard of a friend's home. I was always an adventuresome child, so it surprised no one when I leaned over to get a closer look at the deep end of the swimming pool and became so mesmerized with its crystal beauty that I simply jumped in. I didn't know how to swim, of course, so I had no idea of the danger I was in. My mother ran to the edge of the pool to grab me, but a friend quickly intervened.

"Wait a minute," he said. "Look what she's doing."

The adults stood transfixed as I made my way across the pool. I was actually walking along the bottom. I would push myself up for air, then go back to the bottom and walk along a little further until I needed to come up for air again. I continued all the way to the shallow end of the pool, where I climbed out, completely unruffled. Everyone was awestruck, but I took it all in stride, with no realization whatsoever of the miraculous event that had just taken place.

When my mother told me this story, I was amazed. It reconnected me with the extraordinary magic that lives within all of us. I realized for the first time that no matter what calamity in life pulled me under, I had the innate ability to find a way to surface once again.

We all have this extraordinary ability, but somehow our inner magic collides with our outside reality and we forget the strength of our inner resources. Fear takes over, and our natural ability to create our own solution gets lost in the mire of the circumstance. But, if we can learn how to stay connected to our natural source of magic, we can use the abundant, blissful energy of the universe that is available to us at every moment. We can literally create "heaven" right here on Earth.

The true challenge of life, as I see it, is to stay connected to this natural source of energy. In my book, I refer to it as "dancing in the Bliss Zone." By living life in the rarefied riches of its air, we can see, live, and experience ourselves from a whole new perspective.

Our personal magic begins when we find our own method of staying connected to this source. And by simply awakening to, understanding, and flowing with this connection, we begin to reach the full depth, richness, and potentiality of our lives.

In my new book, *Let the Magic Begin*©, I tell the story of how I unwittingly re-entered the Bliss Zone and stepped into this dance of the Universe. Within its natural rhythm, you will find every gift you've ever dreamed of just waiting to be discovered. So, awaken to the energy, trust the coincidences that come forth, live from the core of your heart and *Let the Magic Begin*©.

Fear controls us or we control it; it is just a matter of degree. When cave dwellers were confronted with pterodactyls, fear saved their lives by pumping adrenaline into their circulatory systems. They then had the strength to stand and fight or run as fast as they could.

In the thousands of years since then, we humans have had more time to get creative about fear. Our sophisticated and complex lifestyles have given us much more to be afraid of.

Today, when fear triggers an adrenaline response, we have the same physiological reaction as our ancestors. Our pulse will accelerate and make us dizzy, shaky, or sweaty; our muscles will tighten. Delight heads out the door. Our reaction is the same as the cave dwellers', but we don't have to go for our spears. There are other ways to deal with our natural, elemental processes.

The reaction to fear needs to be dealt with on two levels: physical and emotional. Physically, if you don't fight and you don't run, you still have to do something! Our shaky legs and sweaty palms can be brought under control with some kind of a fast workout—a brisk walk around the block, taking several deep breaths, running in place, playing a comedy tape until you laugh your way out of it—anything that will satisfy your body's need to rid itself of the adrenaline. Tell yourself this is a normal reaction, and thank your body for being responsive to your feelings.

The emotional part can be more difficult. The first thing to do is to ask yourself this: "What are my fears, and do they prevent me from being successful in my job or career, from enjoying my free time, or from having fun with my family and friends?"

Most fears cannot withstand the test of careful scrutiny and analysis. When we expose our fears to the light of thoughtful examination they usually just evaporate.
Jack Canfield

List your fears according to the degree of immobilization that you experience when confronted with each one. For instance, fear of falling: 10 = completely immobilized, 1 = barely aware of sweaty palms. Erase or cross off the fears that register under 5. You can live with them.

Look at the fears that are left. Ask yourself "What is the worst thing that can happen to me when I experience this fear?" List the answers under each fear. List as many as you can—let your imagination run wild. Once you have completed your list sit back and really look at what you have written. If the "worst" things are projected into the future, you could be fantasizing a negative future, but none of it is real yet. You can imagine and project a better outcome. It's no more difficult than imagining calamity.

If the worst thing is happening right now in this present moment, ask yourself two questions: (1) "Can I survive this?" If it isn't going to kill you, it isn't the worst thing. (2) "Is it necessary for me to overcome this fear in order to have the lifestyle I want?" For example, if you are terrified of heights, and you feel that you can enjoy a full and healthy life without climbing any mountains, by all means stay on level ground.

> Courage is doing what you're afraid to do. There can be
> no courage unless you're scared.
> Eddie Rickenbacker

Mary Manin Morrisey's mother told her time and time again that no matter what happened, she could do whatever she dreamed, for the dreamer of great dreams in her was greater than any of her fears. Mary always believed her because she lived her own advice. But one day, when her mother was no longer young, the circumstances looked truly overwhelming.

Stepping Out into the Blue

When my mother was sixty, she developed severe pain in her pelvic region. It came out of nowhere, overnight. Exploratory surgery revealed osteoporosis so severe it was disintegrating her pelvic bone. The doctors told her her condition was beyond treatment. She would spend the rest of her life in a wheelchair.

Mother chose not to believe in these limitations, so she began to read books on visualization and healing. I stopped at her house three or four times a week to bring her flowers and food, to clean for her and help any way I could. Most days she lay in bed or was wheeled to the living room to gaze out the picture window. Then one day, about three months after her release from the hospital, she said, "Mary, unless you are just coming for a cup of tea and a chat, stop coming over here."

I was confused. "What do you mean?" I asked.

"I want you to stop cleaning my house, stop bringing me flowers, stop cooking for us."

"But why?" I asked. "It's one way I can give back some of what you've given to me."

Her response pulled me out of one frame of mind and renewed the beliefs I had spent years embracing in preparation for my ministry. "Because your help is a positive benefit I'm getting from being sick. I want to let go of everything that looks like a reward for being sick. I've read that secondary gains, the nice things that happen when you are sick, actually can inhibit healing. I've had enough of this. I want to heal. I'm going to put all of my energy into getting well."

Within six months of her announcement, the doctors were amazed because Mother's pelvic bone had begun to regenerate and knit itself together. A few months later, she was walking so well that no one would ever guess she had once been told she would never leave her wheelchair.

When she turned sixty-five, my mother announced, "I think I should start a new club; I'll call it the CMT club."

"Good. What is it?"

"CMT stands for Can't Miss a Thing. I don't want to live worried about squeezing the last little drops out of my later years. I want to live them fully every moment. I'm going to practice not missing things I think I'm too old for."

On her seventy-fifth birthday, with pins in her hip and a fragile pelvic bone, she decided to go skydiving to celebrate three-quarters of a century of living.

My dad and I were amazed. "You want to go skydiving?" Part of me wanted to shout, "You shouldn't go skydiving. You're seventy-five years old!"

In private I asked my dad how he felt about it. They had been married for more than fifty years. He responded with his eyes misting over, "I don't want anything to happen to your mother, but I'm not going to tell her she should narrow her life or limit her experiences because of fear. I'm just not going to do it to her! I'm going to be at the airfield to give her moral support."

So Mom took up skydiving, training for a tandem dive with

the instructor. Then she got suited up and went to the plane four days in a row for her jump, but there wasn't enough wind. The fifth day was her lucky day.

When I got home there was a message on my answering machine: "Mary, I did it! I did it! I did it!" When I called her back, she was vibrantly energetic and alive. "I took that step. I was standing at the door of that airplane, twelve thousand feet in the air, and I stepped out. It's a symbol of my life now. I'm seventy-five and I'm stepping out."

"What did you learn, Mom?" I asked.

"I learned I can do anything I decide to do. I've got a whole life in front of me now and I'm going to live it."

What a great model my mother is. How many of us stand at the edge of our own airplane but because of our fears, hesitate to step out?

Mary Manin Morrisey

Sometimes fears arise that we do not even know we have. The elevator door shuts, starts to go up to the next floor, shudders . . . and then stops. There you are, looking at the other six people around you. Surprise! Suddenly you have an overwhelming fear that the other people around you are going to breathe all the air, and there will be none left for you. The walls seem to close in on you—claustrophobia, the fear of enclosed spaces, has hold of you. What can you do until you are rescued?

Close your eyes for a moment, and see your body overlaid and protected with a glowing white light. This light is much like a shield of spiritual armor that will serve you in any situation. You can wrap yourself or your car in white light, an airplane you are traveling in, your house, your children—anything or anyone you want to protect. The more you fill your world with light, the less your fears will appear. The light is the spiritual goodness that you are, projected outward and upward.

If, in your hour of need, you can fill your mind with the thought and belief that you reside within the heart of God, that God operates through you—as you—you will feel protected. Repetitively say, "God and I are one."

All of your fears do not need to be conquered—only the ones that keep you immobilized, locked up, and that may prevent you from enjoying life. Many times, just acknowledging that you have a fear and then taking action in the face of that fear can be exciting and exhilarating. If this was not true, all the amusement rides and rollercoasters in the world would go broke. There is a thin line between excitement and fear, and many people thrive on it. If you feel that there is a fear that you *cannot* survive, please find a professional who can help you.

Reach for the Stars

> If I were asked to give what I consider the single most useful bit of advice for all humanity it would be this: Expect trouble as an inevitable part of life and when it comes, hold your head high, look it squarely in the eye and say, "I will be bigger than you. You cannot defeat me."
>
> Ann Landers

The ability to reframe our experiences and the guts to overcome our problems can lead the way to inner and outer success. Mary Lou Retton won the All-Around gold medal in gymnastics at the 1984 Olympics. When she met a young woman named Gina, the experience gave her a new view of overcoming obstacles.

The True Hero

We all encounter thousands of people in our lives. But only a few really impact our hearts forever. Shortly after the 1984 Olympics, I met such a woman.

Gina was born with spina bifida, a severe condition of the spine that meant she would probably never walk without braces or crutches.

By the time she was thirteen, she had endured seven operations to rearrange her muscles so that she could walk as normally as possible. Still, she couldn't do anything without using crutches.

Her mother took her to every physical therapist in the area, but nothing seemed to work.

"What's the difference," Gina would say, "I'm always going to be disabled." The physical therapist was doing her best, but had very little hope.

The only thing that made Gina want to try her best was the sport of gymnastics. She joined Project Happy, a program for the physically disabled, and signed up for gymnastics.

When Gina and I met, she thanked me and told me that watching me perform at the Olympic games inspired her and helped her to understand that she can do anything if she wants to badly enough. Her mother took her to see me perform every time I went to New York. Two years later, she started to train at a regular gymnastics center. Within two months she could walk around the gym without braces or crutches. A few months after that, the doctor told her that her body had improved so much she would never have to wear braces again.

Gina told me that watching me inspired her to accomplish in less than a year what she never thought would happen in a lifetime. Well, I think Gina is the true inspiration.

I'll always be grateful to Gina for sharing her determination, her heart, and her zest for life with me. She touched me in a very special way and put my accomplishments into a brand-new perspective. The way she faced and overcame incredible obstacles makes her a true inspiration to us all.

Mary Lou Retton

We all have fears to overcome, problems to solve, troubles to get through, although maybe not as serious as Gina's. With everything in perspective, is it as bad as you think?

Even the great Norman Vincent Peale, one of the most brilliant speakers of all time, had to overcome his own negative attitudes and limited sense of himself. He went on to publish *The Power of Positive Thinking*, which has sold more than 15 million copies—so far. It was from wrestling with his own failures that he discovered the path to success. "You can have peace of mind, improved health and an ever-increasing flow of energy. . . . [L]ife can be full of joy and satisfaction," he said, and made it come true.

You have every right to reach for the stars, to aspire to greatness, to improve your life any way you choose. To aspire to go beyond our circumstances is a natural human urge—we hope for more, we'd like to expand in positive directions mentally, physically, spiritually, and emotionally. Everyone wants to be happy and has some idea of what would bring happiness to them.

Stairway to the Stars

> Don't be afraid to take a big step if one is indicated. You can't cross a chasm in two small jumps.
> David Lloyd George

When you make the commitment to live in delight, obstacles become steps on your stairway to the stars. "The mountain lifts me as I climb," poet Jean Burden wrote. When you are in motion, you can take in stride annoyances that might have flattened your spirits when you were idling along. And your spirit grows with each step. "The great awareness comes slowly, piece by piece," Scott Peck said. "The path of spiritual growth is a path of lifelong learning. The experience of spiritual power is basically a joyful one."

As you start your climb, inner resources you forgot you had will come into play—all of the knowledge and experience you've accumulated over a lifetime. Nothing is wasted. When you worked at the carwash on Saturdays as a teenager and learned to be fast and thorough, or when you volunteered at the hospital and held the hand of an old woman in pain—everything you ever did taught you something, and it is a part of you.

> Problems are only opportunities in work clothes.
> Henry J. Kaiser

If you think you can avoid obstacles by spinning your wheels and going nowhere, it won't work. Solving problems is one of the ways your soul develops. Your soul is always trying to expand. Aspire to the heights, climb your personal mountain, and receive the rewards heaven has in store for you. Take the scenic route. Reach for the stars!

4

The Sky's
the Limit

Most of us have jobs that are too small for our spirits.

STUDS TERKEL

I'd rather be a failure in something that I love than a success in something that I don't.

GEORGE BURNS

$\mathcal{Y}$ou have everything you need to make your life a total delight. You were born to be incredibly rich—rich in making full use of your talents; rich in creating a better world; rich in meaningful relationships; rich in spiritual growth and development; rich in contributions only you can make; and rich in delight for life and passion for living fully.

Most of us spend a great part of our lives working. When we're not at our place of work, we think about work, worry about work, plan careers, look for jobs, or retrain for better jobs. If life is to be a delight, then we need to feel our work is worthwhile.

> If you do not feel yourself growing in your work and your life broadening and deepening, if your task is not a perpetual tonic to you, you have not found your place.
> Orison Swett Marden

Part of that happiness comes in the form of financial rewards for a job well done. But there are other rewards to consider. Equal delight comes when work is in harmony with your highest purpose, when you believe in your work, enjoy it, and know that what you do makes a difference.

There are elements of spiritual delight even in ordinary activities if you bring your highest intentions to them. We believe this is true of our friend and life insurance agent, Al Sizer. Al spends hours every day with his clients. He has had friends criticize his "obsession," but he doesn't feel as though he is working. He believes in the security that life insurance gives his clients and he knows he is helping them. Al loves his work and it is his path to delight.

Work Is Delight

When I was sixteen years old, my father died unexpectedly of a heart attack leaving my mother and me penniless. He had had no life insurance and consequently my family was forced into involuntary bankruptcy. My mother, devastated and emotionally unequipped to handle the turn of events, had a nervous breakdown. I vowed then and there this would never happen to anyone else I loved.

The first thing I did was to save enough money to buy a life insurance policy on me, naming my mom as the beneficiary. By the time I graduated from college, I owned $101,000 of life insurance on myself. My mom cried when I told her.

As soon as I was out of school, I entered the life insurance business with the clear intention that none of my clients would suffer as my family had done. Today, I have over five thousand clients that I am in service to, and I have written over $51 million worth of life insurance. My purpose in life is to provide the best coverage possible and to service my clients with my heart, soul, and expertise.

The best example I have that my job is worthwhile happened about four years ago. I had contacted a small family-run business owner who told me he didn't believe in life insurance. I continued to talk with him, and finally my persistence worked and I wrote a $1 million policy for him. Four months later, he went for a walk with his brother in the park. Feeling a little tired, he sat down to rest on a park bench and immediately died. Because I had been persistent and I believe in what I do, his business is still flourishing and his wife is well taken care of. When things like this happen I know that I am fulfilling my purpose in life and what I do is important.

Al Sizer

The Spirit of Work

A motivational speaker we know asks his audience, "Is a woman whose organization has a $500 million annual budget and five Lear jets a capitalist or a spiritualist?"

The audience always laughs and shouts, "A capitalist!"

"No, she's a woman of the spirit. It's Mother Teresa and her Missionaries of Charity. She started fulfilling her life's purpose with three pennies and God's help. Mother Teresa is following the delight of her heart to care for the poorest of the poor with grace and a gentle sense of humor. She says, 'God never sends us more than we can handle. Sometimes I just wish He didn't trust me so much.'"

If you don't think there is a place for spirit in the world of money and work, you're just as mistaken as this audience. Taking care of your material needs has the potential for being as spiritual as any other department of your life.

Ideas from Out of the Blue

Many inspirations that come to us are ideas for making the material world work. The Latin root word for inspiration is *inspirare*, which means to breathe in. When we are inspired, we literally breathe in the spirit.

> We must be steady in ourselves, to be open and to let the winds of life blow through us, to be our breath, our inspiration; to breathe with them, mobile and soft in the limberness of our bodies, in our agility, our ability, as it were, to dance, and yet to stand upright. . . .
> Mary Caroline Richards

Everyone gets a wonderful idea once in a while. Out of the blue, a great notion lands in your lap. Your creative genius has knocked on your inner door of opportunity and wants you to open it to inspiration.

This great notion of yours strikes a deep chord in your being. It can work on many levels for you and for others. "But," you think, "but . . . but . . . but. . . ."

Instead of finding a million reasons why you shouldn't follow through on your idea, treat it like a precious gift. It probably is. Don't let procrastination cause your inspiration to fade away!

You are never more than three people away from finding someone to help you fulfill your idea. Ask everyone you know to assist you. If they don't know how, someone they know knows someone who can help! Ask, ask, ask until you obtain the answer you are seeking. Your sources are infinite, you are the only one who can stand in your own way. Believe in your ideas and inspirations and others will too.

Even if you are busy, remember that there's no end to what you can accomplish. Think of yourself as an instrument of divine completion, here to manifest God's ideas in the material world. Act on ideas that bring you spiritual wholeness and help you make a living as well.

Rudolfo Bernardo might have found a million reasons to quit Allen Elementary School, but he stayed for only one; in his heart he truly loved his vocation. His passion and belief have brought spiritual wholeness to himself, his school, and the country.

The Thirty-Eight Words of Delight

Rudolfo Bernardo spends most of his time sitting in his beanbag chair in the lobby, beaming approval at children who race up to show him A's on their arithmetic and spelling papers. On the wall above his head is a poster with *joyfulness* lettered in vivid colors. Mr. Bernardo is especially happy today. Citywide academic test results are in and the Allen Classical Traditional Academy has taken first place. They're the best school in Dayton, Ohio.

You're probably thinking, no big deal—a private academy with a kind, grandfatherly principal at the helm. Well-behaved children with joyfulness posters all over the place are certain to be number one. But what about our inner city schools? Think again. Allen is an inner city school, and these are our at-risk children.

Just a few short years ago Allen Elementary School was near the bottom academically and the children were unruly. Things were so bad even the teachers had high absentee rates. Principal Bernardo's blood pressure was sky high. Students were sent to his office for misbehaving on the school bus, on the playground, in the classroom. His life was one long line of troublemakers. To make matters worse, parents were not cooperating.

He thought hard and decided to try something new—there

was nothing to lose. He'd read articles in professional journals about character building and they sounded fine, but there were no materials available, nothing practical that he could put his hands on. He called a meeting of teachers and sketched out his ideas. They'd have to figure out the details themselves. The teachers rallied with ideas of their own. They decided to step back and work on themselves first, and developed an eleven-point program which they took one step at a time. Trust Building was a step. Seeing the Good in Everyone. Focusing on Service. Brainstorming. Team Building. On their own time, teachers met and explored these avenues of self-awareness. They discussed things like fairness and justice and bringing the best they could to their students. They began working together, helping each other, communicating.

As the program began its painstaking development, the teachers were aflame with ideas. They would teach manners. They would teach character traits. Teaching values is controversial—in a diverse population there's always a question of whose values to teach—but some valued traits of character are universal to every human being. That's where they'd start. They came up with a list of nineteen traits they could help children develop.

Someone had the bright idea of having a word of the week. Someone else said, "Let's write it on posters."

Of course there was extra work involved, but by this time the teachers were inflamed with enthusiasm and wanted to try out their ideas. They even volunteered to eat with the children at lunchtime so the kids would be able to learn table manners.

"There's a certain sense of dignity and self-respect you get just from dining at a nice table," Mr. Bernardo says. "Most of these children had never seen a tablecloth or even a place mat. We decided to make place mats for all the kids with the word of the week on it."

The nineteen character traits grew to thirty-eight. Each week a different one would be on place mats and posters, would be discussed in class. On Fridays a skit or a choral reading by a group of students would illustrate its meaning.

| Citizenship | Confidence |
| Cleanliness | Consideration |

Cooperation	Patriotism
Courage	Perseverance
Courtesy	Politeness
Dependability	Promptness
Fairness	Punctuality
Generosity	Readiness
Goodwill	Resourcefulness
Helpfulness	Respectfulness
Honesty	Responsibility
Independence	Self-Control
Initiative	Self-Discipline
Joyfulness	Self-Reliance
Kindness	Sportsmanship
Loyalty	Thankfulness
Neatness	Tolerance
Obedience	Truthfulness
Patience	Uniqueness

Attitudes began to change. Parents were called in and the program was explained. They were asked to sign pledges to help. Merchants in the neighborhood cooperated by becoming partners and donating printed place mats and posters. The local hospital sent volunteers to help the teachers. The first year the character building program got off the ground, Allen's academic score went up 6.5 points.

As the program grew, scores continued to climb, and the word of the week spread to other schools, churches, and Sunday schools. Posters went up all over the neighborhood. Meanwhile, classroom behavior was changing so much, the teachers had time to teach. In 1994, Allen was one of the best schools in the city—fifth in academic achievement.

By this time the whole town was abuzz. The ABC and CBS news programs in Dayton started each day with, "Good morning, the word of the week is —." The character building program itself, owned by the teachers who developed it, was heralded in education circles and spread to several states. No one was surprised when Allen reached the top in 1995. It had more than five thousand children on the waiting list for first grade. Certain statistics hadn't changed from the beginning: Almost 60 percent of the kids come from single parent homes, 78 percent were on welfare, about 60 percent were African-American, 39.5 percent were Euro-American, 5 percent "other."

The ambiance at Allen Classical Traditional Academy, for that's what they changed the name to, has shifted from negative to positive. The teachers and the well-mannered, well-educated students freely express warmth and love. They are one big happy family, presided over by a soft-spoken man in a beanbag chair in the lobby whose blood pressure is normal and whose love for children lights up the sky.

Barbara Nichols

When you believe in your work and you are following your path with your heart, you will find that you have extra energy to make things happen. If you feel exhausted after a good night's rest and hate to get up in the morning, then you are in resistance to your life as it is, and you need to take a critical look. Being in resistance always causes a feeling of depletion and fatigue—you are using all of your energy to fight your reality. It is time to take stock; besides making a living, are you creating delight for yourself and others? Does your everyday life make your spirit sour or soar? When you are in delight with what you do, your inner radiance glows and you share that glow with everyone around you.

We see in the workplace, more clearly than in any other area of life, the incredible changes that are taking place in the world. Information written five years ago, policies set then, even people hired then, may be totally irrelevant today. Our basic assumptions about working for a large company until retirement are challenged; our ideas about economic security are shifting rapidly. There are new rules for working in a "postcorporate" environment.

The postcorporate world may well be a blessing in disguise. It gives us a sort of cosmic kick in the pants to custom-design a life around our wealth of talents, abilities, and skills rather than shaping our million-dollar capacities to fit into a corporate slot. The scent of entrepreneurship is in the air. Even at IBM, once a bastion of career security, thousands of jobs have been eliminated and former employees are leaving "Big Blue" to start their own businesses.

Victoria Downing got her MBA when her family was young, and launched her career as an independent consultant, hoping that having her own business would give her more time with her children than a regular job would. Her first assignment took her to the heart of Africa, a long way from Dallas in every sense.

Women of the Cloth

"What am I doing here?" I wondered, as the plane landed in Africa. "How did I get chosen for this? I don't know the first thing about it."

I had been sent to Lesotho to examine a Dutch development for the World Bank, which was looking into micro-enterprises in the years that everything was geared to building dams and other huge macro-projects. I started the assignment with excitement, but now a shudder of fear went through me. It was a clear case of "be careful what you wish for—you may get it."

When I arrived at the Royal Weavers of Lesotho I discovered that they were managed by a cool, aloof young man who didn't know anything about the weaving part of the business and certainly didn't know how to market it. My trepidation grew. What was I going to do?

All of a sudden, I heard women in the next room singing— and it sounded familiar. I was so delighted, I said I'd like to go in there, and when I did, I found all these beautiful women sitting on the factory floor weaving and singing under their breath an old familiar Methodist hymn.

Suddenly, I knew I was in the right place and it wasn't so far from Dallas after all. We're all connected. I relaxed and my assignment went very well.

On the way home a week later, I stopped over in Zurich. I had never been away from my husband before and I could hardly wait to call him and tell him about my trip.

When he heard my voice he didn't even say hello. "Where are Michael's soccer socks? He has to have them or he'll be thrown out of the game."

"Look under his bed. He always leaves them there. You have to fish them out and wash them."

"Don't have time. The game's in thirty minutes."

We hung up and I knew my life and my marriage and my new career were going to be all right. Between the weavings in Lesotho and the socks in Dallas, the fabric of life would hold.

Victoria Downing

More and more blue-collar work will disappear as robots and automation take the place of human beings. What a divine chance for us to use our gifts and talents in creative and beneficial ways! Although the prospect of radical change may be frightening initially, remember that what you may perceive as a crisis can actually be a great opportunity. The ancient Chinese understood this principle so deeply that in Chinese the character for *crisis* is a combination of the figures for *danger* and *opportunity*.

Find a Need and Fill It

A British schoolteacher opened a small cosmetics shop in a London neighborhood a few years ago because she needed to support her family. She was tired of spending too much for glitzy packaging and promises and believed other women were as "hyped out" as she was. She put lotions in plain plastic bottles and jars that her customers could refill again and again from her larger vats. Passionate about the environment, she made sure that they were recyclable. Anita Roddick's shop reflected her high personal standards. She believed that cosmetics should be pure, that salespeople should be educated about the product rather than about pushing sales, and that everyone who worked for her should share her dedication to service and be involved with soup kitchens and other worthy projects in the community.

The response was beyond Anita Roddick's wildest dreams. The Body Shop is now one of the most successful international corporations, with stores in thirty-seven countries. Customers are as loyal and enthusiastic as the people who work there. *Vogue* called Roddick "the queen of the beauty industry."

This former teacher is still inventing herself and her company with great delight every day. She tells us, "We still don't know the rules. Instead, we have a basic understanding that to run this business, you don't have to know anything. Skill is not the answer. Neither is money. What you need is optimism, humanism, enthusiasm, intuition, curiosity, love, humor, magic, and fun and that secret ingredient—euphoria. None of this appears on the curriculum of any business school."

Ordinary People

Ordinary people do the most extraordinary things when delight leads the way. Ray Krok, a milkshake machine salesman, absolutely loved hamburgers and french fries. He came upon a small hamburger stand in northern California that made the best burgers and fries he'd ever tasted. The owners were not interested in expansion, so Krok, at fifty-seven, took over McDonald's recipes, added his milkshake expertise, and the rest is history. Today McDonald's is the number one franchise in the world.

Julie and Bill Brice, a teenage sister and brother, enjoyed their summer jobs at a Dallas yogurt shop so much that they purchased a small shop of their own with $10,000 borrowed from their college fund. Their company, I Can't Believe It's Yogurt, grew to have more than two hundred outlets.

At the other end of the age spectrum, a sixty-three-year-old retired insurance agent, Tom Duck, formed an unusual car rental company featuring low-cost older cars: Ugly Duckling Rent-A-

Car System. Today the Tucson-based brainchild of this humorous insurance agent is an $85 million business.

High school teacher Peter De Yager took his German class to Europe where they ran into some candies that brought them great delight. Instead of just munching them, Peter and his wife, Betsy, set up an office at their home in a small Iowa town and began importing the candies. Their enterprise grew to be Foreign Candy Co., which now operates nationwide and grosses almost $10 million annually. The candy? Gummy Bears.

Work As Healer

There is great healing potential in any work you choose. You can bring wholeness to yourself and others by doing your work with kindness and care, no matter what it is.

> The highest reward for a person's toil is not what they get
> for it, but what they become by it.
> John Ruskin

Distinguished Hollywood writer and producer Fern Field Brooks has worked hard to fulfill her own dreams. Because of her own strong self-image, she has been instrumental in helping others find career opportunities that shape and heal them.

Cousin Geri

In 1979 I was honored with an Oscar nomination for *A Different Approach,* a live action short subject I had produced and directed, which took a comedy-musical approach to encourage employment of people with disabilities.

From the beginning, it was a magical project. Everything went right. It not only touched and changed the lives of those of us who worked on it but had global ramifications as well, and gave birth to the Media Access Office and the Media Access Awards under the auspices of the California Governor's Committee for Employment of People with Disabilities.

I was suddenly perceived as the unofficial champion of every disabled singer, actor, dancer, and musician within five hundred miles of Hollywood. So it wasn't surprising when someone called and said, "Fern, there's this wonderful comedian with cerebral palsy. You have to see her. Her name is Geri Jewell and she'll be on TV Saturday afternoon." Come Saturday afternoon there we were, my husband and I, glued to the television set and falling in love with an incredible young woman who was making us laugh so hard the tears were rolling down our cheeks.

I called my boss, told him about Geri, and asked for a meeting. We met and much to my delight he sat down and worked out all the beats of the story right there. I went back to my office, called the producers of the show, and told them Norman Lear had just written a story for Geri Jewell to guest-star in *The Facts of Life*. That show, entitled "Cousin Geri," resulted in a recurring role on the series for the young comedian.

A year later, Geri popped in to see me.

"You know, Fern," she said, "being in the series has changed my life. I just want to thank you for helping."

I thought I understood exactly what she was saying. Of course it had changed her life. She now had a regular income and was paying the rent. Fortunately, I didn't open my mouth, and Geri continued.

"It used to be, when my father was asked about his children, he'd take out photos and say, 'This is my son, so-and-so, and this is my daughter such and such, and this is my daughter Geri-she-has-cerebral-palsy.' It was as if it were part of my name. But now, when he speaks of us he says, 'This is my daughter Geri, she's on *The Facts of Life.*'

"And that's not even the best thing," Geri continued. "All of my life, what made me most unhappy about having cerebral palsy was that children were afraid of me. But since the show, if they see me on the street or in the mall, they come over, ask whether I'm Cousin Geri, and we talk."

She stood up and we hugged. Then Cousin Geri-who's-on-

The-Facts-of-Life headed back out onto those streets where people now smiled at her instead of staring.

Fern Field Brooks

Something on the Side

One approach to staying in delight in an economy in flux is to have more than one source of income. Start something on the side. You might open a small florist shop if you love flowers, or bake and decorate beautiful cookies to sell. Many people are joining multi-level marketing companies, which offer opportunities to learn about and sell herbal remedies, makeup, or many other products that offer value to the consumer, along with the chance to supplement their income.

The time may come when your sideline becomes your main delight. The sideline occupation you choose because you really enjoy it may take off and replace your "just for the money" job. It happens all the time.

Getting Better

You can always improve on what you do best. For the professional, school is never out—and anyone who wants to do a good job is a professional. At this time of accelerating change, you need to be ready to move in any direction. Besides learning new job skills, learn about yourself. Find your spiritual center so your body and mind remain in balance in case you have to change direction in a hurry. If you are centered and paying attention, you will be prepared for dramatic shifts. You can avoid disaster. Statistics show that most of us will change jobs or careers on the average of every seven years. Learn as much as you can to prepare yourself for your next phase, the next chapter of your life.

New possibilities are in the wind, not just for financial success but also for creating the kind of jobs—and world—you really want. Go to your public library and consult with someone in research.

Ask for the career section. There are several publications available with descriptive entries to inform and enlighten you, including *The Dictionary of Occupational Titles*, distributed by the U.S. government, listing over 46,000 different job and career opportunities. Spend the day, and try to match your gifts, talents, genius, and interest levels with more than ten eye-catching jobs. Even if you are not planning on changing occupations now, the knowledge that there is something to fall back on if your situation ever changes can hearten you.

You never need to feel as though there is nothing available that you are suited for—or that you would love to do. The truth is, there is more available than any one person could ever hope to accomplish in any one lifetime. This is where delight gets factored into the equation. When you work at what you love, you can bring the same delight to work that you bring to play . . . and work *becomes* play. So choose an occupation or career that sets your spirit sailing—you don't have time to do something that gives you no reward or growth.

Here is one man who can say for certain that his job is rewarding. He took the gift of advice and turned it into one of the most successful television careers in history. The reward is not only for himself but for all the children whose hearts he has touched through the years.

One Little Buckaroo

My first job was at NBC in New York City in the early 1950s, working on the music programs—*The Voice of Firestone, The Hit Parade, The NBC Opera Theater, and The Kate Smith Hour*. I had just graduated from Rollins College, with a major in music composition. Working with creative people in music through television was exciting because television then was a new, challenging instrument.

I had never planned to go into television, but during my senior year of college, I was home for spring vacation and happened to see some children's television programs. What I saw was slapstick and nonsense, people throwing pies in each other's faces, and I just hated it. I felt children deserved better and I decided to go to New York to learn more about television.

During that time in New York, one of my most important lessons came from the "television cowboy" Gabby Hayes. Mr. Hayes was a famous movie personality, a beloved old "codger," who had a huge following for his Saturday morning children's program (one that I floor-managed). Mr. Hayes's program featured his own library of cowboy films, all introduced by him. He'd look out into the television camera and chat with the viewers before and after the film would roll.

One day when we had just completed a telecast, I asked Gabby Hayes what it was that he thought about when he looked out into the camera and knew that hundreds of thousands of children were watching. I'll never forget what he said to me. "Freddie, you just think of one little buckaroo."

What a gift he gave me that day! Gabby Hayes just naturally understood that television is a very personal medium, that it can give us a way to relate one on one.

A decade later when I developed *Mister Rogers' Neighborhood* for educational television (after adding graduate work in child development to my television background), it became even clearer to me that it's through relationships that we grow best. So it was only natural that if I wanted to offer really meaningful communication that could help children and their families, I would need to think of our program not as a "show," but rather as a television visit . . . with a television neighbor who cared about that one little buckaroo.

Fred (Mister) Rogers

Forget to Retire

One of the great benefits of using your unique gifts to create the kind of work you want is that you never have to retire—unless you want to. There have always been people who loved their work so much they simply forgot to retire. Many went on to do their best work after retirement age. Yetta Bernhard, a counselor in Chicago who loves her work, is still working in her mid-eighties, helping to train therapists. When her own daughter was accepted for a psychiatric residency, she called and asked, "Ma, will you help train me?" It was one of the greatest delights ever. "I felt like I'd received an Oscar for professional and parental competency," Dr. Bernhard said.

The Institute of Noetic Sciences in Sausalito, California, was founded by astronaut Edgar Mitchell to investigate the connection between science and spirit. It is headed by Willis Harman, a professor and member emeritus of the prestigious Stanford Research Institute. Being president of the Institute is a second career for Harman, who, at seventy-seven, works a full schedule, delivers lectures in various parts of the country and continues to write books. His work is too interesting for him to contemplate retiring, and his contribution continues unabated.

Serving and Growing Through Volunteering

Your job is one vehicle for your personal and spiritual growth. Another equally challenging vehicle is the world of volunteering. If you have been forced to retire or have not been available to enter the workplace, that doesn't mean that you are not in a position to contribute, or that you have to stop growing in spirit. Volunteering can be the best thing that has ever happened to you, and through you.

Sometimes an inspiration to connect with someone we don't even know enters our hearts like a bolt from the blue. A decision to volunteer can make all the difference in your life and the life of another.

Maria's New Shoes

Our city newspaper carried a story about a young girl from Bosnia-Herzegovina who lost both of her legs in the war. She and her father were struck by the same mortar shell while helping to distribute food from the United States to their countrymen. Her father had died in front of her. It was impossible to try to imagine all that she had been through.

I remember looking at the news photographs over and over again during the course of the day. I'd put the paper down only to find myself returning for another look an hour later.

By that evening, I decided to write Maria an upbeat note. I told her about happy times I've enjoyed on horseback, at dances, while attending college, bicycling with my daughter on the beach, and in my career and married life. I also mentioned that I, too, had been fourteen years old when I began to use an artificial leg.

Before sealing the envelope, I added that I would be happy to send Maria a gift of new shoes. I pledged to take my daughter along to ensure the shoes would be "cool" and said how much having great shoes had meant to me during similar days.

I felt good about making the offer, but felt sure that I would never hear back. I couldn't have been more wrong. Two days later I received a call from the prosthetics firm where she was a patient telling me that my card had already been selected and read to Maria through an interpreter. When I voiced my surprise, the woman said my letter was "the best one" Maria had received.

She then explained that they were going to have a national press conference for Maria the following Tuesday, and asked if I could send a pair of shoes that weekend. We launched into a discussion about the color of the outfit Maria would be wearing. She then suggested that I fly up to meet Maria and be a part of the occasion. I assured her that Maria would have her shoes in time for the press conference, but I would need time to think about making the journey.

My daughter and I traipsed from store to store the next day in mad pursuit of exactly the right pair of hot pink tennis shoes. We ended up buying two pairs of shoes, hair ornaments, an assortment of socks, and a purse before dashing off to mail our gifts to a young girl we'd never met.

By that time I knew that I would make the trip to meet Maria. When I arrived at the prosthetics center I was amazed by the number of press and media professionals there. It reminded me of a press conference I'd attended for Nancy Reagan several years before. Television and cable crews, radio people, writers, and photographers jammed the room. I could tell that many of them had covered national and international events for many years.

As Maria was wheeled into the room in a wheelchair, I looked into her face and felt as though I knew her. Moments passed before I could bring myself to look down at the hot pink tennis shoes we had selected so carefully. I felt humbled at the sight of them. They were such a small part of what she faced each day.

Word passed through the crowd that her mother and sisters had not seen her wear or walk on artificial legs. And that, until recently, they really didn't understand what artificial legs were all about. I saw her family sitting across the room. Maria answered questions through an interpreter. I stood out of camera range, yet directly in front of her. When she looked at me I did my best to give her a small smile, and the smallest of smiles began to cross her face. Her eyes sought me out again and again. I felt a powerful connection. Then they wheeled her into position in front of the walking rails. Her strength and determination were palpable. I found myself thinking that she is exactly the human being she needs to be to live out her destiny.

Memories flooded my mind and tears came into my eyes as I watched her reach out her arms to take hold of the rails. I understood that moment. As she pulled herself up, there was an audible gasp and sounds of quiet crying from the area of the room her family occupied. And then she began to walk. Slowly at first, with spotters on either side, but with a coltlike grace. She was amazing.

Newsmen and women throughout the room were quietly shedding tears—even the men I had pegged as seasoned veterans of nearly everything were forced to lower their cameras and wipe away tears before going back to the work at hand.

Pretty young Maria finished her exercises standing alone, without support, with her arms raised above her head. A remarkable achievement for anyone who has only been "up on their legs" for a matter of hours.

After the ceremony, I was introduced to her as the woman who sent the shoes. "Thank you very much," she said, in almost perfect English. We talked through the interpreter about how to wear miniskirts and high heels with prosthetic devices. Our visit ended with hugs and kisses.

Maria's mother and I hugged wordlessly for a minute. There wasn't a sound in the room. As we ended our embrace, I tried to conjure up a way to tell her that Maria would be all right. Was all right. Is all right. I tried saying in a voice much too loud that Maria was "OK." No response. "She's fine!" Again no response. Finally, I gave her the "thumbs-up" hand signal. As a look of understanding crossed her face, we both broke into broad grins and the kind of laughter that defies differences of language, continents, and even war.

She knew then that Maria would be all right. And I understood how much Maria helped me connect once again with the frightened fourteen-year-old I had been so long ago and appreciate her courage—perhaps for the very first time.

Mary-Pat Hoffman

There is such a wide range of opportunities for volunteering that it may be difficult for you to choose your path. Make a list of your gifts and interests. When you see yourself on paper, it becomes easier to match who you are with what is available. Do you like to read? Would you be happier outdoors or inside of a building? Would you rather work closely with other people or do work benefiting others without their knowledge? Do you want a consistent schedule or would you rather participate in short-term projects?

If reading is your specialty, you can volunteer to read to older or blind people, to children in a library program, or to assist immigrants with language skills. You could assist in writing letters to friends and families of bedridden residents in hospitals or nursing homes.

Volunteer your business skills, deliver meals to the housebound, plant trees, or clean up our beaches and parks. Whatever your interest level is, there is a place for you to be in service to your fellow humans and to all of the world.

No man has ever risen to the real stature of spiritual manhood until he has found that it is finer to serve somebody else than it is to serve himself.

Woodrow Wilson

A dynamic minister from Oklahoma City didn't know he would be sending tons of food around the world until his meeting in Haiti with a special person who came out of the blue and very gently pointed the way.

No Wrong Way to Feed a Child

I took a group of pastors to Haiti in 1979 to do some missionary work. We stayed in a small motel with no air-conditioning. Even though it was January, the temperature was 95—and so was the humidity.

I got out of a cab in front of the motel, eager to get out of the heat, when a wide-eyed little boy came up to me. He must have been about nine years old.

"Hey, mister. You got a nickel?"

"Yes," I laughed. "What do you want it for?"

"I haven't eaten all day," he replied. "If you give me a nickel, I can go to the store over there and buy a roll."

He regarded me appraisingly as I reached into my pocket. "Do you have another three pennies?" He looked hopeful.

"Well, sure. Why?"

"For three pennies, the store man will cut the roll in half and butter it."

"OK," I said. "How much is a Coke?"

"Twelve cents, mister," he replied.

I handed the little boy twenty cents. He thanked me and lickety-split he ran across the street to the store. I stood there watching and thought, This is terrible. This child hasn't eaten all day.

When I got into my motel room, a scripture came to me. In Matthew 25 the Lord said, "When you've done it to one of the least, you've done it to me."

Haiti was the second poorest country in the world, and that little boy was one of the poorest of the poor. That sure qualified him as one of the least.

"What am I going to do with this?" I wondered. It would make a great sermon, but there was more to it than that. I came from Oklahoma, where we had tons of surplus wheat. It cost the American taxpayers millions of dollars just to store all that grain.

When I got home I told the story of this little boy on television, and mentioned the tremendous surplus we had. "We shouldn't be paying taxes on it," I said. "We ought to take it and feed hungry children."

People responded from the goodness of their hearts in all kinds of ways. First, farmers gave me truckload upon truckload of wheat. I don't think I'd ever sent a package overseas, let alone truckloads of wheat. When I was puzzling over this, a cross-country trucker called from Florida who usually came back through Oklahoma empty, and he volunteered to haul wheat from Oklahoma City to Miami. From there it could be put on a boat and sent to Haiti.

And so it began. For two years, our effort didn't even have a name, but we got very good at sending food to hungry children. We learned as we went along and discovered there was no wrong way to feed a child. Then someone suggested that we call our organization "Feed the Children."

Today, thanks to the inspiration we got from that hungry little boy in Haiti, we feed one hundred thousand hungry children around the world every day.

Larry Jones

Make sure that you do not make a commitment that is too heavy for you emotionally, or takes more time than you are ready to give willingly. You will defeat yourself, and others will lose the benefit of your good deeds. Choose an organization that feels right for you—including the objectives, goals, plans—and the people running it. Don't let yourself get easily discouraged. Don't expect everyone to act as if they have been waiting for you all along. Not everyone will even say thank you. What you need to remember is that you are doing this from the center of your being, from your heart. It *is not* a hook to make others feel gratitude toward you—it *is* a vehicle for you to develop your true spiritual nature and benefit others while you do so.

> One thing I know: The only ones among you who will be really happy are those who will have sought and found how to serve.
>
> Albert Schweitzer

This Miss America was anchor on the nightly news in Oklahoma City where she worked on human interest stories as well as hard news. One of the things she learned was that happiness can be found in the most modest of places when the richness of the soul shines forth.

Edith's Home

The tiny house had been a one-car garage in a neighborhood that most people would consider undesirable, yet it had the glow about it that comes when someone cares. It was most certainly someone's home. Flowers surrounded it, tinkling chimes hung from every tree branch, and empty plates on the porch had clearly fed every stray cat in the neighborhood.

Edith lived alone. She had retired from a lifetime of secretarial work and now had a severe case of arthritis. She needed a wheelchair, but one wouldn't begin to fit into her little home, so she had learned to maneuver by "scooting" around the floor. Her arms lifted the lower part of her body and her legs would follow. Although it was awkward, Edith moved with surprising efficiency and grace.

The main room of her tiny house was crammed with papers because Edith was one of the most dedicated volunteers in the city. She helped several agencies with mailings and other paper projects that she could handle from her home. Staff members of nonprofit agencies brought her the work and she turned it back in no time. Her walls were covered with awards, certificates of appreciation, and letters of heartfelt thanks from hard-pressed charities she had helped.

When I asked Edith about the hardships of her own life, she only spoke of the joy her involvement with other people gave her. She would not complain. She was surprised when I asked her why she didn't live closer to her one child, who lived in another state.

"I couldn't leave," she said simply. "This is my home."

I left Edith's home filled with delight, knowing that joy comes to those who understand that to give is more blessed than to receive, that being an integral part of a community gives a sense of belonging, and that joyful people live their lives finding ways to celebrate what is and not what could have been.

Jane Jayroe

Check volunteer centers in your area, your local newspaper for listings of volunteer opportunities, and your phone book for Community Service numbers. Your inner creative genius is willing and ready to explode with new ideas and ways to serve as soon as you have made your decision. The world needs you and your gifts.

Head for the Sky

Find the blessings in today, accept the challenge of change, and find the possibilities in tomorrow. You are exactly where you need to be right now. The grand adventure is to create a path to your highest and best self using the materials of your everyday world. That may be the most important lesson on earth.

Put your best efforts into what you do best without focusing on the outcome. You can't always control the outcome, but you can control your attitude. When you live in delight, there's always another idea, another dream, another opportunity. Life has the most delightful way of bringing us a new day every morning, no matter what. Fresh starts abound.

Trust your spirit to show you the way to delight. When you live a centered, optimistic life, your spirit will soar over limits and seek the possibilities beyond. The sky is the limit, quite literally.

5

The Delight Between Us All

We are one, after all, you and I. Together we
suffer, together exist, and forever will recreate
each other.

TEILHARD DE CHARDIN

$\mathcal{E}$ach of our souls is like a candle in the darkness, emitting warmth and light. There are times when all of us try to cover our light; times when we feel imprisoned by fear and doubt. However, like a lit candle when held close to the flame of another lit candle, when we are in the presence of a loved one our combined lights flare up and become much bigger than the light of two separate candles. As we join with others in the spirit of delight, the world becomes a brighter place for everyone.

Our relationships with others hold for us the deepest and most intense of our emotional experiences. Our highest highs and lowest lows are felt within the context of our relationships, be it romantic love, friendship, or family. Every relationship that you have can serve to turn you toward all that is good in life—great relationships give you great joy, and even not-so-great relationships can open us to the most profound spiritual growth available to us as humans.

Everything is a gift of the universe—even joy, anger, jealousy, frustration, or separateness. Everything is perfect either for our growth or our enjoyment.
Ken Keyes, Jr.

Delight can be found in everyday activities we share with others. You can create it from daybreak to sunset and turn ordinary moments into fulfilling memories. Look into the eyes of the people that you greet on the way to work, share smiles with strangers, have lunch with a friend that you haven't seen for a while—everything that you do to make life more enjoyable for the people you come in contact with is worthwhile. Every day you can make a new decision to serve love, truth, and delight and allow the small delights in our lives to strengthen the bonds between us. When we give strength to our relationships, we can draw upon that strength to help keep us in balance during those inevitable times of grief or stress.

Our primary experience with relationships is with our family. Our parents, siblings, grandparents, and other family members are the mentors who lead us into either a positive or negative first impression of life.

During our early childhood we established a self-perception based upon our experiences with our parents. Parenting can be challenging and confusing for anyone. There are those of us who experienced deeply abusive relationships with our parents, we do not deny this. But the majority of us had normal ups and downs with parents who were having their ups and downs of life at the same time. All of us remember, at one time or another, thinking to ourselves how unfairly we had been treated by one or the other parent. The most important thing to remember is that our parents did the best they knew how to, given the circumstances of their own childhood and experiences of life before we came along.

We have heard it said that it is never too late to have a happy childhood. We can all achieve this by shifting our perception of our parents—try to look at them as people with normal weaknesses and failings, yet also with many inner strengths. When we can come to a place in our hearts where we accept our parents the way they are, or were, and forgive them for the pain they caused us, then we will have the strength to break the chains that bind us to the past.

It's never too late to heal old relationships. Here a woman rediscovers the benefits of kinship years after her father died.

Bird-of-Paradise

Nora had never forgiven her father for being rageful and, she felt, neglectful of her needs. She was so angry with him that she would not go to his funeral. In the twenty years since his death, she had never once visited the cemetery.

Eventually Nora came to realize that her own spirit was choking on old resentments. Finally, after months of trepidation, she felt ready to get rid of them. With a combination of fear and joy, she bought an armload of birds-of-paradise, which had been her father's favorite flowers, and went to the cemetery. There she held a private funeral for him, and cried as if her heart would break, releasing all the anger she felt for him—even the anger she felt about his dying and leaving her, which she didn't realize she was carrying.

Nora's heart broke open and she was filled with great love. Memories came flooding back of all the fine things her father had done for her and the good times they had shared. The more she cried, the brighter the birds-of-paradise became. Their vivid orange and golden hues seemed to reach her soul, igniting her own inner glow.

Nora has made several trips back to the cemetery, always bringing a bird-of-paradise with her. She never fails to get a message of love when she goes.

"It feels like my father is on my side now," she says. "He's always been my ally, even when I didn't know it."

Nora was a member of a twelve-step group, and when she told her fellow group members what she had done, several of them went off to visit their parents' graves too. Great healing took place as they discovered that forgiveness is one of the most important keys to living a life of delight.

"Every time I see a bird-of-paradise, I remember that souls can be united in joy even when circumstances seem insurmountable," Nora says with a smile. "If I could get over twenty years of anger, it gives me hope for the whole human race."

Barbara Nichols

The Power of Forgiveness

Nothing blocks your happiness more than resentment, anger, and guilt. No matter what someone did to you or how much they were at fault, if you don't forgive them, you are the one who carries the effects. Forgiving others rids your life of immobility. Holding on to resentment and anger uses up energy that you could direct toward delight. You could be contributing more to life and feeling wonderful about yourself and others if you would only forgive.

In *A Course in Miracles*, we hear, "Through forgiveness the thinking of the world is reversed. The forgiven world becomes the gate of Heaven, because by its mercy we can at last forgive our-selves. Holding no one prisoner, we become free."

Forgiveness heals. It opens our hearts, frees our emotions, releases dammed-up energy in the body, and allows the life force to flow freely through us.

When we take the necessary steps to make peace with our parents, we open the heart path to unconditional love between us. This love without judgment is the beginning of the inner harmony that we all seek.

Making Peace with Mom

For most of my adult life, I either tried to be just like Mom or I rejected her completely. Either way, I was still under her control, locked in an eternal power struggle that never seemed to end.

Judging from old photographs taken of me in my twenties, we could have passed for sisters. I had the same short hairdo and wore the same baggy clothes. I talked the same politics and values and marched to the same party lines.

When I moved to California in my thirties, I totally rebelled against her. I permed my already naturally curly hair, wore a leopard-skin bikini, and used too much pink eye shadow. I stopped eating red meat, went to juice bars, and espoused the virtues of the West Coast lifestyle. I ran from everything she held sacred and chased other things I would have done well to leave alone.

In spite of my best efforts to carve out my own identity, I was utterly lost, stuck in this dance of emulating or rejecting her. The more I resisted her, the stronger the pull to be like her. It took Mom's imminent death to motivate me to truly reconcile with her during the last six weeks of her life.

When Mom was alive, she was bigger than life to me and could intimidate me with the slightest look or gesture. She was not only a big woman, but she also took up a lot of space with her persona. She had so much moxie that most of us just got out of her way when she was on one of her life missions.

The doctors told Mom that her cancer was progressing quickly and she had less than six months to live. She tried chemotherapy, but it made her so sick she decided against further treatments. By the time I saw her, she'd lost most of her hair, and her skin had turned a pale, chalky white. Because she had been bigger than life to me, I was shocked to see her 60 pounds lighter, a mere shell of the mother I remembered.

So there I was, sitting by her bedside at St. Lawrence Dimondale, the nursing home where Mom was the first hospice patient. I was quietly doing needlepoint, looking up every now and then at Mom, and listening to that awful wheezing sound she was making as she slept. Mom woke up, smiled at me, took my hand and said, "It's so good just to have you here, Den."

At that moment, I looked into her eyes and saw God's light, and then I understood that this woman, bigger than life, was vulnerable too, and there was as much strength in her vulnerability as there had been in all her bravado. I only remember fearing my mother. Now, when I looked at her, I saw so much more. I saw that spark of divinity, that spark of holiness in her and knew instantly that it was in me—and my daughters—and all of us.

I sat there thinking about this newfound awareness when I felt it come over me like a wave of warm energy—unconditional love. Suddenly, I remember what I must have felt as a child, but somehow forgot as an adult—this was love.

I sighed with relief—all things were possible in this place of unconditional love. It had an easiness, a warmth, a flow that I had rarely felt in my life. I took a breath and leaned into it—I cried, kissed her forehead, stroked her hair, and told Mom just how much she meant to me. I told her I would pass on the stories to her granddaughters and all the wisdom she had taught me. Then I just sat back and felt that new sense of love washing over me, taking away the pain, and leaving me with a peace I had never known before.

When Mom died six weeks later, I was so glad I hadn't missed a moment with her. Since her death I have had many more moments of reconciliation in which I've been able to embrace the gifts of her life, gifts that often came wrapped in incredible pain. But none of these moments can match that one at her bedside, when all time seemed to stop and I was given a cosmic wake-up call.

Seeing that spark of divinity in my mother has made me very aware that we are all divine and here to live God's purpose for us. It has given me a sense of urgency to get on with my destiny and make a contribution to others.

Denise McGregor

I have decided to stick with love. Hate is too great a burden to bear.

Martin Luther King, Jr.

Jesus was the perfect model of forgiveness. He told Peter to forgive his brothers who sinned against him "not seven times, but seventy times seven."

Declarations are words that we repeat to ourselves to change our self-perception, perception of other people, or our perception of the world at large. To create a leap from our existing consciousness to the desired new perception, the repetition works best when done according to the numbers that were stated by Jesus two thousand years ago.

Written declarations can create almost instantaneous results since we are so visually oriented. When you realize that you can change a lifetime of negative feelings about yourself, your parents, or anyone else that you need and want to forgive, it seems amazing.

You will need a notebook to keep by your bed. Before you go to sleep on the first night, write "I forgive myself" thirty-five times. You must forgive yourself before you can go on to forgive anyone else, as everything starts and ends with you. The next morning again write "I forgive myself" thirty-five times. Do this for seven days and seven nights—it may be the most powerful thing you have ever done to free yourself from your past.

Nancy Kerrigan, the Olympic ice skater, learned how to forgive herself long before she went on to win an Olympic medal. She said, "I used to be very negative toward myself. If I'd fall, I'd tell myself I stunk. But I have learned that after making a mistake, I should just forget it, block it out. I may have made a wrong move, but that doesn't mean I'm stupid."

Most of us are not very gentle with ourselves and think we should be able to do more, be more, and have more than we currently do. When we have forgiven ourselves for judging unfairly, we can use this very powerful declaration to improve our self-esteem. "I'm beautiful, lovable, and capable." Devote the time you need to make this declaration a reality, and soon you will see all of your experiences through beautiful, lovable, and capable eyes. Then forgive your mother, your father, sister, brother—anyone else that you feel the need to include. Once you have finished your book of forgiveness, you can close the chapter of your life that had you stuck, and move forward with boldness and delight.

Sibling Strength

The interaction that we have with our siblings during childhood can deeply affect our feelings of self-esteem and help us develop social skills that will carry us through the rest of our lives. We learn how to comfort and empathize with another person, how to make jokes, resolve arguments, even how to irritate one another. All the things we learn with and from our siblings we use later in life when we are in the job market, marry, or have children of our own.

There may never be anyone more intimate with your strengths and weaknesses than your sibling. Our brothers and sisters can be our strongest allies in times of need, and will be there to share joy and sorrow throughout the years. From the moment that he or she appeared in your life until the day that you are separated by death, there will be no one who knows as much about you as your sibling—and no one who can be a better friend.

This brother and sister believe that they have been blessed with each other, and have created a strong friendship that has lasted throughout childhood and beyond, through all of the great adventures that life has presented.

Brothers and Sisters

When I was a child, it was my sister, Arline, seven years older, who took me to and from school. With my hand securely held in hers, I felt safe as she first looked left and then right before crossing the street. On one of those same streets, it was "Arl" who once thrust herself between me and a menacing German shepherd. And it was Arl who taught two left feet to dance, took me to my first baseball game, and bought me the red truck for Christmas the season our parents were broke.

As adults, with Arline's hand held securely in mine, we buried my father, and it was my shoulder she leaned on when our mother later died.

Through life's hardships and joys, my sister and I have been more than just siblings. Most people seem surprised when we each claim the other as a best friend. They do not expect two opposite-sex siblings to be so close and say we are unusual, the rarity, but we think not. Arline and I both believe that the brother-sister relationship is just largely unacknowledged and undervalued.

Alan Ebert

Siblings have been known to travel halfway around the world to reestablish a severed bond. Adult siblings who were separated at birth have gone to extreme measures to reunite. Sisters or brothers who confess to years of childhood bickering turn to their so-called antagonists with love and affection later in life. There is something within our very souls that yearns to see the familiar face, hold the hand that may have protected or teased, and to relive shared bittersweet experiences.

Time or distance apart do not make a difference in a relationship between siblings. And sometimes, as in this story, even death cannot prevent a brother from sharing a gift of hope.

Mike's Dream

My brother Mike and I shared our dreams. From the time we were children we woke up each morning and told each other about our inner movies. As we grew older, we discussed their symbols and subtleties, meanings and themes. I went on to study dreams for a living as a psychologist; he went into business. We continued as adults, calling long-distance to interpret each other's vivid dreams.

He was thirty-seven when he was diagnosed with an inoperable brain tumor. A few months later, he called me with a dream. Like his illness, it was simple and straightforward.

In the dream, Mike saw two rooms joined together by a door. In the first room, elegant leather-bound history books with gold-embossed titles lined the wall behind an intricately carved desk. A stately but well-worn brown leather chair stood next to the desk. The adjoining room was plain and simple, all white with no furniture. There were windows but the view was obstructed by pure white light which shone through the panes. This room was open and inviting, yet mysterious. One of the most curious aspects of the dream was a large lump of black coal which held open the door between the rooms.

The psychological interpretation of the dream was uncomplicated and forthright: The room with books represented this world and the knowledge and ideas of humankind. The white room represented the next plane, the afterlife and the spiritual wisdom of the eternal. The unconscious mind was unveiling what fate had in store for my brother. He was both comforted and disturbed by the explicit nature of the dream—it was so matter-of-fact and inevitable. Yet we were both puzzled by the coal in the passageway between the two worlds.

Nine months later, after a heroic struggle, my brother died. My wife and I went to Florida for his funeral. At breakfast in our hotel the day of the funeral, we noticed several people coming into the dining room with black spots on their foreheads. It was Ash Wednesday, the beginning of Lent. These people had been to church and were marked with ash. My mind dashed immediately to Mike's dream and the chunk of coal that held open the door between the two worlds. In that moment I understood that the black coal was a truly significant part of the plan, and remembered that Ash Wednesday was related to the time when Christ retreated into the desert and learned of the inevitability of the crucifixion.

Overwhelmed by the intensity and duration of my brother's illness, I decided to retreat and rest for a while in order to heal. I made a commitment to myself that I would follow the course of Lent to its natural conclusion and attend church on Easter—something I hadn't done for fifteen years.

I awakened early on Easter Sunday and dressed quietly. I left my family asleep and began the two-mile walk to church. Atlanta had never looked better to me. The sight and fragrance of the dogwoods and freshness of the light breeze were wonderfully intoxicating, the brilliant colors of the azaleas, stunning. Soon I felt peaceful and content and acutely aware of the life in the world and how vital every blade of grass was. I was enchanted with spring. Suddenly a rabbit hopped out from behind a tree and stopped within a few feet of me. I looked at the rabbit and the rabbit looked back. Our eyes met and held for a long moment; we encountered each other in every sense of the word. After what seemed an eternity, the rabbit hopped away.

I walked a few steps toward church, but couldn't continue. A tingle of delight started at the bottom of my feet and surged upward through my body, and I laughed a great belly laugh. I had just encountered the Easter Bunny. And I understood. I was brimming over with joy and more aware than I'd ever been that the earth is alive and vibrant. It was opening up and blossoming after the bleakness of winter—and so was I.

I never made it to church that Sunday. Instead I rested against the tree and wept and laughed for hours. This was the end of Lent and the rebirth of hope, and I had the joy of resurrection in my soul.

Robert D. Simmermon

Erica Goode, in an article in *U.S. News and World Report*, explains, "Sibling relationships—about eighty percent of

Americans have at least one—outlast marriages, survive the death of parents, and can resurface after quarrels that would sink any normal friendship. They flourish in a thousand incarnations of closeness and distance, worth, loyalty and distrust." No one on the planet knows how to find and push your emotional buttons as easily as your sibling—whether it be to encourage, challenge, or cause you heartache. Goode goes on to say, "A time comes when it makes sense to rework and reshape such 'frozen images' of childhood into designs more accommodating to adult reality, letting go of ancient injuries, repairing damaged fences. In a world of increasingly tenuous family connections, such renegotiation may be well worth the effort."

When you are called to the path of delight, delight can open your heart to new possibilities of interconnectedness with brothers or sisters. It doesn't matter what has happened or hasn't happened with your siblings—only what you want to have in your relationship from now on. See your brother or sister in the quiet of your mind tonight, and bless them—love them. You will never have a better chance than now.

Positive Parenting

Novelist J. B. Priestley felt very keenly the delights of parenthood. "To show a child what has once delighted you, to find the child's delight added to your own, so that there is now a double delight seen in the glow of trust and affection, this is happiness," he wrote. "How good it is to recapture old and fast-fading delights, to see them anew through love and to find them sparkling and glowing now like jewels." One of the deepest joys we can experience as parents is sharing with our child the experiences that brought us happiness and fulfillment in our own childhood. Learning to whistle, weaving daisy chains in spring, sharing family secrets, being caught up in a fit of giggles together—these are the golden moments that hold rapture and enchantment of their own.

When a child is born, the whole family falls in delight. Tiny babies, in whom we see our future, are the greatest joy and blessing we will ever have. And they are very easy to love. These small beings have the ability to bring out the best in us and we want to make them happy. It is the one relationship that literally demands that we love unconditionally, from the very second our child is born. That tiny baby that we hold in our arms can do nothing more than eat, sleep, and expect the creature comforts. We can do nothing less than to love them totally and without reservation or judgment.

Deepak Chopra shares this with us: "Attachment is not a component of real love. A mother is not waiting to be complimented by the baby, she feels love that's totally without conditions. When you feel that kind of love, it radiates from you in all directions, not just to the baby but everywhere. It's like a light radiating from a bulb."

The love for our child enlarges our spirits, expands our hearts, and allows us to feel the essence of our higher selves. The highest delight, the very stuff of heaven, comes through when we love a child.

Bridge to Heaven

When my fourth child was due I made a commitment to experience this thing called birth. Throughout my wife Christine's pregnancy we called the baby "Miracle," because that's what I believe about birth—it's a miracle. I attended all the doctor appointments with my wife. When the doctor put the stethoscope up to her stomach, I heard Miracle's heartbeat speeding away—dumdumdumdum. What a revelation! When you look at a pregnant woman you don't realize how much life is going on inside her.

At the moment of Miracle's birth, a blissful feeling came over me—I could feel the presence of God in the room. It was so joyous to see my little girl come into the world.

After the baby was cleaned up, we sang Happy Birthday to her because it was really her birthday, and I played the kazoo. It was a wonderful celebration.

We named our baby Sarah, but we also wanted to give her an Hawaiian name. In Hawaii the custom is to ask a special person to do the naming. We called a very spiritual woman named Nana—she was my first call after we sang Happy Birthday.

Sarah was born in Kapiolani Hospital. "That's it," Nana said. "Her Hawaiian name is Kapiolani. It means 'the bridge to heaven.'" Yes, I thought, that was the context in which we saw Sarah.

When I started sharing Sarah's birth at my lectures, I realized what an incredible insight I had received. Seeing another human being come into the world gave me a new appreciation for life and a deep understanding of the oneness we share on a spiritual level, a God level.

On another level it helped me strengthen my faith in God to realize that first she wasn't and then she was. Sarah weighed 8 pounds, 8 ounces. I could hold her in the palm of my hand. I thought, there will be a time when she will be no more. And that is the continuum of life. She started from a drop and within that drop was everything—her hands, her eyes. God begins that evolutionary process and it happens in such an orderly way.

God created your heart that pumps thousands of gallons of blood through thousands of capillaries throughout your body, 24 hours a day. Do you think He can do that and not help you find the right mate? Or help you get a house? Or pass an exam? He created your brain, which records everything. It's the computer of all computers. Only God can do that.

To have faith is to know that I am constantly being cared for. The fact that I'm still breathing is confirmation that God is not finished with me yet. I still have more work to do. And if I'm still breathing, He will provide all the things that are necessary for life.

Sarah's birth brought us incredible delight. She's been a great teacher for me.

Wally Amos

We will never have any greater teachers than our own children—they look at the world with new eyes. When we set aside the judgment that only age brings wisdom, we begin to understand why the Bible tells us "And a child shall lead them." Listen, and discuss with them their observations. We are sure that you will find, just as this father did, that wisdom can come in small packages.

A Little Piece of God

After tucking in my six-year-old son Chris one night, I tapped his chest and asked, "Do you know what you have in there?"

Chris looked puzzled and responded, "My guts?"

"No, you have a piece of God," I replied.

After a brief silence he responded, "God is in my guts?"

"No, we all have a piece of God inside of us; it is God's gift to each of us."

He smiled, tapped my chest, and asked whether I had a piece of God in my guts. We laughed and together we began to ask this same question about the rest of the family.

"Does Mommy have a piece of God?"

"Yes," we answered, laughing.

"Does Matt have a piece of God?" we asked about his older brother.

"Yes."

I knew that Chris attended a day care center with a little girl named Mary who was so spoiled she made the people around her miserable. I said, "You know, even Mary has a piece of God."

Chris looked stunned, and then he said emphatically, "No, not Mary."

When I insisted he said, "Daddy, I have been with her more than you. She doesn't have a piece of God."

I told him that God never missed anyone; everyone has a piece of God inside.

He pondered this awhile, and then said, "Well, her piece must be all covered up with junk!"

I have tried—not always successfully—to remember this lesson: Even people I dislike have a piece of God. My task is to move the junk out of the way so that I can find it.

Robert P. O'Brien

Give your children the one thing that no one else can—your time. It is easy to get caught up in our busy world and forget the things that are important: companionship, understanding—most of all, attention.

Performance Under the Stars

They slouched in foldout chairs in a semicircle, eyeing me suspiciously. Their ages ranged from fourteen to sixteen, and they were there because they loved drama. I was a new teacher, and I had absolutely no experience in directing drama. My background was in teaching and writing and literature.

No problem, I thought.

That was how I found myself in chaos late that fall, staging the musical *Godspell*. I spent countless nights at rehearsals coaxing my Jesus to sing louder and my Mary to tone down her body language.

My three-year-old, Breana, was the least of my worries. She was a sweet child, undemanding and easy to please. Usually I left her at home with my husband. But when he couldn't watch her, I'd throw her in the car and take her to rehearsals. She wandered about the stage with her bottle in hand.

When I was wrapped up with responsibilities, I would pass Breana off to students. Her word for bottle was *baboo*, and it was common to hear the pitiful cry of "Baboo!" from some corner of the drama room. The student nearest to her would then hunt it down.

As rehearsals for the play progressed, the integration of the acting with the choreography and the music became extremely time-consuming and intense. Breana seemed to accept my hectic schedule with characteristic charm. Once the play was over, I reasoned, I would give her back the time I was taking from her.

On the way home from one particularly good rehearsal, I asked lightheartedly, "Do you love Mommy?" She turned to me and said simply, "No." Wounded, I drove on in silence.

Opening night. We played to a sold-out crowd. My Jesus sang like a dove. The crucifixion scene had the audience in tears. At the last song people were on their feet, wildly cheering for more.

Our reputation apparently mushroomed, for the next night an even bigger crowd appeared, and we had to bring in more bleachers to handle them. Those who couldn't find a seat crowded shoulder to shoulder in the back.

Breana came both nights. The first night, she sat on her dad's lap—dutiful but fidgeting. As everyone complimented me for a job well done, she fell asleep.

The second night, she was bored. I sat her in a corner where she played quietly. Then she came over and pulled on my arm.

"Go outside," she whispered.

I looked in vain for her dad.

"Go outside," she whispered again.

I glanced down. Breana was looking especially pretty in a red dress with petticoats. Loose hair from her pigtails trailed softly down her neck like tendrils. I relented. My cast could be without me for a few minutes.

There was a slight chill in the air. I let her pull me wherever she wished. We ended up outside the cafeteria, where there was a small amphitheater.

Breana pushed at my waist. "Sit, Mommy!" I did. She looked at me with sparkling eyes. "Watch *me*!"

Marching up on the stage, she put her arms straight out to her sides and began to twirl. Her red dress lifted up, revealing white tights that were bagging a little. I leaned forward and chuckled. She threw her head back and laughed gleefully as she spun.

Around and around she twirled like a plane out of control. I could hear the noise from the auditorium but it began to subside as I focused on my daughter.

I remembered my countless hours at rehearsals. I remembered

handing Breana off to anyone who would take her because I didn't have the time.

A rousing cheer from the theater, but that was only background noise now. I was at the best performance—sitting under the stars, watching my three-year-old revel in her delight. She spun. She skipped. She finally bowed. And straight-backed on a wooden bench, I sat alone and clapped and clapped.

Rayleen Downes

Choose daily to convey love and compassion to your children and you can rest assured that you will always be doing the very best that you can. Be a conscientious parent in every sense of the word—you can choose to emulate your own parents, or not. Strengthen and prepare your children for our wonderful world. Let the love you feel for them overflow from your heart to theirs, tell them you are proud of who they are, and that with the power of delight—all things are possible.

Romantic Love

You always remember the first time you fall in love. You have a song in your heart and walk on air—you want to dance down the street. No one can fail to notice your mood—it is infectious. Everyone seems to smile at you. You feel openhearted and generous with yourself and your gifts. In the generosity of love, you wish for the "other" to reach their own higher self and are delighted with their uniqueness.

> When two people relate to each other authentically and humanly, God is the electricity that surges between them.
> Martin Buber

When we first are in love with another, we are at our best at loving unconditionally. Judgment is suspended the moment you look into your loved one's eyes.

Deepak Chopra states, "I think the reason people seek romance is that they want to step into the field of infinite possibilities with someone. They want to share the experience of another world in which two people share the unknown together." He suggests that romance is a daily choice between the couple. "If I see you through the eyes of the known, I already have a story about you and so I can never see you with fresh eyes. The known is the past. But if I'm willing to shed all of the past, and see you as if for the first time, then I'm in a state of bliss. The known is just an image of self. The reality, which is the real you, is the infinite possibility that exists beyond ego."

When a daily choice is made to retain those first feelings of longing, the moments of love turn into months of love, the months to years. Mark was participating in a seminar recently, waiting in the hallway outside of the room for his turn on the platform. An older man came down the hall and asked if Mark had seen his wife—she was about five feet, four inches tall with blond hair, and the man further explained his wife's shapely figure with his hand gestures. "No, I'm sorry, I haven't seen anyone matching that description," Mark answered. Just then, the gentleman turned and said, "Oh, there you are, honey, I've been looking everywhere for you." A rather elderly woman with gray hair was coming down the hall. "Is this your wife?" Mark asked, somewhat surprised. "Why, yes, isn't she a beauty? We've been married for thirty-four years." This charming incident showed that when we love, and love for the duration—not just the moment—we continually see our beloved through the eyes of a romantic.

Magda Krance, in *Redbook* magazine, describes romance: "For me, it's a gesture or a moment born of surprise and imagination, something that leaves me breathless, giddy, and flushed with love or lust or both. Breaking the barrier between interest and passion—the hand tentatively touching the knee, the first quivering kiss, and all that follows—is the essence of romance. But so is an unexpected nuzzle on the neck, a spontaneous shared laugh that lights the eyes, a slightly salacious grazing of our bodies as we pass in our daily chores. These are the embers of our romance in our day-to-day lives, and they still warm."

In these days of sophisticated relationships it is rare for a man to express his deepest desires and longings with poetry to a woman he is dating or hoping to impress. Our friends Jon and Lisa Williams are an example of outright delight with their relationship.

When Lisa started working for Mark, his office was under construction. The assistant foreman, a young man by the name of Jon Williams, seemed to spend an extraordinary amount of time hanging around Lisa's desk. Although Lisa was dating another man at the time, Jon's gentle persistence, backed with showers of flowers and the poems he wrote, gave Lisa such delight that within a year they became man and wife.

Lisa

Awake, shake dreams from your hair my pretty child
Rise, for life is just beginning . . .
I want to tell you
Now it's true, the feeling in my heart
Has now become the feeling in my soul.
Where once I walked as half a man
I now am walking whole
I can't regret the days gone by
When you were just a dream
For dreams beget reality
To which life is conceived.
So take away my emptiness
And hurl it through the sky
For without the love we share together
My heart would surely die.

Jon Williams

What if Jon had never written what was in his heart for Lisa, or worse yet, written his poems and been so immobilized by the fear of rejection or of appearing foolish to Lisa that he never shared himself with her? Perhaps she would have granted him one of her dazzling smiles and gone on with her life, never knowing the delight she could have shared with Jon. There would be no Jon and Lisa Williams or beautiful little Sabrina Williams, their baby. When we learn to share our true feelings without fear of rejection we are in for our most delightful romantic experiences.

A one-on-one relationship can be our greatest source of personal growth. It is a daily challenge to struggle to be all that we can. Our partner in love is our closest mirror—we learn faster and more accurately within the bonds of our relationship all of our faults and weaknesses. But we can also learn to love more deeply and accept more freely, and to give without expectation of return. It can be one of our highest spiritual experiences.

Ken Keyes, in *A Conscious Person's Guide to Relationships,* explains it this way: "We discover that whenever our ego expects something in return, we lose the essence of love. For love cannot be like a business deal based upon barter or equal exchange. Our own life can demonstrate that when we give selflessly and openly to other people, we begin to create a loving field around us in which we get back much, much more than we could ever give. But this magic of love will not happen if we take a bookkeeping attitude."

Our love relationship is not just an interaction between two people. It is a model that exemplifies who we are as partners—to our children, parents, friends, and to the world. Our model can be a curse or a blessing in this human family we share. We can choose to stick to the old model of power, which relied on control and domination—or be pioneers of empowerment, love, growth, and encouragement. When Mark asked his ten-year-old daughter, Elisabeth, what was the most important thing she could tell him about relationships, she replied, "It needs to be about love, not about power." From the mouths of children! It is time in our family and business relationships, in all our relationships, to be about energizing others rather than "keeping them in line."

Communication

One of the easiest ways to empower others is to give them our undivided attention and listen to them. This is the receiving end of communication, and can be the most important. Of course, we know it is important to share our thoughts and feelings, to be consistent in our guidelines for our children, and to be gentle and honest with each other. But by listening and giving understanding, most of which can be accomplished without words, we encourage our loved ones and friends to feel important and cherished.

In our complicated and busy world, it can be difficult to find the time to listen to the rattling of a child. If we don't find time now, when will we? If your children feel important enough to share little things with you now, later in life they will feel comfortable sharing the bigger things. We need to encourage our loved ones to talk—and we need to listen.

The best time to do this is during the meals we share. Turn off the television. Share the love on your face with your family, not the back of your head while you watch your programs. There is no greater insult than to be made to feel less important than a television program. A program can be taped. During meals we can create memories that will become anchors of love to see us, and our children, through difficult or lonely times.

A Perfect Dinner Together

Papa had a rule that before we left the table, we had to tell him something new that we had learned that day. We thought this was really horrible—what a crazy thing to do! While my sisters and I were washing our hands and fighting over the soap, I'd say, "Well, we'd better learn something," and we'd dash to the encyclopedia and flip to something like "The population of Iran is one million. . . ." We'd sit down and after a dinner of great big dishes of spaghetti and mounds of veal so high you couldn't even see across the table, Papa would sit back and take out his little black cigar and say, "Felice, what did you learn new today?" And I'd drone, "The population of Iran is. . . ." Nothing was insignificant to this man. He'd turn to my mother and say, "Rosa, did you know that?" She'd reply, impressed, "No." We'd think, "Gee, these people are crazy." But I'll tell you a secret. Even now going to bed at night, as exhausted as I often am, I still lie back and say to myself, "Felice, old boy, what did you learn new today?" And if I can't think of anything, I've got to get a book and flip to something before I can get to sleep.

Leo Buscaglia

Read to Each Other

Mark recalls that when he and his wife, Patty, were first married they purchased tons of love books to read to each other. He would read one night and she the next: Books of poetry and passion were shared in the quiet hours before sleep.

Reading bonds the reading partners with the vicarious experience they share and inspires imagination. Love partners who read to each other share a special world with other lovers throughout history. Families who read together are stronger, get along better, and have more time to laugh or cry over a shared experience. Read more, watch television less.

Get Physical!

During one entire year of his speaking career, Mark conducted a hug survey. At varied professions and income levels, he surveyed all of his audiences. He wanted to know how important hugging is to people, in what instances they were hugged as children, and how often they now hugged others.

What he discovered was that 85 percent of the people surveyed were given less than one hug a day during their childhood. Hugs were usually given for comfort—for scraped knees, bumped elbows—and during departures and arrivals at home. For the majority of people, hugs were not given simply to show affection.

Yet 97 percent of these same people said that they would like more hugs than they were now receiving. We are a nation of people starved for a simple show of affection and comfort—a warm embrace, a touch of the hand, a friendly hug. Leo Buscaglia shares with us, "Love touches, fondles. Physical love is necessary for happiness, growth and development. . . . [T]he infant needs to be fondled or he will die even if all his biological needs are met. . . . Even a handshake may be classified as sensual gratification. No matter the degree . . . man needs to be touched. There are some, of course, who find it, in a pathological way, unpleasant. 'Please don't touch me.' It is their right, which must be respected. Nevertheless, love is physical, it touches."

We suggest that you hug everyone you come in contact with on a daily basis. Start with your own family. Hug your loved ones, just for the heck of it, for no particular reason—just to let them know that you care. Hug and kiss your kids before they go to school—sure, they are going to say, "Come on, Mom, Dad, cut it out! My friends are watching!" Do it anyway—what their friends will see is love—your child will figure out a explanation. "My folks are crazy," they will share. But they will feel loved. Your children want to assert their independence—let them know it's all right to do so and still be hugged.

> The moment you have in your heart this extraordinary thing
> called love and feel the depth, the delight, the ecstasy of it,
> you will discover [that] for you the world is transformed.
> J. Krishnamurti

Ask your friends if you can hug them. It may feel uncomfortable to both of you at first, but it won't take long until it becomes second nature. With their permission, hug your co-workers. Your boss. The principal at your children's school. You will never know how important your willingness to reach out to others may be, or how one hug can totally change an otherwise lonely existence. All you have to do is open your heart, and reach out.

A Special "Other" Person

> Treasure the love you receive above all. It will survive long
> after your gold and good health have vanished.
> Og Mandino

Some of us have been lucky enough to find a close and trusting relationship with someone special in our families; someone who is always willing to listen, to comfort, and to love us. This certain person with whom we feel especially bonded may be an aunt, uncle, cousin, or, as in this case—a grandparent.

Looking for Grandma's Swing

"I want to swing."

My own voice awoke me and a sense of urgency and loss spread through me one hot Dallas morning in May. I understood. My ninety-year-old grandmother, Nana, had gone blind shortly after my son was born on New Year's Day and seemed to be giving up hope. Ever since then, a part of me was grieving and missing her in preparation for her death.

Nana is the person I loved the most for as long as I could remember. When I was growing up, she was a haven during times of turmoil, a cheerleader during times of challenge, and in many ways, my security blanket. I remember half-teasing her when I was a child, telling her she could never die because she was the only person in the world who loved me for me. I don't know why I believed that, but I did.

One of our favorite things was to sit on her front porch and swing for hours at a time, and now I was homesick for that place of the heart. I grabbed my favorite CDs, put down the top on my convertible, and set off down the highway in search of a front porch swing. Grandma was far away and her swing was long gone, but I needed the comfort of seeing an old swing again.

For two hours I drove around feeling sadder and sadder. There were pretty flowers everywhere, but not a front porch swing in sight. I could hear my watch ticking, warning me it was time to start the ride home. Suddenly a sign caught my eye. "Fresh strawberries," it said, with an arrow. My husband loves strawberries, so I followed it telling myself that at least the day wouldn't be a total loss.

I found myself on a little road that wound through tall pines.

The air was ten degrees cooler here and the honeysuckle was fragrant. Each twist brought a new flower smell along with a fresh sign pointing the way to the promised strawberries. I began to have a dreamy, Alice-in-Wonderland kind of feeling.

I finally arrived at an old wooden gate. There sat an old woman behind a small stand covered with red straw buckets. At this stand, she explained, people pick their own strawberries.

I selected my bucket and headed out into the strawberry field. My heart was already beginning to feel lighter as I danced among the berries.

Just as I thought I had explored the entire field, I changed direction and suddenly encountered an old oak tree—the kind of tree that looks as if it's been there for hundreds of years and will be there for hundreds more. And underneath that tree hung the most beautiful wooden swing I had ever seen.

I sat under that huge oak tree, eating strawberries and swinging with Nana until I was ready to go home. I could feel her presence and hear her voice as if she were beside me. I told her all about the strawberry patch and the beautiful tree. I told her how much she had meant to me for so long and cried over how I missed her every single day. I thanked her for living long enough for me to learn to love myself so I wouldn't have to depend on someone else to love me.

An incredible feeling of peace settled over me. Then, in a flash, I understood the miracle of finding that swing in the middle of nowhere. For the first time, I realized that just as long as there are memories to cherish and swings to swing upon, Nana would be with me. Always.

Joni Johnston

Animal Friends

Sometimes the easiest beings to bond with are of another species. There are times in our lives when our relationship with an animal can be the most rewarding of all our relationships. Most of us delight in pets of all kinds who bring us affection and companionship.

As long as Homo sapiens has walked upright, people have

enjoyed animals as companions. We shower attention, love, and care on dogs, cats, and other animals. We make them members of our families. They move right into our hearts. In their own way, they share their lives with us, bringing us immeasurable joy. Nearly everyone remembers a shining moment when a pet came to the rescue of a broken heart. Or bad days when only the dog really seemed to understand. Or surprising moments when the cat jumped into your lap and purred your sadness away.

Animals often do for us what we cannot do for ourselves. Guide dogs lead the blind. Dogs and other animals are trained to respond to audio signals such as doorbells and telephones for hearing-impaired people. We rely on the keen senses of dogs to guard our homes and fields; we depend on cats to get rid of mice. By living true to their own natures, animals serve our needs. And, of course, they love to cooperate in the family chore of removing leftovers from our dinner plates.

Many kinds of animals become pampered pets. Finny denizens of fishbowls get names and the finest fish food. Birds remind us of our soul's urge to take wing and fly. Hamsters and guppies, snakes and lizards find their places in someone's heart. They provide delight, amusement, and enchantment. Tuning in to their ancient rhythms allows us, for a moment, to remember the tranquility of our souls; watching their antics makes us smile.

In ancient China, sages carried around crickets in cages believing that crickets brought good luck. Today, it is not uncommon to see people in the Orient take songbirds in cages wherever they can to listen to their delightful song.

Sometimes love can happen even to those of us who have been totally committed to hating dogs, cats, or rodents. In spite of our strongest intentions not to share our lives with a furry pet, God may have a bigger and better plan in store for us.

Puppy Love

I'm in love. He's broadchested, hairy and extremely intelligent. His big brown eyes and sweet face make my heart melt. There's only one problem: He's not my kind. Really.

This is not a religious or ethnic problem; it's species.

As it happens my adored one is a yellow Labrador retriever named Rockne. So you can see the complexity of the situation.

To make matters worse, this is my first out-of-species live-in affair.

In the brief span of six months I have gone from being a raving speciist—"I'll have no livestock in my home"—to fluffing pillows and stuffed toys for my canine love. Let me explain.

As a person convinced that every dog lived only to have the opportunity to tear out my throat, I assiduously avoided all contact with furry quadrupeds.

I'd call ahead when going into a home that might harbor non-human life forms.

"Excuse me," I began. "You don't happen to keep a dog, do you? You see, I'm extremely allergic and could throw up if confronted with your pet." That usually did the trick. No argument.

I had learned to not even hint I hated dogs. Feared them. Was repulsed and revolted by their disgusting smells, obnoxious manners (i.e., "He only wants to smell you") and poor bathroom hygiene. No, sir.

I was "allergic" to them. That's a statement a pet owner could accept without feeling the need to defend the creepy critters.

Such was my state of mind when God's dog plan was first revealed. It was not a good one. But nevertheless, one that required me to open my home—if not my arms—to a living, breathing, tail-wagging puppy. I was duty bound to make him welcome.

Now, as I write this, he sits at my feet.

This day alone I have taken him on five errands, including a research trip to the library. His reward for being so good in the car is a one dollar noisy toy and a romp in the park.

My reward is having the joy of watching him gallop up and down the grassy knolls, joyously crunching his newest toy. It is an exercise in pure exuberance. I feel blessed to see this. The sun is shining and Rockne DeCarlo is gallumping along at full speed, like the puppy he still is. All ninety-two pounds of him.

Last week when Rockne and I were attacked by the vicious chow dog that lives on the next block I screamed in terror for my beloved, not myself. I was heartsick that I had failed to protect this sweet creature against such a Philistine. So swift was the mad dog all I could do was bray, "Go away, you disgusting dog."

Too late. Poor Rockne was mauled. Many stitches were required to patch him up. I was shaken. My docile Lab wouldn't dream of defending himself against a mere twenty pound Storm Trooper.

Over the past months I have learned Rockne has a range of emotions that closely mimic human characteristics. Except that he's a lot sweeter.

He can't bear suitcases. One peek at them and he's melancholy for days. In his experience bad things happen when suitcases appear.

So when one of us must be away, we make sure he's in another room before we sneak downstairs and out the front door with the bags. We've made it a rule that he can't ride to the airport for departures, but he's welcome to pick up a loved one returning from a trip.

In our short time living together he has trained us to play fetch in the backyard swimming pool and to understand about sixty dog commands, including "get your baby" (the plush toy he got from Santa), "get your teddy" (the golden teddy bear he sleeps with), "get your ball" and other essentials of dog life such as a "do peep" or "do poo."

Remember, I didn't suggest he is Einstein. Merely intelligent. In fact, I am sometimes startled when I look at him and notice he is a dog.

For me his corporal structure has completely transcended. Love has made him real. I guess he is my Velveteen Dog.

Angela Rocco DeCarlo

The Nature of Love

Pets help us understand the nature of love, for that is what they bring to us. We give lovely, furry little creatures to our children as a reliable source of unconditional love. Through owning pets, our children learn about love and how to care for others.

Jimmie Weasner, a four-year-old San Francisco boy, got clear on the concept right away. When he adopted Tarzan, a dachshund from the Society for the Prevention of Cruelty to Animals, he wanted to do something for all the sweet dogs he couldn't bring home. He began to collect pennies form his friends and class-mates to purchase rawhide bones and treats for pets awaiting adoption. His fund has grown right along with Jimmie. Last year, when he was nine years old, he collected $289.58 to bring a little delight into the lives of animals who bring so much happiness to humanity. The San Francisco SPCA now administers the fund for him.

Studies show that when a person with high blood pressure pets a favorite dog, it works as well as biofeedback or hypnosis to lower the pressure. People in health care facilities come to life again when the facility adopts a pet—hearts that have long been sealed shut from the inside open again and the residents begin to communicate. People who uncontrollably stutter when talking to other people do not stutter when they talk to their pets. It is incredible the healing power that animals can have.

All of us subconsciously know our pets will love us, no matter what. Even if we are considered by others as too old, too stupid, too worthless, too damaged—our animals love us. It is the purest form of unconditional love. If we could love as unconditionally as our pets, it would be a far different world in which we live.

You've Got to Have Friends

Everybody needs friends. Friends are our allies in times of internal conflict, our comfort in times of grief, and our companions in times of stress. The laughter that we share is as important to friendship as the tears. A friend can be made in a minute—there are times when you feel an instant connection with someone. You may not be able to explain it, but it's there. Friends from child-hood can remain friends through adulthood.

It has often been said that in order to have a friend, you must first be a friend. Treat your friends as you would your family—hug them, listen to them, spend time together. The best thing about a great friendship is that you can be separated by time or distance, and pick up right where you left off.

The Joy Is in the Journey

If Jack left at six in the morning he should make Grand Junction by seven tonight, assuming Whiskey Pete's and all the other casinos in Nevada burned down last night. It's a long trip and we're all excited that my friend Jack is coming into town for a visit. As I'm warmly appreciating his willingness to drive so far to see me and my family, my thoughts drift to memories of our shared past and I begin a journey of my own over the landscape called friendship that we have shared for almost thirty years.

I remember the times we laughed, and the times that we cried. Even though he's seventeen years older than me, I feel like we grew up together. Because I was too shy to ask a girl out, he arranged my first date . . . he even came along. I comforted him when he gave his love to one who didn't return it. He comforted me when my football career ended. He shared his parents with me, which was a wonderful gift, and I have drawn from the richness of their presence many times over the years, even though they are gone. I shared my family with him and he knows there is always a place for him with us. He was with me at my wedding and the birth of my children. I was there at the birth of his new career as a writer and motivational speaker. He told me my children were wonderful and I told him his writing would inspire the world. We always tell each other the truth. There are no secrets between us.

I was with him on the day his mother went up to help God run the universe, and a year and a half later I was with him when his father, a man of great integrity, went to be with the only woman he loved. Jack was with me on the day my dream to build a nationwide business collapsed. Most importantly, we have shared ordinary days and common moments that help shape and define a friendship.

The journey I'm on today brings back so many sparkling moments from the past. I am anticipating many more to come— our friendship is not a destination. It is an ongoing, wonder filled journey and it makes me happy because the joy is in the journey.
                                    Martin Crowe

When you begin to show the effects of delight, your friends may challenge your new behavior and results. Be gentle and honest. Remember what brought you together at the beginning. As you grow in delight, some friends may grow along with you. Others will fade away. Release yourself from the attachment that your friendship has to be a certain way.

Deepak Chopra describes his friendships this way: "It is blissful for me to have relationships which are full of love and detachment at the same time. When I have made an agreement with myself to be totally nonjudgmental, to be totally silent, to be with nature, then it's great to share it with someone who's also in that state of mind." We may find it is easier to love a friend unconditionally than it is anyone else in our experience. Be grateful for the times you have together, and bless them.

Strangers and Friends

"Strangers are just friends I haven't met yet," said Will Rogers. How many of us really believe this? Most of us are afraid, in our age of violence and street crime, to look at another person, much less look into the eyes of a stranger and call him friend. Somewhere along the way, we have stopped realizing that almost everyone we come in contact with wants the same things we want—love, understanding, companionship, acceptance.

The only time we can see and experience the oneness of humanity is during sporting events and other performances. The crowd at the Olympics rises and cheers as a unit when a performance electrifies them. The delight generated by an outstanding performance cuts through our illusions of separateness and stirs all hearts in unison. We are united for one glorious moment as energy flows from heart to heart.

"We have arrived at an age where our voices and images carry across the planet riding on beams of light. Today, the touch of the remotest human is not further away than tomorrow. Try as we may, how much longer can we maintain the illusion of separateness? It is time to believe that humans are, once again, one community. The bonds of compassion that held us together as a tribe are calling to be reestablished so they can hold us together as a world," Ari Siletzw wrote in *The Mullah With No Legs.*

This teenager learned a very important lesson about himself, strangers, and the tribe we call the brotherhood of man.

The Angels of San Luis Potosí

I had been awarded my driver's license just a few months before my family took their annual big vacation. The four of us, my father, my mother, my sister, and I, were to drive through Mexico for two weeks in the family's Pontiac to see Mexico City, Acapulco, and the towns and countryside along the way. I was seventeen and about to go away to college, my sister was thirteen, and this was one last chance to travel together as a family. It was 1962, I knew little about driving, less about Mexico, and nothing at all about angels.

The first day's driving was through the harsh Coahuila desert in northern Mexico. For five hundred miles, the highway ran as straight as a ruler's edge through parched, thinly populated land. The Pontiac's giant engine had been tuned down to run on the lower octane gasoline in Mexico, but still ate up the miles easily at the highest safe speed.

At the southern end of the desert, the small mountains of San Luis Potosí climb out of the desert floor. They too are arid and brown, with only the gray-blue manguay plant breaking the monotony. This offshoot of the Rockies was a welcome change after the flat desert land we had crossed. We stopped for a rest and gasoline at a village at the edge of the mountains, and then headed on toward our planned stop for the night. The day had already been a long one. The thought of stopping for the night was welcome to all of us.

We were well into the mountains when water first appeared on the windshield. It was midsummer in these desert mountains, and there was not a cloud in the sky. It was only after I had run the windshield wipers that the rust color of the water became apparent. This was not rain. Something was wrong.

We pulled over to the side, and opened the hood of the car. Neither my father nor I knew much about car engines, but the problem was easy to spot. The radiator cap sat neatly on top of the air cleaner cover, right where the station attendant at the last gas stop had left it. The huge engine had boiled all of its water out over the miles of mountain driving. The one cup of drinking water we had steamed away as quickly as I poured it into the car's radiator. The car was crippled. We could go no further.

For hours, we had been the only car on the highway. There was no other car in sight now, and we had no reason to expect one, perhaps ever. Our family sat on the side of the highway with the hood up, stranded in a place we did not know, where we did not speak the language, and with no idea what to do next. We were lost and frightened.

Then, suddenly, we were surrounded by eight or nine men who materialized from nowhere. They were dressed in canvas pants and smocks the same color as the dun and scrub mountains around us. They were *campesinos*, men who worked the land we had been traveling through. They could be there to help us, or they could be *bandidos*. No one in my family spoke Spanish well enough to find out.

I could not explain what was wrong with the car, but the plume of steam coming from the radiator spoke more eloquently than any words I could have used. With much pointing and nodding, these *campesinos* led my father and me to a small rock wall and over a timber stile into the adjoining field. Not fifty yards from the roadside was a small pond. The one thing we had needed, water for the car, had never been more than a short walk away.

We had with us two paper cups, one small water jug, and a plastic bag that could carry about a pint of water. With only these, my father and I and one of the *campesinos* hiked back and forth with water for the Pontiac's radiator. Our other roadside angels escorted us on each trip, with much talking in words we could not understand and much broad smiling and bowing. When words fail, the language of a smile and open hands, a nodding head and encouraging wave, fill the gap.

I was nervous when I started the car. Had there been more damage? The giant engine jumped to a start immediately, and the car settled into a comfortable idle. It appeared we would be able to go on. There was much handshaking, with more head nodding and smiling all around. And then our angels disappeared into the countryside just as they had appeared. In less than a minute, we could not see a single one. They just faded back into the mountainsides that were theirs and had been for centuries.

I have never forgotten that whatever I need most in my life may be only a short walk away. Nor have I forgotten those angels who appeared from the brown scrub brush that summer day, who conquered an uncrossable language barrier, and gently helped a family of stranded strangers on their way.

H. Dee Johnson, Jr.

One Community, One Family, One World

> Gardens are not made by singing "Oh, How Beautiful"
> and sitting in the shade.
>
> Rudyard Kipling

This world is full to the brim with opportunities to create delight for ourselves and others. In our families, neighborhoods, schools, on the streets of our cities, we are offered a hundred different ways to "move the junk out of the way" and reach out with compassion. There are no problems that cannot eventually be solved by good people acting in a positive spirit of service and joy.

We need to see and believe in the possibility. The world can work for 100 percent of humanity. It is up to us to help make it happen.

> The human spirit is so great a thing that no man can express it; could we rightly comprehend the mind of man nothing would be impossible to us upon the earth.
>
> Paracelsus

We are all interconnected and bonded by this thing called life. Every idea, every intention, every action contributes to the whole—to the energy that life is.

> A human being is part of the whole, called by us the universe. A part limited in time and space. He experiences himself, his thoughts and feelings, as something separate from the rest, a kind of optical delusion of his consciousness. This delusion is a kind of prison for us, restricting us to our personal desires and to affection for a few persons nearest to us. Our task must be to free ourselves from this prison by widening our circle of compassion to embrace all living creatures.
>
> Albert Einstein

If we choose to express appreciation, gratitude, compassion, and all of the positive emotions, we open the door to new levels of spiritual understanding. We can help create a glowing network of joy and love that will embrace every other being. The great unifying force of delight can open our hearts so that they can be read by others, and gifts of love and mercy will flow between us. We can see divinity in one another. Our joyful interactions with those whose lives we touch will send beams of delight beyond the land and sky—into forever.

6

Clear Skies Ahead

Imagination is the beginning of creation.
You imagine what you desire; you will what you
imagine; and at last you create what you will.

GEORGE BERNARD SHAW

*C*reating a delightful life for ourselves and those we love is what we all want. Yet there are times life just doesn't seem to work for us. We feel lonely or depressed—as if our hearts and minds are filled with heavy, dark clouds.

When this happens, you need a way to clear the clouds and find the blue sky beyond. Just as nature uses a breeze from the ocean to dispel the clouds that obscure the sun, you can use the strength of your imagination as a power to help you find clear skies ahead.

> Surely as I have thought, so shall it come to pass; and as I have purposed, so shall it stand.
> Isaiah 14:24

Our imagination is a gift from God—it is the bridge that connects our desires to our realizations. The use of imagination fulfills dreams and allows miracles to come into our lives. It is the source of all creative power.

The dual principles of visualization and masterminding help us utilize the power of our imagination in a resourceful and creative way. Masterminding allows us to explore our imagination with others who are interested in the same things we are, and visualization grants us passage to our inner resources. Both principles come to us naturally.

As a very young child, you thought almost entirely in images. When you entered school, the emphasis of education was on developing verbal and visual skills. Little time was allotted during the day for you to use your imagination freely, and if we did, we were accused of "daydreaming." We were actually visualizing—recalling memories and projecting our dreams into the future. Your ability to visualize may have been little used, but you have not lost it.

> A man is not idle because he is absorbed in thought. There is visible labor and there is invisible labor.
> Victor Hugo

The Principle of Masterminding

Masterminding is forming a group of like-minded people to achieve a common goal. It is using the collective energy of several people's minds to create synergy so that the total effect is greater than the sum of individual efforts. Masterminding comes quite naturally to us. We enjoy working in groups to uphold a common purpose or achieve a common goal. Many of us learned masterminding in Boy Scouts or Girls Scouts, without knowing that we had learned it. We met for fun and companionship and reached significant goals together. In the same way, business partners, religious groups, community groups, twelve-step groups, and garden clubs meet and share their expertise and energy, and great things take place.

Throughout time, mastermind groups have shaped the course of history. Jesus had a mastermind with his disciples; each knew their purpose with the group, contributed to the whole, and supported the common good. Because of the mastermind between Charles Schwab and Andrew Carnegie, Carnegie became so successful that he was able to found the American library system. Rich DeVoss and Jay VanAndel created a multibillion-dollar business with their mastermind—the Amway Corporation. Walt Disney would never have been able to fulfill his dreams if it hadn't been for the participation and cooperation of his mastermind partner, Roy Disney. In sports, every winning team is intrinsically a mastermind group. America was founded by a mastermind, fifty-seven men who worked in harmony to create a new government. When Patrick Henry spoke the words "Give me liberty, or give me death," he spoke not only for himself, but for all the mastermind members. The presidential cabinet gives strength and guidance to the president and is an example of a mastermind at its best.

> Never doubt that a small group of committed citizens can make a difference; indeed, it is the only thing that ever really has.
>
> Margaret Mead

A mastermind may be called by different names—organization, group, team, or club—as this young lady discovered.

The Making of an Organization

At nine years old, many kids do not know how to spell organization, much less know what it means, and this was certainly true in my case.

In 1989, I had written a letter to President Bush asking him to help stop pollution, and he had ignored it. I figured if my letter was really big, like on a billboard, he wouldn't be able to ignore my pleas and he would have to respond. So I had written and asked LaMar Advertising for a free billboard, and they sent an application form to me. I had to include the name of my organization.

I had to ask my mother what the word *organization* meant.

My mom said that an organization "is a group of people who get together for a certain cause or reason—like a club, who share the same interest and work together for that cause or interest to help make a difference."

I thought about this idea of a club. I was interested in the environment and helping nature and I felt there must be other people, especially other kids, who felt the same way and would want to be in a club for the environment. So when I filled out the form for LaMar, I wrote down *Kids for a Clean Environment*. My brother pointed out that the name could be abbreviated to *Kids F.A.C.E.*

The first thing I did was to call existing environmental clubs. I explained that I wanted to be in their clubs and to help the environment. They told me I was too young—"You will have to wait until you are older to help." I didn't like this answer. I didn't want to wait, and actually, I thought that if I waited until I was older, it would be too late because the pollution would have already damaged the earth.

I talked to several of my friends and classmates about my idea of a club, *Kids F.A.C.E.* Some of the kids weren't interested.

Others were too busy. A few told me it was dumb. But five of my friends liked the idea. So we started our club with just six members at Percy Priest Elementary School in Nashville, Tennessee.

We met once a week and did things to make a difference. We planted trees, picked up litter, and learned to recycle. Another thing we did was to tell other people about our club. We wanted kids around the world to know that they could join us and get involved helping to protect nature.

We found out there are lots of kids who care and want to be involved. Kids want to make a difference! These kids wrote to us asking how they could join and the things that they could do, too, to help clean up our world. And now, seven years later, *Kids F.A.C.E.*, the club that started with six members, has over three hundred thousand members in all fifty states and several foreign countries.

Melissa Poe

As we harmonize and combine our imaginations with others, our power to achieve becomes complete. As Melissa found out, the power of one individual's idea combined with a burning desire to accomplish a desired goal, when transmitted to others helps us achieve a much larger desired outcome.

None of us can be totally successful alone. We need other people to energize our outlook and find the best that's in us. We grow in delight from the people and projects we are involved with. The better they are, the more we transcend ourselves. A mastermind, at its best, will help you feel an elevated sense of well-being, a connection to a higher spiritual source, and will help you clear away those clouds when they arrive.

Mastermind at Home

Create a mastermind with your family. Once a week, set aside a designated time to be together and discuss family principles and goals. Discuss individual problems and common goals and give each other support. We all need it from those closest to us. A mastermind group "encourages individual initiative, imagination, enthusiasm and leads to continuous personal growth and development," said Andrew Carnegie.

Once you form one successful mastermind group, you will probably form others. Each group will have its own particular benefits. Masterminding is practical and beneficial to any human relationship.

Your strongest mastermind partner can be your spouse. It is important to create new goals with each other as the years go by. Staying in alignment with that special person in your life will bring years of unfolding delight. Sharing time with each other and working toward common goals, using the mastermind principle, will keep a couple united despite the challenges of our modern lifestyles.

Have a mastermind group with your close friends. Create a common goal—for example, to bring more delight into our lives, increase our income, help solve a community problem. Talk over ways to help each other. See each other's strengths and weaknesses, and give valuable feedback. Share your weekly results and accomplishments. We need others to work with us, encourage, and empower us to fulfill ourselves and our greater purpose.

Mastermind to Business Success

You can form a business mastermind with people in the same work arena to help you network, exchange ideas, and support business growth. Once the members start to accomplish results, they will get new energy and it will activate everyone to be more successful in their careers.

Masterminding always starts as an idea in one person's mind. This person enrolls another on-purpose individual; Melissa Poe's first mastermind partner was her mother. From there, attract other individuals who want to expand their lives into delight for themselves and for others. That is the vital essence of masterminding.

Meet once a week. The meetings should be upbeat and beneficial to each member and to the group's collective purpose or purposes. Each individual must use their abilities, resources, and talents to contribute to the good of the group. The average group works best with from two to six members, no more than twelve. Time is the constraint. Have each member share something positive that happened since the last meeting. Then, each person should share problems or opportunities that they are facing and ask for the support they would like to have. Give each other open support that will help all members to leave the meeting feeling revitalized.

Visualization as a Tool for Transformation

When you visualize, you are telling your mind what thoughts you want it to think, and you are sending those thoughts out into the universe with positive energy. This energy is like a magnet that attracts "like" energy, and the energy responds by manifesting itself in physical form. Mark says, "Whatever you want, wants you!"

The process of visualization involves creating time to go into the inner spaces of your mind during a relaxed and meditative state. Imagine your life exactly the way you want it to be. It is like daydreaming with a focus that you keep reembracing with feeling until the pictures on the inside of your head match the pictures on the outside. You can imagine having the kind of career that you really want, a satisfying relationship with a loved one, a beautiful home that's just right for you—whatever you want and believe that you deserve, you can have by using visualization to bring it into your life.

> We have been endowed with the capacity and the power
> to create desirable pictures within and to find them auto-
> matically printed in the outer world of our environment.
> John McDonald

Visualization is important to your growth and life balance because it gives you direct access to the right side of your brain—the nonverbal, visual, artistic, intuitive, creative, and feeling side.

It is the home of your creative genius. The right side can show you new and creative ways of doing things, and is attuned to new patterns. For example, if the left side is organizing the alphabet into ABCDEFG, the right side could be singing an alphabet sonata. Major creative breakthroughs come from new patterns. As Albert Einstein said, "Imagination is more important than knowledge." Einstein claimed that his most important ideas were developed using visual images, not words and numbers.

Changing your beliefs changes your world, and visualization is the easiest way to bypass the conscious mind and get to the subconscious where your limiting beliefs can be easily changed. When your conscious mind and your subconscious mind are in alignment, seemingly miracles happen.

The clarity of your mental visions determines the speed and ease with which you will realize them. Your mental clarity through visualization can give you personal power—power to create your perfect mate, job, relationship—simply, your life.

Margaret Mead used visualization extensively and gave it credit for much of her original thinking and success. Faced with a problem, she would often ask herself, "If this should happen, what would follow?" Then she would sit back and watch the images unfold.

Betty Edwards, the author of *Drawing on the Right Side of the Brain*, remarked that becoming good at drawing "is not a matter of 'talent,' but a process of developing and turning on the perceptual skills available in the right hemisphere."

Jonas Salk used visualization to fight polio. He visualized himself in his mind's eye actually *being* a polio virus, doing what a polio virus does, thinking what a polio virus thinks. He said visualizing this was a major step in his developing a vaccine that saved millions from being crippled by polio.

Carl O. Simonton, M.D. has helped thousands of people overcome cancer using visualization. He teaches his patients to see their white blood cells attacking the cancer cells as if the white blood cells are an army defending their home territory. Some people see their "army" as traditional army-type soldiers, others see knights in shining armor, and still others, Ninja warriors.

Whatever gives them the feeling of power over their own disease is the most effective.

Maintain Relaxed Awakeness

Quiet yourself, close your outer eyes, and open your inner eye. You can see with the inner eye the way you want your life to be. Jesus said, "Go inside your secret closet and shut the door." Shut the door on lack, doubt, fear, what you can't be, can't do, and can't have.

You need quiet time. As you go into this meditative state, let your face relax into a peaceful and soft smile. Tilt your closed eyes up at a 45-degree angle. This may feel strange at first, but remember that anything new is uncomfortable and can help turn on your creative juices. The best time to visualize is right before you go to sleep at night or right after you wake up in the morning. At those times, you're already relaxed and in a receptive mood, so it can be easier.

Visualization is a process to allow your mind to expand and play. If you feel as if your visualizations are forced, or that you're "not doing it right," you won't enjoy your time inside your mind. There is no correct way to visualize. For some it is clear pictures—but not for all of us. Some of us see only indistinct forms, or swirling and shifting colors.

Theater of the Mind

About 87 percent of our mind is visually oriented. That is why television is such a powerful enticement and why movie theaters draw crowds. In the theater of your mind, see yourself involved with your heart's desire in the greatest and sharpest detail you can imagine. If you want a new job, *see* yourself getting recognition from your co-workers and boss. If you want a new home, *see* it exactly as you desire it to be, right down to the doorknobs and the artwork. Picture yourself as already having your miracle, whatever it may be, and by the very act of envisioning your dream you will be that much closer to realizing it.

A student of Mark's named Leta had this to say about her experience visualizing herself speaking in public: "I used to picture myself at Toastmasters stumbling on stage, forgetting what I had to say, and getting booed off the platform. Needless to say, my presentations as a result were pretty bad. Then I decided to take charge and I pictured myself speaking confidently and engagingly and getting standing ovations every time. Something happened that's hard to explain. I became the speaker I imagined—confident, charismatic—and at the last meeting I did get my first standing ovation!"

> By visualizing your goals, you can get your subconscious to work toward making these mental pictures come true.
> *Success* magazine

If you change your vision, you can change your life. If you can see it, you can have it. You can have it all right here and right now—if you'll just take the time to visualize. This well-known professional speaker looked into her heart—and her mirror—and decided it was time to change her life.

The Picture of Success

I used to be an overweight, depressed housewife sleeping eighteen hours a day. One day I decided I'd just had enough. I was either going to kill myself or get out of bed and change my life.

I began listening to self-help tapes over and over, all day long. When the tape said to repeat my affirmations three times a day, I did it five times a day, ten times. When it said to fix in my mind a picture of the person I wanted to be, *I did it all day long*! I stuck that picture of Farrah Fawcett on the wall, but with her head cut out and mine in its place.

I pictured myself being outgoing, trim, confident—and I'd run that picture over and over in my mind. And in time, the picture and I started to match! I never was any competition for Farrah, but I lost most of the extra 50 pounds I had been carrying and I even started becoming a little athletic.

I got a job selling health club memberships, and visualized myself becoming the top seller. Before long, I was!

I decided to switch to radio sales, and visualized myself working at one particular station. But the manager of that station said he had no vacancies and wouldn't see me. I really wanted to work *there*, and so I camped out in front of his office until he agreed to talk to me—and I got a job that didn't exist before I came along! Using visualization, affirmations—and plenty of hard work, I became the top seller there, too.

Before long, they made me the sales manager. This truly was a surprise from out of the blue and was not anything I had visualized getting. But I taught my salespeople everything I knew, especially visualizing getting those orders. One exercise I remember was to set sales goals for the month for selling, and then visualize reaching those goals, and how happy you'd be when you did. At the end of the month, everyone sold almost exactly what they had visualized! One salesman remarked, "If I knew it worked this well, I'd have had a higher goal!" And so he and everyone started picturing selling a lot more next month. Our monthly ad sales exploded from $40,000 to $270,000! What made this all the more extraordinary was that our station wasn't very good and hardly had any listeners. We had no listeners, but all the advertising you could imagine!

In less than two years, once again out of the blue, they made me vice-president for the entire Disney-owned Shamrock Broadcasting!

I came so far, from absolutely *nowhere* to the kind of success I only dreamed of. And what I loved best was helping other salespeople achieve their dreams. So one day I decided to do what I did best and become a sales trainer. Today, I'm president of my own company, Lontos Sales and Motivation, in Orlando, and I travel the world teaching people how to picture success in their minds, affirm it, and get it.

Pam Lontos

When you're visualizing, if you find yourself in the prison of a limited reality, it's time for you to break free. Get beyond your fears and start thinking BIG.

Come from the End Result

Dr. Denis Waitley worked with a very famous gymnast before the 1984 Olympics. He had her write on her goal card "Practice doesn't make perfect, perfect practice makes perfect." She went over and over and over the following visualization ten thousand times: "I see myself go through every motion letter perfect. I see myself coming off the high bars victoriously and valiantly. Mama is coming unglued out of her chair, tears streaming down her cheeks. The digital clock reads out a perfect ten. I see the audience giving me a tumultuous standing ovation. I see a contract from Wheaties for $3 million." She won the Olympic Gold Medal *before* she ever stepped onto that floor in Los Angeles. It happened in her mind first, and then it happened before the astonished eyes of the whole world.

Motivational speaking pioneer Jim Rohn says, "You shouldn't start the day until you finish it. Don't start a year until you finish it." By that he means you should know exactly how you want it to come out. One of the world's all-time most successful insurance salesmen, Ben Feldman, always knew how much insurance he was going to sell the next day. Every night before he went to bed, he wrote out a list of the ten people he was going to see the next day and how much he'd sell them. Sometimes the amount he'd imagined a given person buying didn't work out, but the totals quite consistently did equal his vision.

Have an Attitude of Gratitude

Your imagination can work to bring ever-increasing delight into your life. Be thankful in advance—adopt an attitude of gratitude. When you send gratitude for your many blessings to God, your hopes and dreams will rise to the realm where they take shape and become reality.

What blessings did you accept today? Did you notice the scent of spring in the air, the birds' laughter and songs of delight—just to be alive. Our friend Naomi Rhode says, "If you didn't recognize them as blessings, it is not because they weren't there for you. They only become a gift if you reach out, accept them, and take them as your own. The receiving of gifts is as vital to the equation as the giving." Reaching upward toward the gifts creates a connection with divinity.

Sit in a quiet place and reflect on the blessings you have. This is advice we have all heard many times before, but how many of us actually do this daily? Look at what you have, not at what you don't have, and thank your Creator from the bottom of your heart.

Give of Yourself

When you operate from your heart, you know and understand that the door to delight is opened from the inside. Your heart becomes an open channel through which giving and receiving flow—you give of yourself, and blessings and unconditional love flow back to you.

Many of us have been afraid to give. We will not offer a smile to a stranger, or donate money to charity. This creates a hardened exterior shell that is difficult for us to break through—an attitude of "I'll give only if someone else gives to me first." You must break through from the inside out. A verse in Scripture says, "The measure you use to give your gifts in, is the very same measure that is used to give gifts back to you." Personal transformation will always precede world transformation.

Giving gifts to people that you come in contact with can magnify and amplify your good in unending ways—ways that you may not be able to conceive of right now. It can be the simple gift of looking into someone's eyes as they speak to you, or a hug—or, as in this story, a special dress for a special person.

A Very Special Gift

My husband and I have been in a very rewarding profession for many years. We are professional speakers and give seminars in the healthcare and business arenas. One of our favorite places to give seminars is Hawaii. A number of years ago at one of these seminars a very special "gift" experience occurred.

It is our tradition to have meals with different couples to get to know them and hopefully to be facilitative with their life challenges. One of the mornings of the seminar we had breakfast with a delightful young couple. Having never met them before, we enjoyed hearing of their family, their dreams, their challenges, and bonding our interest with many of their endeavors. As we left the breakfast on the way to the seminar, Judy said, "I'll be there in just a moment—I want to stop at the dress shop. I've looked at this beautiful dress many times. It was a real stretch for us to expend the funds to come to this seminar—so I mustn't buy it, but it's fun to just go and look." After she came into the seminar and Jim was about to start his presentation I had this wonderful "message" enveloping my soul that I was to go and buy the dress for Judy. I whispered this strange message to Jim and as he usually does, he totally reinforced my intuition (God's leading in this case) and I gratefully slipped out on a wonderful mission. I went into the dress shop asking the manager if there had been a beautiful blond lady in here looking at a special dress with quilting on the sleeves and quilting around the bottom (an explanation she had shared with me).

"Oh, yes," she said, "she's been in here many, many times looking at this dress," pointing to the one in the window.

I said, "Oh, wonderful. Please wrap it up for me in a beautiful box with a beautiful bow. I want to buy it for her as a gift."

She looked at me aghast and said, "Is it her birthday?"

"Not that I know of," I answered.

"Did she do something very special for you?"

"No," was my reply.

And then she looked at me and said, "Well, she must then be a very, very good friend."

I smiled and told her that we had just met, but that I felt God had told me to buy her the dress. This was enough of an extraordinary message that she obviously was not going to argue with it. She quickly wrapped the dress in a gorgeous box with a beautiful bow and I left the gift shop rushing to the front desk.

"I need your help, I need to know the room number of Judy and Carl Anderson. I have a very special gift to deliver," I said.

"Oh, that room is 407, up the elevator, down the hall to the right," they said and off I went. When I got into the hallway I found a maid and said, "I'm going to need your help—I have a very special gift for the people in 407. Would you please open the door for me so I can put it on their bed."

Amazing, amazing, the door was opened and there I was in their hotel room trembling with excitement as I placed the gift on the bed.

Rushing back to the meeting room I looked across the room at Judy and had a very awesome thought. She is sitting there enjoying the meeting and has no idea of the beautiful gift that has already been purchased, wrapped, bowed, and delivered for her. If she were to check out of the hotel without going back to the room she would miss that gift entirely. It caused me to muse on all of the "gifts" that I may have missed in life that were prepared specifically for me because I had not been on the right road.

The seminar finished and several hours passed. We were relaxing in our room, having almost forgotten the very special "gift" when there was a knock on the door.

Opening the door we saw Judy and Carl with almost white faces. "Do you know anything about the dress in my room?" was Judy's question.

I smiled and said, "Oh, what dress?"

"The beautiful dress that I've been longing for—you bought that for me, didn't you? Why would you do something like that when you hardly know me?"

"Because I believe God told me to."

She started to cry. She said, "You really need to know the 'gift' that you really gave to me. I was born the older of twins. I was always told that I was to be the big girl and take care of my 'younger' sister. Somewhere through my teenage years I stopped crying and literally have not been able to shed a tear for the last fifteen years. When I realized that you had given me this lovely gift without even knowing me I was overwhelmed with the gift of tears."

I asked, "How did you feel about God leading me to give the gift?"

Judy answered, "Well, that's very interesting because Carl and I do not have a spiritual faith—but we've been seeking one, and would love to know about yours."

Through that experience they found spiritual faith, which is the greatest gift anyone could receive.

Naomi Rhode

Hold the Vision

Once you have begun visualizing your success on a daily basis, you may come in contact with situations or people that will try to discourage you. Be aware that this could happen and you will more easily overcome these delight dampeners when they show up.

Our friend Chris knew what she wanted, and despite advice from other people, she continued with the vision that held power for her.

The Knight on a White Charger

My marriage of twenty years had broken up four years earlier. My life as a single mother working full time was busy and fulfilling, but I longed for a companion with whom to share my life journey.

I was deeply involved in my church, working as a counselor in a divorce recovery workshop with single women like myself. As a group we were often told that the perfect mate was out there for each of us, but for whatever reason, the timing wasn't yet right. The best thing I heard during those sessions, and it serves me well today, is that God has three answers to prayer—yes, no, and wait.

One well-meaning friend, a clergyman, told me that I wasn't doing enough to actively seek a mate. "That knight on a white charger isn't going to come galloping through your bedroom while you're reading your Bible," he said. But I was working on it in my own way. I wrote a detailed list of qualities that I felt I needed in a life partner, including age limits and height and weight requirements. I listed all the characteristics important to me—honesty, spirituality, an earthy sense of humor—someone who, no matter what his work, does the best job he can and values family and relationships above everything else. At night, just before I would go to sleep, I visualized those characteristics—I let my mind wander through the feelings I had when in the presence of someone with a great sense of humor or a deep sense of spirituality. And whenever I visualized the qualities, I repeated the following words: "I, Christine, deserve to love and be loved perfectly."

It was the day before Easter, in the seventh year of being single, and the kitchen drain was stopped up for the fifth time in as many months. I scanned the local paper and one ad caught my eye—"Any drain cleared, $15." I was instantly captivated by his voice over the phone, and twenty minutes later he came striding into the kitchen, all six-foot-five of him—in total control. He solved the problem in five minutes, holding up a handful of green leaves and saying, "Well, the first thing you can do is stop putting artichokes through the disposal." I wanted to crawl under the counter.

As he sat there on the floor, absentmindedly putting back all the things I kept under the kitchen sink, we talked. I learned that he was single, didn't have a current girlfriend, his young wife had left him two years ago, and she had taken their two children to Nebraska. He was also a writer who had a long string of acting and song-writing credits. His sparkling blue eyes seemed to dance, and every so often he would glance up at me to catch my reaction to what he was saying. When I mentioned that I did typing on the side, he went to his truck and brought back one of his short stories for me to read. As he left, he said he would be in touch about a possible typing job.

I sat in my kitchen and wondered, "Why do I have flutters in the pit of my stomach?" I was attracted to this stranger and yet he didn't match the physical description I was attracted to—he looked older than the men I usually dated. Then I realized—I had been visualizing the qualities I had felt were important and how I would feel when I was with that person. I was feeling exactly the way I visualized that I would!

We were married six months later, and after eight happy years, he still marvels at our good fortune in finding each other. But I know that there are no accidents in life—we came together because he embodies all the qualities I envisioned in a perfect mate and the timing was finally right. Chronologically, he is past the limits I had specified on my list—but age is a state of mind. He is younger in mind and spirit than most people half his age. He still does plumbing repairs—and he has introduced me to opera, quotes Shakespeare, and loves me as I deserve to be loved—perfectly. And, every year, on April 18, we serve artichokes in celebration of how we met.

Christine Russell

You will receive lots of attention when your life starts to improve—some of it negative. The delight dampeners will be there to tell you that it can't be done, you can't have it, no one has ever done it before, and you shouldn't try. Other people are always going to have opinions about everything. Their opinions are not necessarily the truth—just ideas that they own. Let them keep their ideas; you have glorious visions of your own to implement.

None of these barriers have power over you unless you give them the power. Ignore them; step over, under, or around them. Negative criticism from delight dampeners cannot stop you from fulfilling your dreams.

The Path to Freedom

> Imagination.... Its limits are only those of the mind itself.
>
> Rod Serling

Anything you want to enfold within your life is possible when you allow your imagination to reach beyond your existing self-limitations and take flight.

The Indian poet and sage Rabindranath Tagore speaks of the freedom that comes from soaring beyond our limits: "To fledgling birds, flight in the sky may appear incredible. They may with apparent reason measure the highest limit of their possibilities by the limited standard of their nests. But in the meanwhile they find that their food is not grown inside those nests; it is brought to them across the measureless blue. There is a silent voice that speaks to them, that they are more than what they are, and that they must not laugh at the message of soaring wings and glad songs of freedom."

The message of soaring wings and glad songs of freedom is clearly understood by those who choose to see what is possible within their imagination—and then to bring it into their reality. With daily visualizations, joy and enthusiasm will beckon us to go beyond our own self-imposed boundaries—to reach for the stars and let our imagination and spirits take flight and soar.

My Vision Took Flight

It was spring. I stood on the Dana Point cliffs, overlooking the Pacific Ocean. Next to me a man attached to a hang glider was preparing to jump. The noise was overwhelming. As the wind hit the fabric it flapped and snapped with such energy that it was frightening to the unaccustomed ear. But the man was unfazed. He simply hooked himself in, checked the wind, waited a few moments, and jumped. As he took off he lifted and soared over my head then headed out over the ocean. Back and forth he went. I had never seen anything like it in my life. I wondered what it felt like to be so free and fly. To my right I could see the sand dunes below the cliff. Several people were learning to hang glide and I watched for a while as they ran with their gliders off the shallow dunes. They would lift off and gently glide a few yards and then set back down, their feet running as they touched the sand.

When I got home my wife could see the excitement in my eyes. I couldn't stop talking about how impressed I was. I immediately got out the yellow pages and looked up hang gliders. I called the first number and spoke to a salesperson who explained that it would probably cost around three thousand dollars to buy a glider and take the lessons necessary to learn. My heart sank. I was a school teacher with a wife, two kids, and mortgage. Where would I get that much money?

That night I visualized I was flying—soaring out over mountains thousands of feet in the air. It was so real I could even feel the wind and the coolness of the air. For the next few weeks I revisited the cliffs and kept visualizing the feeling. I even got used to the noise of the flapping fabric. I wasn't sure how it would happen, but for some reason I knew I was going to hang glide.

As spring turned into summer, I turned thirty-six. On my birthday we went to dinner to celebrate and Jean, my wife, handed me my present. It was a plain white envelope; in it was a birthday card with a wonderfully silly poem. In the message Jean conveyed that she had purchased a tandem hang glider ride for me with an expert instructor. In all of my visits to the cliffs I never saw two people hang glide. It never occurred to me that someone could take you. Jean found out and completely surprised me.

A few weeks later I stood attached to the hang glider with my instructor/pilot. He looked at me and asked me if I was ready. I nodded and we began to run toward the 2,000-foot cliff high in the San Bernadino Mountains. As we lifted to 3,000 feet I found myself yelling with joy and confidence that I had never ever felt in my life. I was flying and the vision was real.

We soared for over an hour, rising, diving, lifting, turning gracefully over the forests, and eventually landing in the valley. When my feet touched the ground I know I was changed forever. I think God knows how to bring our visions into reality if we will not give up. Believe in what you want to do with your life, and life will figure out a way to bring it to you.

Jim Turrell

Imagination is the key. You must aspire to more than you currently have—so that you will have overflowing abundance in all areas of your life; for then and only then can you truly benefit all of mankind.

True genius is being able to see past what is evident to what is possible—and using your imagination to do so. Anything is possible to those who believe.

When you reach for the stars, you stretch your mind and imagination. Your spirit will emerge and grow. Reach inward to your own mind, and reach upward to the universe, to God, to your own goodness. Create a connection with Divinity . . . from which all blessings flow.

7

Under a Mantle of Blue

The pastures of the desert grow moist,
the hillsides are wrapped in joy,
the meadows are covered with flocks,
the valleys clothed with wheat;
they shout and sing for joy.

PSALM 65

*R*enewal is the gift of dawn. Every morning of the world, the sun rises and the sky turns a lovely shade of blue, signaling a new start. If there are dark clouds overhead, we know that just above them the sun shines and the sky is bright. Nature tells us every way she can that happiness is never far away. The gentle wind of our understanding can send the clouds rolling across the sky, revealing a limitless blue.

Wrapped in this mantle of blue is a world of natural delight. We delight in the majesty of mountains, the quiet beauty of forests, and oceans meeting the sky. The astonishing pinks and purples of orchids can open our eyes in a new way; the extraordinary calls of birds can pierce our hearts and take our breath away. What gifts they are!

One of our nation's most revered newscasters grew up on a ranch in Montana. Living so close to the earth and "the big sky" during his early years gave him an appreciation for nature that enriched him all his life. Here he recalls with delight the exuberance of springtime when he was a boy.

The Sound of Spring

Spring was a phenomenon in Montana, and it is yet. It is an explosion of sunlight, burgeoning earth, scents, bursting buds, and a sudden cessation of the raw March wind. The poignant call of the meadowlarks trills across the prairie. It is a season affecting man, animal, and plant.

Spring was such a burst of energy that children were simply compelled, frequently, to jump up and down in their sheer exuberance. Out on some hilltop, I often filled my lungs and screamed . . . because it was spring!

The horses bucked and reared when the harness or saddle was removed following a spring day's work. The lambs played "king of the castle" on a large rock on the hillside, leaping completely over the backs of their complacent mothers. The cows sported themselves in the pasture, and the turkey gobblers almost burst their wattles in apoplectic strutting about.

My parents had provided us children with a small wagon, a

scale model of the big farm wagon. One spring evening, I made a harness out of rope and slipped it innocently on Billy, the pet bull calf. He stood patiently while I hitched him to the toy wagon. Wadine and Marian were observing all these preparations and I invited them to accompany me on the first ride, and of course they leaped at the opportunity.

Marian, my second sister, sat in front, her plump little legs overhanging the wagon. Wadine sat behind her and I was about to crowd into the back when the calf suddenly shot forward as though he had been discharged from a cannon. With the first leap, my sisters were left sitting, unhurt, on the ground. The lines snapped out of my fingers and the calf flew around the corner of the house, bawling at the top of his lungs. A young colt, also kept in the yard, shook his head once and bolted through the small wooden gate, sending it flying in a hundred fragments. With that, one of the horses in the corral took a flying leap over the gate, caught his rear feet in it and kicked it to bits. The cows suddenly went stir-crazy inside the shed, and one emerged, bucking and bawling, with the wooden stanchion locked about her neck. Still the calf was circling the house. Dad stuck his head out of the barn and shouted, "What the hell is going on?"

Mother had her head out the kitchen window, and I was rolling on the grass in hysterical laughter. My sisters were weeping in fright.

The sheep joined the bedlam and poured through the barn area, surrounding bucking horses and stampeding cows. Wire was creaking and straining, wooden gates were being smashed; and the calf continued to circumnavigate the house, with the wagon flying behind him. Grandpa and Dad frantically tried to separate the sheep, lambs, colts, horses, cows, calves, and squawking chickens. The whole farm had exploded into a paroxysm of suddenly released spring energy.

As quickly as it all began, it subsided, and we picked up the pieces.

Spring on the prairie inspired one to creative musings and stirrings. It was as though man, seeing and feeling this astonishing burst of life and new energy on the part of nature, responded by trying in some way to emulate her. Surely, there was, in the soul and capacity of man, something he might do to rival some of the bursting loveliness about him.

I sat in the warm sunshine on top of the hills overlooking the ranch house, the barns, the fields, and the lake bed. I lay down and put my head on the grass. I could hear it! I could hear spring! The ground was a moving, writhing, stirring mass of movement and growth. Millions of tiny shoots were probing at the warm earth, drinking its moisture, absorbing its goodness, and sending their growth to the sunlight. The earth, the sky, the air, the universe were throbbing with life . . . and it was good!

Chet Huntley

We all look forward to relaxing vacations at the shore or in the mountains. We take weekend trips to the country and ask for a room with a view. Waterfront lots and homes at the crest of a hill are always in great demand; just a glance out the window during a busy day connects our soul for a moment with joy. At work, the corner office with the biggest window goes to the person of rank. Whether or not we are conscious of it, something in us wants to be connected with the natural world every day.

Beauty of Life Around Us

Letting us see the beauty of nature is one way that our Creator tells us how much we are loved. Peter Marshall, once chaplain of the U.S. Senate, noted that people wait and hope and pray for a special message from the Creator while overlooking the miracle of God's ongoing communication.

"The natural is ever full of the supernatural," he wrote. "Manifestations of God are lying at your feet, cradled in the soil. They surround you everywhere in the ordinary things of every day. Providence is plucking at your sleeve as you walk down the street. God is speaking to you all the time. . . . Did the cherry blossoms say anything to you? Did the azaleas and the wisteria? Had the trees no message for you? What about this new day? Did it not speak? And the evenings, with their stars?"

A magic moment of transformation in the Connecticut woods is shared in this story. This tough-minded executive believes that joy and compassion might never have surfaced in his life had he not heard God speak to him through the songs of the birds on that special day.

Springtime

After my divorce I couldn't find happiness. One cold spring afternoon I found myself walking on a bluff above the town where I had grown up. It was a familiar place. I used to walk there when I was a child to get away from my troubled home life.

That afternoon I had my journal with me and thought I might do some writing, but didn't have anything specific on my mind. I was mulling over my problems when I came upon a grove of pine trees sheltered from the cold wind. In the middle was an inviting spot covered with soft leaves and dappled with sunlight. As I stretched out on my back in that pile of leaves, I began to notice the birds singing.

Suddenly, from a place I knew nothing about, an overwhelming feeling of peace came over me. It felt as if all of the negativity and confusion of my life were draining out of me, right into the Earth. What was left was peace and the most delightful loved feeling you can imagine. My total being was at peace—every cell in my body. I felt that peace and love had always been there, buried under chronic anger and confusion. All of the things I had written in my journal about my terrible childhood, failed marriage, and the terrors of life became irrelevant. What was left was the real me, a peaceful and loving person. I lay there until the day grew cold, not wanting to move or lose this incredible feeling. Gradually it faded, and I decided to go on with my day and my life.

My life literally began again at that point. I used to look at the negative aspects of everything on my walks in the woods—growing up on welfare, having a raging father, and feeling demeaned because of it. I had been an angry person who had kept coming up with justifications for being mad at the world.

Right after this experience, I walked to the bluff and looked down at my hometown and all I could remember were the good things that happened when I was young—fishing in the river and loving my mother who did the best she could to raise eight children under very trying circumstances. My whole outlook on life suddenly shifted from negative to positive that day.

I listened to the birds that day as if I were hearing them for the very first time. Ever since then, I hear birds very clearly. They are messengers for me, reminding me that this very instant is full of delight. Right now! It's wonderful to hear a bird when I wake up. It loves to sing, loves the morning sun. And it's looking forward to another good day. I'm not sure I can define God, but when I hear birds, I get the sense there's a benevolent presence out there. It loves me. No question about that. I still don't know what really happened that day in the woods. I may never know, but I'm comfortable with the mystery.

Robert Butch

Nature has a voice of her own that speaks to our inner ear. The 96th Psalm suggests that we listen for her message: "Let the heavens rejoice and earth be glad! . . . Let the countryside exult, and all that is in it, and all the trees of the forest cry out for joy."

In these busy days, with so many things to do, you may forget how important it is to stay in touch with the earth. Then you may drive through a forest with lovely trees growing all around you and become soothed. Their cool shade and fresh scents calm you and you remember, once again, that contact with nature is necessary to your well-being. You just naturally begin to breathe more deeply, and tensions give way. Being out in the natural world makes you feel whole. And well it should, for you are a part of that world.

In the fresh, oxygen-rich air, you can imagine every cell of your body smiling as you take in great gulps of its invigorating essence. Against the backdrop of a larger reality, problems melt away and troubles are put into perspective.

Native Americans have long taught of the giving nature of trees and plants. Mysta Hiye, a spiritual elder living in the far north, teaches that trees have great healing energy.

"The longest distance is between our hearts and our minds," he says. "Just being in the woods can help us make that journey. We learn so many lessons about ourselves from nature. Living in the trees helps make us well."

In the soothing green forests we find healing light filtered through the trees and an expanded sense of ourselves as deeply rooted beings living in harmony with all of life.

Walking in a Pine Wood

Near the house, high on a hill, were woods of pine and fir; and, slipping away from the others, I followed a path that led me into one of those woods, through a tunnel of green and gloom and smoky, blue dusk. It was very quiet, very remote, in there. My feet sank into the pile of pine needles. The last bright tatters of sunlight vanished. Some bird went whirring and left behind a deeper silence. I breathed a different air, ancient and aromatic. I had not gone a hundred paces before I had walked out of our English-South country and was deep in the Northern forest itself, with a thickness of time, centuries and centuries of it, pressing against me. Little doors at the back of my mind were softly opened. It was not the mere quickening of fancy that brought me delight then, but an atavistic stirring and heightening of the imagination, as if all my distant ancestors, who were certainly of the North, were whispering and pointing in this sudden dusk.

Any turn now might bring me to the magical smithy, the cave of the dragon; a horn might blow and shatter the present time like so much painted glass; the world of legend, hung about these trees like spiders' webs, was closing round me. No doubt my precious ego, challenged at every step, felt a touch of fear; but my true self, recognizing this enlargement of life, finding its place for a moment or two in that procession which is the real life of Man, drew deeper breaths, lived in its own world during these moments, and was delighted.

J. B. Priestley

The rhythms of the natural world refresh your mind and heart, recharge your batteries, and bring joy to your inner being. We are so much a part of the universe that St. Francis of Assisi addressed our neighbors in the sky as "Brother Sun and Sister Moon."

The surf roars and we plunge into it on boogie boards, splashing with joy and zest. A fresh snowfall sends us crunching down the path to the ski slope. Some people climb mountains or explore the depths of the ocean at risk to life and limb—but to the great delight of the soul. Some of our deepest spiritual connections, our understanding of God's love for us, can only happen when we are beneath God's mantle of blue. In fact, most transcendental experiences, from runners' highs to sightings of saints, take place outdoors.

Avalanche of Love

I had moved from the urban sprawl of Los Angeles to a small town in north Idaho, and the adjustment had been difficult.

One morning Roger, my neighbor, invited me to go cross-country skiing. We loaded the snowmobile with skis and a tasty lunch, and off we went about ten miles into the wilderness to ski on the peak of Gisbourne Mountain. We skied back and forth across the top of this steep slope. A novice skier, I was paying attention to staying vertical, and admiring the awesome scenery. Danger was the furthest thing from my mind. Roger is a forest ranger, a paramedic and expert skier, so I wasn't worried about a thing, even though we were miles from civilization, or even a telephone.

As the sun dropped toward the horizon, our mountain and the snow-covered peaks around us were suffused with a gentle pink glow that faded to deep opalescent purple. We were reluctant to go, but we wanted to get home before dark since the snowmobile had no headlight.

We took off our skis and started down to the snowmobile, when all of a sudden I sank into snow up to my waist. I began thrashing around, trying to get back on top of the snow, when Roger's voice froze me.

"Stop that and don't move," he said. When I saw his face I realized I was in terrible trouble. He was really alarmed. Panic gripped me, and all of the blood in my body seemed to drop into my feet.

"We've hit a weak spot in the snowpack," Roger said as he slowly approached me to take my equipment. He was calm and serious as he told me what might happen next, and what I was to do if I were to survive an avalanche. He extended the end of a ski to me, and very slowly, I inched my way out of the hole.

We stood up and gingerly walked back to the trail. By this time it was nearly dark, and as if on cue a full moon rose over the distant peaks to light our way. Its luminous beams reflected on the snow, turning a threatening mountainside into a glowing vision of ethereal beauty.

I suddenly felt safe and warm, then the feeling intensified far beyond any emotion I'd ever known. I felt as if I were floating on a sea of love and joy, surrounded by a benevolent presence. The moonlight was everywhere, and so was that feeling—the trees, the stars, the night were all part of it. My heart was so full I wanted to sing or cry, but all I could do was to open my hands and receive this incredible blessing.

My inclinations are more spirited than spiritual, so I can't say what that presence was, but I now feel that something watches over me with more love than I knew there was.

Kathryn Kidwell

Nature is the great common ground between the rich and the poor, old and young, athletes and artists. Whether you jump in and swim in a beautiful lake or sit on the shore and paint the scenery, just being outside makes you feel at home.

Walk in the Light

Few men know how to take a walk. The qualifications of a professor are endurance, plain clothes, old shoes, an eye for Nature, good humor, vast curiosity, good speech, good silence, and nothing too much. If a man tells me that he has an intense love of Nature, I know, of course, that he has none. Good observers have the manners of trees and animals, their patient good sense, and if they add words, 'tis only when words are better than silence.

Ralph Waldo Emerson

Be available to experience the gifts and grace of Nature—find pleasure in the outdoors. Choose an outdoor sport that resonates with your innate nature—golf, tennis, horseback riding—anything that will keep you in the sunshine and air for some portion of your day. If those activities do not appeal to you, then take a walk.

Walking in the great outdoors, for any length of time, allows you to experience nature's grace. Park your car in the farthest spot from the market and enjoy the walk. Walk to work, walk your children to school. Walking slows the pace of life, lowers stress levels, and improves our health.

Walking strengthens and tones your muscles while allowing you to communicate with nature's creatures and creations. When we walk, we reinforce our feelings of being part of the whole, the oneness of creation.

By walking, we also do something for the environment. For short trips, we do not need a noisy, polluting engine to get us there. We are the caretakers of the world, and this is just one small and easy way that we can contribute to the health of the planet, instead of to its destruction.

Nature's Creatures

The divine spark in all living beings shines through the eyes of all nature's animals. Our friend Wyland, the ocean artist, told us,

"You will never be the same after you have looked into the eye of a whale and felt the wisdom of the ages that this giant creature of the deep possesses."

Animals have been known to step in to help human beings—to once again remind us that maybe they know, better than we do, that we are all creatures in God's great world.

Recently, teenager Ryan Potton got separated from his group while camping in the Rocky Mountains. As night fell, and temperatures dropped, snow began to fall. He curled up in a ball, trying the best he could to keep himself warm. Sometime in the night, he reported feeling "presences" around him in the darkness. The presences turned out to be two female elk that had lain down with him. Their body warmth kept him alive throughout the night of below freezing temperatures. The imprints of their bodies, next to his in the snow, were visible to the rescuers who found him in the morning.

Animals not only have the ability to astound us with their wisdom and caring, they also can display an enjoyment of the outdoors that can rival our own. During the Iditarod, the dogsled race across the frozen wonder of Alaska, Gary Paulsen, a rookie driver, came upon another musher who had stopped his team and was gazing down a hill with rapt attention. He paused to see what was going on and found, to his great delight, the following extraordinary sight.

Buffalo Games

We were looking down on a frozen lake—one of the Farewell lakes. But it wasn't the lake that held his interest. Below and to the right a group of four buffalo were standing on the shore. Two of them were in the grass at the edge and the other two were out on the ice.

"Somebody told me that there was a herd of buffalo here, but I hadn't expected to see them along the trail."

"Yes," I told the other musher. "Buffalo. I know. They told us . . ."

"No—*watch*."

I turned back, thinking frankly that he was around the bend. So it was buffalo—so what?

Then I saw what he meant.

The surface of the lake was bare of snow . . . and the two buffalo out on the ice were having a rough time of it trying to stand. . . . [O]ne of the buffalo on the shore backed away from the lake, up the sloping side of the ridge, pawed the ground a couple of times and ran full bore for the lake.

Just as he hit the edge of the ice his tail went straight up in the air, he spread his front feet apart and stiffened his legs and slid away from shore, spinning around in a circle as he flew across the ice.

When he slowed to a stop he bellowed, a kind of "Gwaaa" sound, then began making his tortuous way back to the shoreline.

While he was doing this the fourth buffalo came shooting out on the ice, slid farther (also tail up) than the last, made a louder noise, and started back slipping and falling.

I couldn't believe it and blinked rapidly several times, thinking I was hallucinating.

"No—it's real," he laughed. "I was passing when I heard the bellow and came up to check it out. . . . I've been here an hour, maybe a little more. They've been doing this all the time. Great, isn't it?"

We lay there for another half-hour watching them play. The object seemed to be who could slide the farthest and each of them tried several times, tail up, happy bellows echoing on the far shore of the lake as they slid across the ice.

Buffalo Games . . . who would have thought it could happen?

Gary Paulsen

Nature's Patterns

The patterns of nature speak very deeply to our souls. The rising and setting of the sun and the moon, the nightly progression of the stars, the turning of the seasons, the ebb and flow of the tides on our beaches—all of nature's patterns give us a feeling of continuance and security. When we are in touch with the sacred patterns of nature, we become more aware of the sacred patterns within us. The Reverend Lauren Artress discovered this early in life along the banks of the River Chagrin.

The Dance of the Fishes

Across the river from my home was a beautiful shale cliff about 200 feet high. It was green and lush up there and I loved to wade across the river and climb up the trail to the top. There I felt at peace. I think that children have a sense of the sacred, though they do not use words like "spiritual ground." But that's what that place was for me.

One summer day when I was in seventh grade, something caught my eye as I walked along the top of the silent cliff. It looked like someone was standing in the water flashing hundreds of mirrors at me. I moved closer to the edge of the cliff and focused on the water. The source of the shining light was the sun reflected off the sides of little fish swimming in a school of about forty or fifty. These little "shiners" were swimming in formation. First they were a rectangle swimming in one direction. Then, Flash! They formed themselves into a circle and swam in another direction. Flash again, they turned back and swam in a rectangle.

I lay on the cliff and watched them for hours, until sunset forced me to cross the river to home. Later I learned that the Native Americans call this "the dance of the fishes." I felt that I had been let in on one of the great mysteries of the world. It was the beginning of understanding that there is a sacred pattern in life— the hibernation of bears, the flight of birds going south for the winter. Sets of patterns guide our lives and speak to the human heart.

Lauren Artress

Barbara visited Sea World in Orlando and watched the great whale doing its graceful, leaping show. The audience was mesmerized.

The whole place felt like one enormous heartbeat. The entire audience was hushed, awed at the spirit of this great creature so far from its own home, yet performing with such delight. Everyone in the amphitheater learned something about love and connection.

At the same place, nine-year-old Meredith Zinn thought her glasses were gone for good when they fell off as she bent over the dolphin tank. But a friendly dolphin brought them up to the surface and handed them back to her. When Meredith reached out to get them, the dolphin swam away, teasing, as Meredith squealed with delight. The game went on for several minutes and drew a crowd. Finally the manager came with a fish and bribed the dolphin to give up the glasses. A dolphin toothprint on the frame is Meredith's souvenir of this enchanting exchange.

Many people are fascinated and intrigued with our whale and dolphin friends. Their intelligence and sense of play remind us of ourselves at our best.

Member of the Pod

When I worked in the Florida Keys I would take my fins and snorkel and enjoy a relaxing swim in the warm, blue water of the Florida Straits every day at lunch time.

I often ran into a pod of dolphins—usually four or five, but sometimes as many as twelve. They never seemed frightened of me—on the contrary, they allowed me to swim along with them. I developed a wonderful rapport with them.

One day we were playing around in about ten feet of water and a young female that I called "Rosie" kept going under me and standing on her head. I dove and stood on my head too. We did that a couple of times and on the next try I saw a piece of seaweed between us. I picked it and bobbed to the surface. She came up too, and I laid the plant across her lower front teeth. She took off with it, porpoising around until I lost sight of her. A little while later she came back with a different piece of seaweed, which she offered to me. I took it and porpoised around in my clumsy fashion.

Rosie and I really communicated. It wasn't a deep discussion of how to save the world or anything like that—just two beings enjoying each other and exchanging small gifts. Important enough!

One afternoon I was lying on my waterbed attempting biofeedback to relieve the pain of a migraine headache. Suddenly in my mind I was in the water. I could really feel the water going past my eyeballs. Then I felt other shapes around me and I felt as if I were with the pod. My skin felt different, especially sensitive—like getting goosebumps and having no control over your skin. The sensitivity was multiplied a thousand times—as if in our play the dolphins had imparted a more delicate sensitivity to me.

All the while, I knew I was in the bedroom of my house on the ocean. I liken the experience to picking up an extension phone and "listening in" to the senses.

I do not have the degrees or discipline for a scientific inquiry designed to prove telepathy between species. I only know that after that experience I often feel I am in communication with the pod. I can feel the water passing my eyes or skin sensitivity at the oddest moments. It seems to be something that just happens—without my willing it. I feel as if there are delicate threads holding me within the pod—no matter where I am.

Joyce King

Our interaction with the other creatures on our planet can provide a deeper understanding of ourselves and a heightened awareness of our connection with them. This understanding and awareness opens the way for us to be in delight with all of creation. It can also give us the gift of seeing with more than just our eyes—beyond the obvious, to the divinity within.

Two Looks Away

Life abounds with epiphanies. Epiphanies are life's invitations to come out and play. Perhaps for a moment we receive the invitation—from a rainbow or a child or a whale. Like a child afraid of the dark, we may fearfully reject the invitation, and we don't see what is in front of us.

While I was researching the play behavior of wolves, I went on a tracking trip to Montana. North of Glacier National Park, I stopped to visit with a Native American elder. He listened attentively as I told him why I was there. He then spoke earnestly, "Most people don't see wolves because they know only how to look with their eyes. Some are trained and can therefore look better than others. Some of these people say that they see wolves. But they don't. You white men use science to improve your eyesight, as if better scopes will help you find wolves. But even with these machine eyes you cannot see. It is not good vision alone that allows one to see a wolf." Then he looked at me and thrust his hands straight out from the middle of his chest. "One must take a second look, and this is done with the heart. The real wolf is two looks away."

With the "first look" we perceive the world rationally, order it according to fixed values, and attempt to master and manage it systematically.

With the wisdom of a second look, we see the truth beyond appearances. The second look puts us in touch with the Greater Life within, the spark of divinity that dwells in all living creatures. In this seeing the divine grace of life is experienced.

At Wolf Haven, a wolf sanctuary where I continued my research, a two-year-old wolf named Sybil often rested on the ground with her head on her crossed forepaws, watching me intently. Her deep amber eyes encompassed me without the least trace of aggression or confusion. From my seat on a nearby tree stump, I glanced at her every so often. After a time, she walked over, put her forepaws on my lap and rested her head on my shoulder. I leaned against her gently. In a few minutes she left as quietly as she had arrived.

Sybil sauntered back to her special spot among the six other wolves, nosed the ground and spiraled slowly downward. I stood up and began to move slowly about the enclosure. Almost immediately, Sybil trotted over. She jumped up and put her paws on my forearm which I held out in an arc in front of me. She mouthed my beard and I jostled her head with my free hand. Our faces were very close. Then we caught each other's eye. Suddenly there was neither Sybil nor Fred, just light. For just a second, something powerful penetrated me and was gone. I had experienced myself and Sybil not as man and wolf, but as two creatures created by the same master's hand.

Afterwards, tears ran down my cheeks as I realized that Sybil had shared with me a deep communication. I wondered if she felt what I felt. If she had been human, I would call her or at least write her a letter. But how would I let her know that I knew? I smiled at my human thought. Sybil already knew that wolves and all creatures, including me, are part of nature.

My experience with Sybil that day made me realize that life is *the* epiphany. We are, each of us, born belonging. Our together-ness is the Creator's all-embracing gift. Everything is a part of everything. My intention is stronger than ever to see all of nature's creatures with the second look, and to recognize that spark of divinity within us all.

O. Fred Donaldson

We expand into the larger life of delight as we learn to love and respect the animals and plants that make this planet both special and sacred. Our consciousness grows and souls expand as we delight in the gifts of the Creator.

How countless are your works, Lord,
all of them made so wisely!
The Earth is full of your creatures.

Psalm 104

Unending Delights of Gardens

Anyone who has ever planted a garden and watched it grow knows the joy of blooming things. Angela Lansbury, star of the TV thriller *Murder She Wrote*, has been a gardener since she was a child.

"There's nothing like the unending delights of a garden," she says. "No matter how small my garden is, to me it is a place of tremendous peace and inspiration. I find that gardening releases my mind to drift away from whatever has been bugging me. I try to create a beautiful landscape, and I want my garden to inspire feelings of tranquility in the people who see it, just as it does for me."

It's simply amazing to watch a tiny seed become a flower. It seems an incredible miracle. From a tiny brown seed, a bold marigold plant sprouts up. Flower after flower blooms in astonishing color. Then suddenly, out of the blue, butterflies of the same vivid golden hue begin landing on the flowers—butterflies who have never visited your yard before, summoned, it seems, by nothing more than color. How did they know? What a wonder!

I bud forth delights like the vine.
Ecclesiasticus 24

Popular Buddhist teacher Thich Nhat Hanh describes the seeds within us that help us grow our personal gardens of delight and the seeds we must plant within ourselves: "When I smile, the seeds of smiling and joy have come up. As long as they manifest, new seeds of smiling and joy are planted. But if we don't practice smiling for a number of years, that seed will weaken, and I may not be able to smile anymore. Every time we practice mindful living, we plant healthy seeds and strengthen the healthy seeds already in us. Healthy seeds function similarly to antibodies. Each of us needs a reserve of seeds that are beautiful, healthy, and strong enough to help us during difficult moments."

From a windowsill garden in Manhattan to the tropical rain forest in Costa Rica, plants bring us tiny impulses of joy. If we are paying attention and living mindfully in the moment, we can receive great happiness and insight from the gardens of the world.

Elexis Rice visited Costa Rica's rain forest and rode the aerial tram that travels into the canopy of trees far above the ground. There colorful birds nest and monkeys swing in the trees.

"Very little sunlight reaches the ground because the canopy of trees is so thick," she reported. "Because human beings are tied to the ground, we don't realize how much is going on over our heads.

"A multitude of seeds fall to the ground and wait for light. It might take twenty years, but when a break occurs in the canopy—a branch falls or a tree dies—out of the blue the sun's rays shine through and the seeds suddenly awaken. They work fast, for the light will not last too long. In a few days, they leap from the forest floor and shoot skyward, photosynthesizing with gusto as they drink up the light."

Rice went on to reflect, "Like those seeds, we may lie dormant until something happens. You lose a loved one or a job, and into that hole light begins to shine. Your light may come in the form of a book, a meeting with an enlightened person, a class or workshop. Perhaps, like the Buddha, you overhear a scrap of conversation at the right moment when your ego takes a break and your soul is listening. Whatever the cause, everything opens up and you begin to grow, like the rain forest, in delight."

The tropics hold exceptional beauty and opportunity to delight in creation. A glorious beach on a perfect day was the setting for an insightful discovery.

Gift of a Feather

I'd never known a bird "up close and personal" and birds could not have been further from my mind the day I went to Cape Romano, the last outpost of civilization on Florida's southwest coast before the mangrove swamps and Everglades take over.

I went on a boat trip with friends to this place of staggering beauty, which seemed to be made more of glimmering light than of land and sky. We moored our boat and walked up the long white beach and were surprised to see a house with a large outdoor aviary. Within a sturdy chainlink fence were trees and shrubs and parrots and macaws, whose vivid colors glowed like neon against the turquoise sky. I had no knowledge of birds whatsoever, except a vague belief that big birds bit.

I walked to the fence, and a blue and gold macaw climbed up to meet me, foot-over-beak, until we could see each other eye to eye. I admired it aloud. "What a beautiful bird you are." We exchanged pleasantries for a few minutes. "My" macaw hopped down and selected a perfect feather from the ground—apparently one of its own. Then it climbed up again, reached through the fence and handed it to me. And I swear it smiled. I was enchanted, and felt that I had been let in on a very special secret. Birds radiate delight. It was a holy moment.

That macaw feather is one of my most cherished possessions, a beautiful reminder of the love that comes to us out of the blue from the miracle of creation.

Barbara Nichols

Learning and Healing

Every plant and animal, every blade of grass, is a celebration of creation. Being out in nature connects us to the beauty and power of the universe and lets us know we belong. The beauty and richness of being reveal themselves every moment if we but pause and pay attention.

All of the forests and fields of the earth offer us the ongoing blessing of healing and wholeness. We are enriched immeasurably by being out in nature and feeling the pulse and joy of the land; we can be healed by plants and herbs if only we have the wisdom to recognize their properties. All of nature, from bees and butterflies to flowers and trees, is the "Garden of Delight."

Tenderly plant trees and flowers, raise animals with love and care, do what you can to keep our water and air clean. The natural power of the universe is on your side.

"Heaven and earth are in us," Mahatma Gandhi said. We live in paradise on this beautiful planet sparkling with oceans and lakes, engraved with mountains and plains. The gifts of our Creator are here for us to enjoy and to remind us that the ordinary kind of delight we take in a flower or an exquisite sunset is a part of the joy of God's creation.

8

Out
of the
Blue

Spiritual energy flows in and produces effects in
the phenomenal world.

WILLIAM JAMES

ometimes we come in contact with spiritual energy when we least expect it. Something comes out of the blue into our lives and engenders a state of consciousness beyond ordinary awareness, and in some cases, beyond our wildest dreams. Near-death experiences can create a spiritual awakening, but you don't need to die to become attuned to the spiritual side of life. Although these "happenings" may occur after we go through life-threatening danger, more often than not they come unexpectedly to ordinary people during ordinary times in their lives—and leave them with a deeper, richer sense of purpose and a feeling of being part of a universal plan.

A man on vacation with his family was surprised when for no apparent reason he experienced an astounding shift in perspective.

The Night the Stars Reached Down

After midnight on New Year's Eve, I was standing on a beach in Mexico, squiggling my toes in the sand. I shifted my four-year-old son on my shoulder as I listened to the ocean's raucous scrape and roar and searched for starry dippers in the sky.

The champagne-guzzling, horn-tooting, new-found-friend-kissing crowd with whom my wife and I had celebrated at our resort two hours before had all gone elsewhere, leaving the long, wide, moon-shadowed beach to me and Jeremy, who had suddenly awakened and couldn't go back to sleep.

So there I was, singing softly into his ear in the velvet night and trying to absorb the scene. The moonlit waves crashed white on the sand, like ghostly horses galloping in from the unseeable sea; the lingering warmth of the day danced with the breeze-borne cool of the night, swirling around us, trailing a faint and salty perfume; and the wind stroked tender fingers in the palm trees' silver fronds.

Earlier in the day I had been thinking about New Year's dreams and goals, about the path of the country and the state of my soul. In my journal, I had written "I believe more fervently than ever in the gifts of travel: compassion and open mindedness, humility and humor, a sense of perspective and place. Travel puts you in the world, and when you are out there in the swirling, messy, mesmerizing, mysterious, and miraculous middle of it, pomposity and bigotry and intolerance lose their grasp."

I thought about endings and beginnings, about new years and old, about the paths we take and the places we never know, the things we lose and the things we hold. A dull futility—a sense of how fleeting and fragile everything is—filled me.

I gazed up at the uncomprehending, incomprehensible stars, when suddenly the moment crystallized, became precarious and precious. There was nothing but Jeremy and me on an abandoned, wave-washed beach, at the cusp of the continent, on the edge of a new year.

Then something extraordinary happened: the stars seemed to reach down to me, the air seemed to close around me, the wind whispered a low lullaby in my ear.

For an electrifying moment, I felt embraced and uplifted by a sensuous intelligence infinitely greater than my own; for one small moment, frozen in time, suffused in warmth and wisdom, I was born aloft on the shoulder of the night.

In that instant, each piece seemed to stand out in singular clarity, as if I were seeing it, learning its name for the first time: star, palm, sand, wave.

And at the same time, I felt how all these pieces were vastly and intricately interlaced, as were my sleepy son and my own restless soul.

I still can't distill a pithy message from that moment, can't think of any all-connecting conclusion. I just know that I needed to tell you what I felt on that Mexican beach: the solacing shoulder of some cherished—and cherishing—whole.

Donald W. George

Like George, most people who have such extraordinary experiences are hard-pressed to give them a name. One explanation involves our own physical makeup. Author and practicing physician Melvin Morse explains in *Conversations with God*, "Deep within our brain, on the right side above the ear, is an area which allows us to communicate with, for lack of a better word, God. And that is the part of the brain which allows us to have an inner voice, that allows us to have a sense of conscience. It's a quiet part, the nonverbal, intuitive side that every human being has. When we have an unexpected spiritual experience, this part of the brain is stimulated. Many people report that once they have had an experience, or communication with God, they often become highly intuitive, or develop the ability to use what we commonly call psychic gifts."

People who have these extraordinary experiences are touched in profound and compelling ways. While the experiences are all different, they seem to have certain similar qualities. Out of the blue, delight comes into our lives, though in different ways. Some people report feeling a sense of "the peace that passes all understanding" from the scriptures. Or they may find a sudden solution to a nagging problem or have a wonderful idea. They come away feeling loved, with the ability to see life more clearly or understand it more deeply. Many people are strengthened in some important way and see their life path open before them. Whether or not these experiences qualify as miracles, they do leave people changed, and in some cases, completely transformed. These nudges from the universe—unexpected communication with a Higher Force—do not follow predictable patterns, but they tend to fall into certain categories.

Epiphany

An epiphany is a simple or striking event that suddenly brings understanding. It is a flash of intuition that reveals the essential meaning or nature of something. And for some lucky souls, it can be a sudden manifestation of the divine.

When people have an epiphanic experience, they tend to describe it in spiritual terms, whether or not they have religious belief. In fact, epiphanies may be conversion experiences. Some people report a visit from the Holy Spirit, angels, God, or their own higher consciousness. Some say it is like a wheel of light or air coming down from above and circling them, or the feeling of being anointed. Others say they are electrified or lit up head to toe, from the inside out. This exactly matches our description of being in delight. Delight *is* that head-to-toe tingle! People in every country of the world and in every religious tradition report similar experiences, though they may explain them in different ways.

Here a woman who attended a seminary years ago reports a delightful experience in spite of the difficulties she went through with her studies and her status as the only woman there.

Little Flames of God

From childhood I had read stories to comfort myself over the messiness of the world. Stories from the Old Testament had given me models of resourceful, independent children God approved of, like Joseph in Egypt, or Ruth. In college I was an English major. Recalling my childhood pleasure in Old Testament stories, I decided one morning to use the summer to learn Hebrew at the seminary campus. That afternoon I bought a copy of *Learning Hebrew by the Inductive Method* and a Hebrew Bible.

The next morning I had my coffee, took my books out of their bag, and laid them on my desk under the window. I studied chapter one of the grammar carefully. After that, I had another cup of coffee, and I laid the Hebrew Bible in front of me, opening it, as you do all Hebrew Bibles, back to front.

Then, as I stumbled through the first words of Genesis 1:1, "In the beginning, God created the heavens and the earth," I had an epiphany. Why this was so, I do not know, but I still recall the way the shape of the Hebrew letters and the look of the light falling on the creamy paper were mixed up with what I can only call a sense of cosmic goodness and joy in all created things I had never encountered before. It was as though the page itself were alive and the jots and tittles on the letters little flames. For the first time I could recall, life seemed safe and complete, and there was a place for me in it. In that instant I knew that God delighted in creation, in light, in water and mountains, in fruit-bearing trees

and grasses, in water creatures and bugs, in wild animals and tame, in men, and most important for me, in women like me.
Roberta Bondi

Epiphanies may be as common as having a flash of insight about your life while listening to beautiful music, or as astonishing as hearing a voice out of the blue telling you to get off the freeway at the next exit, then learning that you had avoided a big accident by doing so. Sometimes they come gently to soothe our aching hearts and restore our shattered confidence.

Heartstone

It was a year of change. My marriage ended and I was feeling shut down. Perhaps a change of scenery would help. I signed up for a tour of mystical sites in Great Britain, and as I went from ancient places like Stonehenge to magical places like Findhorn, my outlook brightened up.

On the remote Scottish island of Iona, we had a free day. Before we separated to explore this fascinating island on our own, some of us decided to pick an "Angel Card" from the deck. My card that morning was love. What a lovely message for one feeling rather unloved.

I set off by myself to find a souvenir—perhaps a colored stone would catch my eye. The sun was shining, the breeze was brisk, and the ocean rolled to the shore in steady waves.

"Love," I muttered to myself. "Will it ever happen again for me?"

I walked along the beach where the shifting tides continually churned up a treasure trove of stones, and paused at a lonely tidepool. The vivid colors of a coral and quartz stone caught my eye. My souvenir had presented itself, just as I knew it would.

I knelt down to pick up the stone, and then, lost in thought, kept running my fingers through the water. Suddenly a perfect heart-shaped stone appeared on the top of my hand as if it had fallen from above. Where did it come from? It was a black stone about three inches across, smooth on one side and rough on the other.

The message of love surged through my heart. I felt I had been given a gift from the unseen forces that watch over me. Dumbfounded, I sat there for an hour, allowing myself to feel loved and protected.

I have experienced tremendous growth in my life since that time. Now when I pick up my heartstone, I remember how it opened my heart for all the good that was to come.

Janice Capriani

Serendipity

> Chance is the pseudonym God uses when He does not want to sign His name.
>
> Anatole France

Most people have experienced serendipity. A series of mysterious coincidences brings you to a shining instant when things come together for you, and you are at the right place at the right time to receive some extraordinary benefit. You meet someone, quite by accident, and think to yourself later, "How amazing! If I hadn't stopped there and done that, we wouldn't have met—it's almost as if it was meant to be!" Serendipity is the aptitude, or gift, of finding valuable things or making fortunate discoveries by "accident."

Those Conservative Swiss

I'd been in Africa on business longer than I'd expected and was out of money and completely exhausted when I checked into a modest little hotel in Zurich on my way home. I fell into bed and went right to sleep.

About two o'clock in the morning I woke up to the throbbing

beat of drums and cymbals. Was I still in Africa? No, Switzerland, the most conservative country in the world. It must be me. I put my hand to my head to test my temperature and jumped out of bed and ran to the mirror. Was I yellow? Was it malaria? What kind of delusion was this? The drums went on and on.

I called the front desk. "Do you hear drums?"

"Oh, yes, Madame. It's the second day of the second month and the trade groups are having a party. It goes on for the whole weekend."

I threw open the window and looked down. There were people with their bodies and faces covered with gold and silver paint, dancing and singing in the street. They looked like men, but they had on huge hoopskirts. They were construction workers and other tradesmen, celebrating like mad.

I put on my clothes and went out to join the festivities. They were cooking sausage on the corner and passing out drinks. Even though I was broke I could eat until the bank opened on Monday. It was a delightful party.

Years later, I formed a company in Switzerland and was back in Zurich with clients—the very stuffy president of an American company and some of his top executives who had come to examine the potential for a semiconductor testing company. I wondered how in the world I would get them to loosen up. We checked into our hotel and met downstairs for a bite to eat, when lo and behold, here came the tradesmen in their gold and silver paint and hoopskirts. It was the eleventh day of the eleventh month. I said to my group, "Come on, this parade is for you." We spent the whole night out there with those conservative Swiss, dancing and having a wonderful time.

I took a clue from all of that—you don't have to plan everything. I used to try to control everything, but I've had more fun with things I never planned. When I'm in the right place doing the right thing, it's an invitation for delight to come in. We used to use the word *coincidental*, but now I know it's all there, waiting to happen.

Victoria Downing

When delight leads the way, your timing is superb. The most marvelous things may fall into your lap and fortune may smile on your every endeavor. Marcus Bach, in his book *The World of Serendipity*, explains: "In the world of serendipity, chance is no longer chance; it may be the signature of God or good, and every experience is a guideline for a great adventure. We have caught on to some secret attunement. At such times we are relaxed, receptive, inwardly confident. Even if we seem excited on the surface, at a subsurface level there is a most wonderful *knowing*." An experience of serendipity will fill you with a sense of rightness and manifest a feeling of certainty beyond the normal intellect. Sometimes you know what to do even though it doesn't fulfill the laws of logic. Perhaps a higher law is guiding you.

Message in the Sand

When my husband, David, and I were trying to make a big life decision, a message that had been written in the sand dramatically changed the course of our lives.

We were staying at a friend's condominium on the west coast of Florida. We were trying to decide whether to continue on the road as we had been doing on our one-hundred city book tour, or to settle down in Florida.

As we walked on the beach, we were praying and meditating on this question. As I looked ahead I could see words written in the sand. We stopped and read them together, "Gold is here follow up." These unusual words had great meaning to us. The Gold Coast of Florida was the place we wanted to live; gold represents the treasures of life and the treasures of the heart.

We took our message in the sand as a God message and decided to end our tour. With great faith, we followed our intuitive guidance, and settled on the Gold Coast. Within a few short weeks, we began to broadcast on the finest classical music station in South Florida. And we were invited to be a part of a wonderful church, where David is now minister.

We were thrilled that gold had appeared in our lives to guide us to our new home, a loving spiritual community, and a fine radio program. Now we walk the beach regularly. The other day we saw another message in the sand. It was only one word, but it summed up, to our greater delight, all that we have experienced on the Gold Coast so far. It said, in big bold letters, ENJOY.

Gay Lynn Williamson

In the Zone

Top athletes refer to their high-performance episodes as "playing in the zone." You suddenly enter a region of consciousness where time vanishes and barriers dissolve. When it happens, you are able to transcend your typical results, seemingly without effort. You feel highly confident and focused, full of energy and life, and there is a natural flow between your thoughts and actions.

A Larger Life

When I was about fourteen, I had an incredible experience of delight while engaged in a sport. I had been training regularly for some years as a fencer. I regularly won at fencing matches and was being encouraged to train for the Olympic team a few years down the line. My fencing master, Frederick Rhodes, was a Russian who had been taught by a French master, so the tradition I learned was elegant and courtly, with salutes that looked as if you were signing the signature of God in the air with your foil. It seemed that fencing was a sport that was bred in the bone for me.

One day I was participating in a round robin—a match in which you fenced with one opponent after another until you were defeated. My opponents, both men and women, included some of the city's leading fencers, all much older and more experienced than I. As I began to fence, I suddenly found that I was "in the zone." I was no longer just a pretty good fencer. I had tapped into the Essence of fencing. I *was* the sport, anticipating all the moves, seeing all the opportunities. I could not tire; endless waves of energy filled me. There was no possibility of beating me. One after another, twenty opponents came up and were defeated. On and on it went. I was all the great fencers who ever were. I felt as if their spirits were joining with mine for one last great bout, until, after six hours of continuous fencing, the match was stopped and I was declared the winner.

I firmly believe that all human beings have access to extraordinary energies and powers. Judging from accounts of mystical experience, heightened creativity, or exceptional performance by athletes and artists, we harbor a greater life than we know. There we go beyond those limited and limiting patterns of body, emotions, volition, and understanding that have been keeping us in drydock. Instead we become available to our capacity for a larger life in body, mind, and spirit. In this state we know great torrents of delight.

Jean Houston

Dr. Robert Kriegel, author of *Inner Skiing*, suggests that we can control the frequency, duration, and intensity of zone experiences by learning how to make them happen. He labels the experience "the C Zone." "For many people . . . Type C episodes happen by chance. For no apparent reason you suddenly get hot in a tennis match and play way over your head. Or out of nowhere the work you have been struggling to get finished just starts flowing. So people attribute their Type C performance to luck. . . . [I]t isn't a rare peak experience that comes once in a lifetime. It is a high plateau of optimal-performance behavior that we can reach over and over again because it is reflective of our innate ability."

Moments of Illumination

Whether we name divine presence synchronicity, serendipity, or graced moment matters little. What matters is the reality that our hearts have been understood. Nothing

is as real as a healthy dose of magic which restores our
spirits.

Nancy Long

Moments of illumination were once thought to be the exclusive province of saints and mystics. But as times change and a new openness to nonordinary experiences occurs, we hear stories from friends and neighbors that bring us face to face with the truth of a higher power that loves and cherishes us. When these enchanted moments bring life to our spirits and joy to our souls, they also heighten our interest in the spiritual life. They feed our hunger for wholeness and confirm our faith in the ultimate benevolence of the universe.

We may have been praying all our lives for a little hint that God knows we are here. Then, when we least expect it, reassurance comes.

Golden Moment

Did you ever think that if there was really anything to this God business that He would show himself once in a while just to silence the cynics? Well, I did.

But by the time I was nearing sixty I had given up on ever coming face to face with my Maker—at least while I was still breathing.

He'd had His chances to make my acquaintance up close, plenty of them, and apparently had decided it wasn't something that would do either of us any particular good.

It wasn't as if I imagined I had earned an audience, mind you. Lord knows there were plenty of more deserving candidates.

Still, I thought it might be appropriate, since I'd been one of the world's dedicated skeptics. My faith comes and goes, and frankly it's been gone more than it's been here. So if anybody qualified for a burning bush experience, it was me. At least to my way of thinking.

However, as a member of a group who depends on a Higher

Power to help them lead a better life, I was cautioned not to get my hopes up. They said that although one of the group's founders had had a spectacular spiritual experience, few people had ever met, or ever would meet, their Maker in a flash of blinding light. Most experience a more subtle inner guidance, a more gradual kind of spiritual progress.

So, as I said, I had given up expecting anything out of the ordinary. And this September night was no different than any other. I had been reading a good murder mystery and was getting drowsy. As I prepared to crawl into bed, it came to me that it might be nice to go out to the darkened front room and sit for a moment.

As soon as I touched the couch, I knew this wasn't going to be a typical meditation. Because suddenly I was lifted out of myself and into something that I have no words for, and can only call a golden moment.

I no longer felt physical. The hundred and fifty pounds that I normally carry around had no heft. Nor could I feel the cares of the world that usually weigh on me. I was as light as the dust particles in a golden sunbeam.

Job worries? Gone.

Fear of people, places and things? Vanished.

Family responsibilities? Health concerns? Economic insecurity? All taken care of. I was free.

No sound of trumpets rent the air, no booming voice nor tinkling bells. The earth did not move.

But something came to me: This golden moment is what it feels like when you quit trying to run your life (and everybody else's) and turn it over to God. That's all.

It was enough.

I didn't see God's face. But He was there.

H. T. Pyle

For many of us, these brief experiences awaken or intensify our sense of ourselves. We find new dimensions in our souls, new interests and capabilities in our everyday lives. Dr. Larry Dossey, author of *Meaning and Medicine,* assures us that "We're biologically equipped to have things like miracles happen to us. For the first time, we have scientific understanding of the nature of God and the fact that neuroscientists are starting to understand it does not devalue it in any way. It makes it more accessible; it says to people who are struggling with their own spiritual feelings and intuitions, 'Yes, you are right.' You're not just a biological machine; you're a biological machine with something extra, something, for the lack of a better word, that has a soul."

This illuminated state brings a sense of connectedness with others and an awareness of belonging to the universe. For some people, stillness prevails and stress vanishes. In this state everything seems to be perfect just the way it is—there is tranquility and great harmony—and they are a part of the stillness. Many believe they have had a hint of heaven or preview of the supreme delight beyond earthly life.

Hints of the life beyond may come at amazing times and in suprising forms. Disaster clouded the joy of these newlywed marriage counselors until help arrived to overcome their blues.

Wedding Bell Blues

Seana's mother, Bobbie McGee, was born Barbara but preferred her own translation. She was a wonder. At eighteen years of age Bobbie was one of only forty civilian women pilots in the United States. Her idea of a good time back then was to etch figure-eights solo over the Arizona desert at the crack of dawn. For all of her kids, she would be a hard act to follow.

It wasn't until she turned sixty-eight and had been widowed for seventeen years that all three of Bobbie's daughters got married—finally—at ages forty-two, thirty-six, and thirty-five. The weddings took place within two years of each other. Seana was the youngest and the last "to go." Our ceremony, held on a cliff above a California beach called Heart's Desire, was celebrated in six spiritual traditions. The October blue sky, like the entire day, was brilliant.

After the wedding, Bobbie decided to make a proper holiday of her trip out West and set out on a pilgrimage of sites important to her early life in Southern California. The weather was still stunning and every day she'd repeat to her driving companion: "Look at that sky, those clouds! If this were the last day of my life, I'd be perfectly happy."

Horrified, her friend would try to hush her. On a whim, Bobbie headed to San Diego to see if the first home she'd shared with her husband still stood forty-four years later. For a woman whose three-decade marriage could hardly be described as harmonious, this was significant. Resolution was clearly in the air.

Bobbie never did find out about the house. In a crash that left her companion seriously injured, she died before the medics arrived at the scene. Although she seemed content to go, the shock cut deeply into our postnuptial bliss.

Bobbie abhorred seriousness as much as she loved to laugh. Often, her sense of humor lapsed into the outrageous. Yet, when the family gathered in her honor to see her rendered to ash, it was hard not to be infected with the gloominess of the crematorium. And she would have been furious had she known she'd be "viewed" without a hint of lipstick.

We stumbled out into the sun and climbed numbly into our cars. Filing singly from the parking lot, Seana's eldest sister, leading in her shiny black convertible, stopped suddenly. She waved us all to come quickly. "Listen," she urged us. Grinning widely, she turned the volume up on her car radio. None of us could imagine what could possibly cause such irreverence, such gaiety at this fragile moment. We listened and recognized at once the throaty strains of Janis Joplin singing the '60s blues classic, "Me and Bobby McGee."

Incredulous, we looked at each other. We giggled. Our eyes filled with tears yet again. It was so true. Feeling good *had* always been the essence of our own Bobbie McGee. And she used to get such a kick from this song. The timing was flawless. Bobbie must have been behind this, at least in spirit. By singing her own blues, Bobbie broke up ours.

Maurice Taylor and Seana McGee

Unseen Delight

We may like to feel that we are totally in charge of our own lives, and certainly we are responsible for our actions and activities. But feeling that we are part of a larger plan, guided by an unseen hand, brings expansion to our lives and comfort to our souls. According to Marcus Bach, " . . . to realize that there are dimensions beyond the commonly seen and experiences beyond the ordinarily felt, these are enriching qualities."

The tapestries of our lives are woven with threads and yarns we can reach out and touch, but also with the skill and care of the weaver—invisible qualities in themselves, but the most important part of the tapestry. We weave our own lives, but perhaps on a larger loom than we can imagine. There is a higher dimension, a greater plan, and perhaps a more delightful purpose than we know—and the Creator of us all guides our creations.

> Appreciation of life itself, becoming suddenly aware of the miracle of being alive, on this planet, can turn what we call ordinary life into a miracle. We come awake to such a realization when we recognize our connection to a spiritual dimension or perceive the awesome mystery of our journey, its amazing twists and turns, its connections to others, those we meet and those from the past who touch us with their words or art or spirit.
>
> Dan Wakefield

Jim Thomas, a psychologist and Episcopal lay preacher, is more than comfortable with the idea of being guided in life by a higher power. But he was amazed when this incident took place.

Nikki

I was driving home from a speaking tour in Colorado when I saw a sign for a rock shop up ahead and felt compelled to stop. I'm a rock hound and often browse such shops, but I had been away from home for some time and was anxious to get back.

When I saw that the owner of the shop was just unloading the back of his pickup, I couldn't resist. He had just come back from Utah where he had found two large selenite crystals. Coincidentally, I had just been reading about selenite crystals in a *Noetic Sciences Review* article. We chatted as he cleaned the crystals and ground their jagged bottoms so they would sit upright. He didn't want to sell them, but I had a strong feeling that they belonged to me. I finally talked him into the sale and took my prizes back to Oklahoma. One went into my office and the other went into my bedroom at home.

About a year later, on three separate nights, I woke up at exactly three o'clock in the morning and was shocked to find a little girl standing at the side of my bed. It was a very vivid manifestation, more than a dream. I considered that maybe she was a ghost—whatever that is—but she seemed to be more than that. I really felt her there with me. The little girl had blue eyes, white skin, and black curly hair. My heart went out to her—I felt that she had a great need.

A few days later I received a call from a woman in a nearby community who had a strange story to tell about her granddaughter. She had just been awarded custody of the girl, Nikki, who had been living in the mountains in northern California. She had been kept out of school and was living in seclusion and deprivation camped out in the woods with her parents. The child had suffered a fall, cut her foot badly, and had been taken to the emergency room. When the Department of Human Services learned of her condition, they took her into custody and sent her to her grandmother. The grandmother was bringing Nikki to me for evaluation. She needed to know if she was retarded or just behind, and where to place her in school.

The next week I went out to the waiting room to greet my three o'clock patient. My heart skipped a beat because there stood this little girl with curly black hair and pale skin smiling up at me with her enormous blue eyes; my girl of the nighttime visits! I had to work hard to control my amazement. I brought them into my office and Nikki walked directly over to my selenite crystal and put her hand on it. She looked into my eyes and said, "This is how I came to you in the dream, Dr. Thomas." It suddenly became very clear to me the path down which I had been led in order to help this little girl. It is hard to know if I was the instigator of this series of events or if Nikki was, but I was overwhelmed by the feeling that something greater than ourselves had brought us together in this way. I *knew* at a deep level that something was going extremely right in the world and that we are all connected with a loving, caring higher power.

Nikki turned out to be bright and intelligent. After a year of special education she caught up and went on to be a regular fourth grader. The last time I saw her she told me she wanted to go to a woman therapist so she could "learn how to be a woman." I hugged her and let her go. But every now and then when I walk past one of those selenites, I send her my very good wishes.

James M. Thomas, Jr.

When delight enters your life, give your heart and soul over to it, and be prepared for the unexpected. You will be enriched and enlightened, enthralled and excited. Delight is the path from your mind to your heart, from the ordinary to the extraordinary . . . and perhaps even to the divine.

Afterword

Everyone has inside of him a piece of good news.
The good news is that you don't know how great
you can be! How much you can love! What you
can accomplish! And what your potential is!

ANNE FRANK

$\mathcal{W}$e are deeply touched by the authenticity of every story in *Out of the Blue*, and by their authors' willingness to share their experiences.

These extraordinary moments seem to follow a pattern, occurring at times and in ways that were just right for the recipients. We don't claim that miracles took place, but it seems that when delight comes from out of the blue, there is a loving lesson behind it, as if it were a message from above. Perhaps these words of Saint Augustine will help us to understand—or, at least, to be comfortable with the mystery: "Miracles do not happen in contradiction of nature, but in contradiction to what we know about nature."

When you choose the path of delight, everyday life can be full of wonders. Moments of sheer illumination and times of overflowing joy will be within your reach. There can still be experiences of pain—things happen in the real world that can bring us sorrow. It's part of the human condition. When something sad or depressing happens, let your down times be times for learning. If you are willing to see them in a new perspective, they are the best times to grow emotionally stronger and spiritually deeper.

Part of the process of delight is to share yourself with others, and to share your expertise. Feeding other people's dreams and allowing them to feed yours is a way to experience happiness and expansion. When you feed the dreams of others, you are helping to create heaven on earth. It becomes a deep healing for yourself and others, when you help make someone else's dreams come true.

A woman by the name of Anne Sullivan helped make a dream come true for her student, Helen Keller. Blind and deaf, Helen Keller was unable to speak, or even to think coherently. One day a new understanding came from out of the blue and freed her from her darkness and despair. Her teacher, Anne Sullivan, with patience and loving care, brought delight into Helen's life. After this magical moment, the little girl who once was labeled an "idiot" went on to learn to speak, get an education, and graduate *cum laude* from Radcliffe College. With the help of Anne Sullivan, she traveled and spoke to great audiences on behalf of blind and deaf people. Because of her teacher's dedication, she was able to share her mind with others and release some of the most brilliant and expressive thinking the world has ever known.

The Delight of Sight

She brought me my hat, and I knew I was going out into the warm sunshine. This thought, if a wordless sensation may be called a thought, made me hop and skip with pleasure.

We walked down the path to the well-house, attracted by the fragrance of the honeysuckle with which it was covered. Someone was drawing water and my teacher placed my hand under the spout. As the cool stream gushed over my hand she spelled into the other hand the word *water*, first slowly, then rapidly. I stood still, my whole attention fixed upon the motion of her fingers. Suddenly I felt a misty consciousness as of something forgotten— a thrill of returning thought; and somehow the mystery of language was revealed to me. I knew then that W-A-T-E-R meant the wonderful cool something that was flowing over my hand. That living word awakened my soul, gave it light, hope, joy, set it free!

As we returned into the house, every object I touched seemed to quiver with life. That was because I saw everything with the strange, new sight that had come to me.

Helen Keller

In a way, just as Helen Keller was blind and deaf to her own greatness until Anne Sullivan freed her, we are all blind and deaf to our own spiritual nature until the door to delight is opened. Just as Anne Sullivan was the instrument of delight for Helen Keller, you can help free others to their own beautiful awakenings in a gentle and supportive way.

Pass this book on to someone you love—everybody needs the good news. If you are in a position to help those in despair, this book will shed light on the path of authentic delight. Spread the word everywhere you go—life is a delightful event, an adventure waiting to unfold. We want the words *in delight* to describe new and emerging patterns of spiritual growth for everyone on earth.

We are now living in the millennial effect as we race toward the year 2000. Each of us will experience avalanching change. It may be exhilarating or traumatic—yet, with delight, we will learn to live with change by being more creative and innovative. Using the techniques we have shared with you in this book can help you shape your future and let your destiny evolve to greater heights than you dreamed possible.

We urge you to let *Out of the Blue* inspire you to *live* in delight, happiness, and joy, to find satisfaction in kindness and compassion, and to be open to the idea that we are tenderly loved and guided along our chosen paths in life.

Fifty-Two Ways to Ignite Delight

Here are fifty-two ways to ignite delight. You can try one a week for the next year, one a day for fifty-two days, or just choose one when the mood hits you! You're sure to find something that works a miracle of delight for you and for others.

Be sure to try a few delight igniters that don't seem to appeal to you at all. In this way, you can overcome areas of your life where you are stuck, and defeat any hidden resistance you may have to enjoying a fully alive life.

Laugh Out Loud

This is the most important delight igniter of all. Have fun! Don't take yourself too seriously—learn to laugh at yourself. Laugh at your worries and the absurdities of your life. Laugh at parking tickets and long lines and traffic jams. HA HA HA! Keep laughing until it becomes real.

A wise teacher of Zen Buddhism suggests that a good belly laugh at the start of the day puts life into perspective. First thing in the morning laugh out loud. Really loud. Ha ha ha. HA HA HA! Laughing exercises your muscles in a beneficial way and gets rid of annoyances before they happen. It's like a massage from the inside out.

Keep comedy tapes in your car and play them on the way to work—you will arrive in a great mood. If you have a terrible day, laugh all the way home. If you have a great day—laugh all the way home! That's what freeways are for.

Norman Cousins told us we need to laugh every day to release our "inner uppers"—the endorphins, a chemical that our bodies create naturally to elevate our spirits.

Never, never be afraid to laugh out loud. HA HA HA! Celebrate life—make a joyful noise.

M. V. H. and B. N.

Sing Along with the "Ode to Joy" from Beethoven's Ninth Symphony

❧

Turn up your stereo and do your best to sing along with this most inspiring piece of music, and don't be embarrassed if your dog joins you. No single human voice can encompass this thrilling chorale, so don't expect anything other than sheer delight from yourself. If you have trouble singing it (and you will), just think how hard Beethoven had to struggle to compose this master-piece—he was completely deaf.

When he was losing his hearing, Beethoven wrote of his determination to "take fate by the throat," and he continued to compose. His best music was written after his deafness became total—and it wasn't easy. While composing the Ninth Symphony, he behaved in alarming ways, "singing, howling, stamping, look-ing as if he had been in mortal combat."

Leonard Bernstein said this soaring composition "conveys a spirit of Godhead and sublimity in the freest way.... [I]t has purity and directness of communication, is accessible without being ordinary. This is the magic that no amount of talk can explain."

Go for the magic. Let the dog howl, let your family laugh, and be sure to laugh at yourself. Beethoven's magic will come through no matter what.

B. N.

Plant a Tree

Together we can reforest our planet by planting three trees for each of the six billion people that now inhabit our earth. If we were able to add an additional eighteen billion young trees to the existing numbers, we would put a major dent in pollution.

Trees clean our air, provide homes for animals and birds, help regulate the hydrology of our atmosphere, and provide beauty all around us. Go to your local nursery and ask what trees will do well in your area. Also ask about fruit or nut trees—why not provide yourself with a snack while you help depollute the planet?

While you are at your nursery, ask about the care your tree requires. How often does it need to be watered, and does it need any special plant food? Make a promise to yourself and to the trees you plant to do what it takes to assure their survival.

Plant a tree to celebrate your own birth, the arrival of a little one in your family, a wedding or anniversary—or to remember a loved one that has passed on. Plant a tree on Arbor Day, Earth Day, Mother's Day, or Father's Day. Ask your garden center to contact you if it has seasonal trees left over that it wasn't able to sell—sometimes your nursery will be willing to provide free trees if you are willing to do the planting. Ask your city or county where trees are needed in your community, and donate a tree. Make the planting an event—bring your family and friends and provide a picnic lunch.

M. V. H.

Give Flowers

❦

We are attracted to flowers—flowers of all varieties, colors, fragrances, shapes, and sizes. One of the most cherished memories I have is my daughter holding out to me a bedraggled bouquet of wildflowers and weeds and saying "Here Mommy, these are for you! I picked them myself." Flowers inspire memories and signify appreciation—and when given with love, they are instant heart-openers.

Give flowers for all occasions: birthdays, anniversaries, new arrivals, graduations—and just to let someone know you are thinking of them. For a real surge of delight, give flowers to yourself!

Get acquainted with a local florist and ask if they would set up an automatic program for you. Give them the names and addresses of the important people in your life, along with the dates you wish the flowers delivered. Ask them to call you for the message you would like to include one day before delivery, so it can be a current thought.

Even if you do not feel you can afford expensive flowers, one rose, or a daisy from your garden will do as much as a costly bouquet from a florist—sometimes even more.

Give flowers anonymously to someone you haven't been getting along with and watch the change. It may take more than once—but flowers can crack even the hardest shell.

Suzanne McCardle

Create a Dream Team

Dream the dream onward.
                    Carl Jung

Some people call this concept your Personal Board of Directors. We call it our Dream Team.

Close your eyes, take three deep breaths in and out, and completely relax. Envision a boardroom table, oval or round, and see yourself in one of twelve chairs. In each of the eleven chairs, see a person that you greatly admire, love, or respect. It can be anybody, a person living or deceased—your parents, grandparents, or spouse. If you have always admired Eleanor Roosevelt, invite her to join you. Albert Schweitzer, Abraham Lincoln, Helen Keller— you may choose any person who has ever lived.

Once you have filled the chairs, open your eyes. Write down the names of the persons on your team. Next to each name, write down the quality or attributes that attracted you, and why you chose that person.

Call a meeting with your Dream Team whenever you have problems. Change the members of your team if someone will suit the problem at hand better than someone else. Announce the problem, and imagine how each person would help you.

You will be delighted and amazed at the wisdom that will come out of your Dream Team meetings. And you can have a lot of fun "meeting" people you could never meet any other way!

M. V. H.

Give Blood

In America, every two seconds someone needs blood. If you can give blood, please do. Make it a goal to give a pint of blood each year. Someone's life depends on you. If you saw someone hurt and dying in front of you, you would do whatever you could to help—this is not much different.

Once I was presenting a seminar for an association of insurance agents, and I learned while on stage that one of the members had been injured and needed a transfusion. In the middle of my talk I made the commitment to donate blood and asked the audience to join me. Four hundred people lined up at the blood bank after the speech. They did not want to miss the opportunity to bring the gift of life to others.

On behalf of everyone you love, give blood. Personally enroll your friends.

M. V. H.

Worry Next Saturday

This is a concept that I learned from the great Norman Vincent Peale.

Write down all of your worries. Make a list as long as you can, of everything that worries or concerns you. Don't leave anything out.

Fold up your worry sheet and seal it in an envelope. Put it in a box and hide it in a place known only to you.

Leave it there until next Saturday at four o'clock. Do not worry about your worries until then.

At four on Saturday, take out your list and resolve each worry in one of three ways:

1. Take immediate worry-solving action.
2. Cancel the worry permanently.
3. Postpone your decision until next Saturday at four o'clock.

M. V. H.

Practice Optimism

One of the main characteristics of delight is optimism—having the capacity to make lemonade when life hands you a lemon.

Optimistic people don't stay down for long. Years ago, an up-and-coming young soccer player in Madrid was gravely injured in an automobile accident. He lay paralyzed in his hospital bed, when out of the blue his nurse brought him a guitar. Julio Iglesias gave her a dazzling smile and launched his new career that very day. He is the eternal optimist.

Some people are naturally optimistic, like Julio. If you aren't, you can learn to be optimistic too. Practice seeing the glass as half full rather than half empty. School yourself to be happy. Create new habits that will bend your attitude toward optimism.

Read something positive before you go to bed and before you go to work in the morning. Listen to self-help positive tapes. Listen to uplifting music.

Most of all, discipline yourself not to read the paper or to watch the news for at least thirty days. All of the bad things fit to print do not help you improve your life one bit. Once the thirty days are over, you will not feel it as imperative to let all of the bad news be your news.

M. V. H.

Exercise

❧

There are many benefits of exercise—you will look better and feel better, it is another way to stimulate the release of endorphins in our bodies, and a way to relieve our body tissue of unneeded adrenaline. All of this adds up to an activity that will help you create a more positive physical and mental state of being and help you live a longer, more enjoyable life.

Covert Bailey, the PBS fitness comedian and best-selling author of *Fit or Fat,* says, "Exercise to the point of perspiration to rid the body of adrenaline shock." At sixty-something, he says he still occasionally fights with his wife. Immediately after the argument, he goes for a run. If he runs for fifteen minutes, he can't remember why they argued. It has been a good way to keep his body and his relationship with his wife in great shape at the same time.

We all need to exercise aerobically for twenty minutes at least three times a week. Walking, running, skating, rebounding, bicycling, singles tennis, rowing, jazzercise, or low-impact aerobics are some aerobic exercises.

Any of the martial arts, yoga, or tai chi are great for flexibility, balance, and general health. Weight-lifting is wonderful for building strength.

Choose the exercise that appeals to you the most, and stick with it. It will be a delight igniter for the rest of your life.

M. V. H.

Try Timelessness

At least one day a week, take off your watch and go timeless. Cover the clock on your car dashboard. Turn the clocks in your home toward the wall.

It is important to get out of time (as we know it) periodically, to refresh, revitalize, and renew your inner metabolic rhythms. During this day, eat only when you are hungry, sleep when you are tired. Try to guess the hour from the position of the sun in the sky. Notice if you feel different than on your "normal" days.

Einstein called it the theory of relativity—time contracts or expands according to your attitude and what you are doing. Thirty seconds of a wonderful kiss can seem way too short—thirty seconds with your hand on a hot stove can seem like an eternity.

Breaking out of our day-to-day clock-bound reality opens a space for other kinds of time to come through. When you go into timelessness you will begin to see things you never saw before. One friend, who is absolutely superior at getting everything done on a very tight schedule, was bowled over when he set aside a timeless day. He finally noticed the flowers along his walkway for the very first time.

M. V. H.

Be There for Sunrise and Sunset

For a spiritual adventure that will fill you with delight, choose to watch a breathtaking sunrise or a sunset. Most people are so caught up in their day-to-day grind, they only see one in a thousand sunrises or sunsets. Break the cycle today.

There is nothing quite as stirring to the soul as waiting in the near dawn for the first ray of the sun to break through. You will feel as if you are the first human alive, and the gift of new beginnings is yours. As the first ray of light shoots into the sky, it seems to penetrate your very soul.

The incredible natural light show of a spectacular sunset cannot be duplicated by any human hand—only the hand of God can create such vivid and shifting colors and forms. When you sit quietly and watch the magic of the show, you will feel as if you are breathing the colors into your beingness, your spirit becomes intertwined with the splendor.

The best thing about sunrises and sunsets is that you can view the show from anywhere in the world. Catch the show in Alaska, the Greek islands, the Caribbean, the Norwegian fjords, the south of Spain. A city sunrise can be lovely, and sunrise over the prairies and deserts is beyond belief. Sunset aficionados often applaud the show when the sun sinks into the bay in Key West; and in Hawaii, as the sun nears the ocean, people in cars pull off the road and watch for the "green flash" that sometimes happens during a Hawaiian sunset.

These visual displays of God's greatest beauty are calming to our souls and uplifting to our spirits.

M. V. H.

Create, Create, Create

Life is creation. You can create joy, create delight. Create your day the way you want it. Create a pollution-free planet. Create blessings wherever you go.

Take up a hobby, paint a picture, become an artist. Sculpt something in clay, grow an herb garden on your kitchen window sill, write a song. Find a new way to approach an old problem.

Do something you have never done before and do it with flair, even if you don't do it very well. Create the dance of life.

Henry David Thoreau had a unique perspective on creation: "It is something to be able to paint a lovely picture, or to carve a magnificent statue, but it is far more glorious to carve and paint the very atmosphere in which we live."

You can create heaven on earth. It's up to you.

B. N.

Write a Personal Mission Statement

Clearly define your basic idea of what your life and work are about, and write it down.

Our personal mission statement defines us and takes us to new levels of self-realization. Once unleashed, your inner genius will expand your horizons and create a future that will be more outstanding than you can imagine. Our personal mission statement has kept us on purpose for years. It may help you to think about your own.

Mark's mission statement: "I want to speak to people who care, about things that matter, to make a profound, positive difference in their lives."

Barbara's mission statement: "I want to live in the precious moment of now, understand life at deep and subtle levels, and to express my truth for the highest good of all concerned."

Patty's mission statement: "To live a conscious life by constantly choosing and re-choosing the good, the beautiful, and the holy. To let others know they can do the same by my example."

Create One Hundred and One Goals

Get paper, pencil, and a timer. Set the timer for twenty minutes.

Write a list of one hundred and one things that you would like to have, be, and do. Pretend you are being paid $1 million to do this. Write quickly, and record the first things that come to your mind. Don't stop to analyze your list. This is a process designed to expand your vision—you want your subconscious mind to speak out.

If you write more than one hundred and one within the twenty-minute time period, great!

Compare this list with the list of goals you were encouraged to write in Chapter Three. Notice any differences and similarities.

M. V. H.

Make Up Songs
of Delight

∞

A good way to get to know your family and friends again is to invite everyone for an evening of silly songs.

Turn off the television and the computer.

Make up words to virtually any melody that people know. Have a contest for the best lyrics, the silliest lyrics, the funniest lyrics, the most inspiring lyrics. Give prizes.

"Row, row, row your boat" might become "Shout, shout, shout delight."

Videotape the party and play it on a rainy day.

M. V. H.

Attend and Support the Special Olympics

The joyful atmosphere at the Special Olympics is contagious, and you will see sportsmanship at its finest. All of the participants are physically, mentally, or emotionally challenged and have come together to outperform themselves. They give 110 percent of all they've got in them, and want the best for their colleague competitors.

There are many incidents like this: In the 400-meter dash, the third fastest runner tripped and fell. The first two runners stopped and doubled back, picked her up, brushed her off, and made sure all was well before they continued. You could feel delight surge through the audience as they rose, as one, cheering for all they were worth.

This is only one example of what will be in store for you when you attend. You will have many more experiences that will renew your faith in mankind and uplift your spirit.

Call the Special Olympics at 800-700–2258 to obtain a date and a city close to you.

M. V. H.

Appoint an Antibummer Squad

You cannot have too many friends with positive attitudes!

Make sure you have at least three friends who ignite your delight. On your terrible days when life is a bummer, call them and ask them to remind you how truly delightful you are. Do the same for them.

Everyone has terrible days; everyone can get over it much more easily when good friends are there to help.

M. V. H.

Walk a Sacred Path

❧

Find a labyrinth and walk this sacred spiral path to your spiritual center. Labyrinths are appearing in many parts of the country following the designs of labyrinths at Grace Cathedral in San Francisco. Grace's labyrinths are based on the sacred pattern of the twelfth-century labyrinth at Chartres Cathedral in France.

You enter the labyrinth at a prescribed place and follow the path, which winds back and forth on its way to the center of the circle. Participants report that they receive many blessings and insights as they do this moving meditation.

The labyrinth is a spiritual tool meant to awaken us to the deep rhythm that unites us to ourselves and to the Light that calls from within. Based on the circle, the universal symbol for unity and wholeness, the labyrinth sparks the imagination, enlivens the intuitive part of our nature, and stirs within the human heart the longing for connectedness and the remembrance of our purpose for living.

Grace Cathedral has information on other labyrinths throughout the world through its Labyrinth Network at 415-749-6358.

Lauren Artress

Live the Golden Rule –
Do Unto Others . . .

When you put the Golden Rule into practice, you not only make this a happier world, but you become a more loving person. When you treat others with politeness, civility, and genuine appreciation, you will find that they respond with gratitude.

David Thomas, founder of Wendy's fast-food chain, writes, "When Grandma Minnie told me I was adopted, I felt my stomach turn. Why hadn't anyone told me sooner?"

Instead of feeling sorry for himself, Dave took a positive position. "Adoption made it possible for me to get Grandma Minnie Sinclair's love, care, and affection. Had I not been adopted by her, I could have ended up as a ward of the state, or been raised in an orphanage."

The day came when Dave was able to "do unto others" in appreciation for the benefits he had received as an adopted child. To express his gratitude and encourage others, the successful businessman added special insurance coverage and financial assistance to employees' benefits if they adopt a child, thus making it easier for other children to find good homes.

B. N.

See "Blue Planet"

∞

This incredible film made under the auspices of the National Air and Science Museum of the Smithsonian, the most popular museum on earth, puts the planet in perspective the way nothing else can.

Beautiful color footage shot from space gives you a look at the earth from the outside. You'll see a glowing ball with blue and turquoise waters covering two-thirds of its surface, wrapped in a thin layer of blue air, which holds off the hard radiation and cold vacuum of space.

This tiny jewel of a planet floating in the infinite blackness of space glows from the inside. Its blueness comes out of the earth itself, from the waters and moisture of our atmosphere, from the cycle of rain and evaporation, from the inhalations and exhalations of animals, human beings, trees, and plants. When you see how uniquely beautiful Earth is, you'll never doubt again that our Creator intends us to live in a paradise of delight.

B. N.

Adopt a Companion for Your Pet

❦

With great kindness and compassion, rescue Everyone.
Buddhist Master Hsuan Hua

Millions of beautiful animals and potential best friends are put to death each year by overcrowded adoption agencies. Please find room in your heart for one of these adorable animals, even if you already have pets in your home.

A friend in Seattle has the right idea. She purchased a pure-bred Persian kitten to show, then went right to the animal shelter and adopted a healthy, lively kitten of the same age to keep her Persian company. The kittens were delighted with each other, our friend was delighted to have two kittens almost for the price of one, and we're delighted with the idea of companion animals for pets.

And we're doubly delighted if you can adopt adult animals, whose chances for finding a home are slim.

B. N.

Make a Date with the Earth

Find one place on Earth where you can go on a daily or weekly basis, and schedule a regular time. It could be beneath a tree in a city park or a special place in your own backyard. Treat the date the way you would treat a date with someone you care about deeply. Take time to really be in that place; notice the changing colors and scents, the plants that grow and die during the year and those that come back again the next.

By going to that one place on the Earth on a regular basis throughout the year, you will see the panoramic changes that happen. Something in you will shift at a very deep level—instead of feeling apart from the Earth, you will develop a feeling of being one with her. Your whole view of life will change.

You will remember that you are a part of the circle, the sacred web of life, and you will never be lonely again. If you keep your date with the Earth, whether or not you have a yard or a field of your own, you will know that you belong.

Marlise Wabun Wind

Sing "Amazing Grace"

Perhaps the best-known hymn in the world, this lovely song has touched millions of hearts. It has been sung for a hundred years in churches of every denomination and recorded in dozens of vocal and instrumental versions. It has unique depth and simplicity and, no matter how it is sung, a special quality of delight.

"Amazing Grace" was written by John Newton, a slave trader who had lost his soul in the search for money, power, and pleasure. When, out of the blue, grace came into his life, he changed completely and was moved to write, "I once was lost but now I'm found; was blind, but now I see." Before his moment of grace, he could not see the truth of love, kindness, and compassion—but after he found his soul, he could see the light. And it was amazing.

B. N.

Treat Your Body to Delight

Get a massage, soak in a Jacuzzi, have a facial. Spend the day in a spa.

Learn about herbs and other natural healing methods.

Sign up for a series of lessons in the Alexander Technique. Often referred to as the "Rolls-Royce of bodywork," Alexander isn't bodywork at all, but lessons that teach you how to use your self optimally in everything you do. For more than a hundred years, the technique has been the secret of actors and musicians, who need their bodies, minds, and spirits to be in perfect alignment to enhance their work. The technique gently enhances posture, relieves pain and tension, and improves health and well-being.

Having a totally relaxed and balanced body can give you a feeling of floating on air, of being ten feet tall, and of being centered and focused all at the same time.

You may feel like dancing down the street. Feel free!

B. N.

Adopt a Zoo Animal

As part of their fund-raising programs, many zoos offer adoption kits to the public. You can adopt a lion or a lizard; polar bear or parrot. You'll know which animal is right for your budget and for your heart.

At the world-famous San Diego Zoo, you can even meet your adopted animal baby in person at special parties. A friend made a gift to her husband of adoption papers for a baby gorilla and he was allowed to have lunch with his adopted "child." It transported him to heaven, she reports. He'd never been so delighted with anything in his life as he was with that little gorilla sitting on his lap.

B. N.

Join the Delight Revolution

Make the word *delight* part of your everyday vocabulary and help the delight revolution grow. Greet people with "I'm delighted to see you," "You look delightful," "It's a delight to be with you again."

When you answer the telephone, say "What a delight to get your call."

Close your letters "With delight."

Use the words *in delight* as you would *in love*; for example, "I'm in delight with you, my friend." It's a great way to share your special feelings.

Instead of saying "I love my new car!" say "I'm delighted with my new car!" It frees the word *love* from being overused and used for the wrong purpose.

Find ways to use the "D" word daily and remind others what a delight life is.

M. V. H.

Attend Church with a Friend

Throughout history, major wars have been fought over religious beliefs. They're still going on today. One of the most important things we can do to create a world of delight is to respect one another's beliefs.

Attend church with a friend who comes from a different religion or denomination, and appreciate the similarities and differences between your religion and your friend's. The freedom to worship as we choose is one of the foundations of democracy, one of our greatest treasures and proudest exports.

I spent one Christmas holiday with a Jewish friend in Turkey, and found the mosque in the city of Bursa so filled with the spirit and light of God that it brought tears to my eyes. I thought I was just touring to see the architecture, but I had an epiphanic moment of truth—with it came an understanding of the spiritual oneness we all share.

B. N.

Swim with Dolphins

<figure>❦</figure>

You can swim with dolphins off the coast of Hawaii at either Oahu or Kona, or off the Florida Keys. Find a guide and bring other delight seekers to enjoy the fun.

After my talk at a church in Hawaii, the pastor asked me to join their group. Bright and early the next morning, four of us entered the water at Waimea with masks, snorkels, fins, and boogie boards.

At that moment, out of the blue Pacific, a pod of seven dolphins jumped up as if to welcome us. They swam gracefully just below the surface of the water, then came up and danced for us. Behind them was another pod of twelve dolphins. Both pods encircled us and let us watch them play for half an hour.

A member of our group, Rutin Lee, told me, "The dolphins are beaming us. They are clearing our negative energy. After swimming with dolphins you will continue to process out negativity for about a week."

Dolphins live in delight and send it out on beams of loving energy. What wonderful role models!

M. V. H.

Climb a Golden Ladder
to the Sky

∞

The One who is full of grace
Will find the ladder to the sky.
                    Rumi

This is a great meditation devised for finding your life's purpose—your greatest delight in life. Before you begin, make sure you have a pen and pad of paper by your side.

Find a quiet place removed from all distractions. Get into a comfortable position and become still. Close your outer eyes and lift your inner eyes upward at a forty-five-degree angle. This puts your mind in an alpha or creative/receptive state. With a gentle smile on your face, breathe deeply and slowly into your abdomen, three complete inhalations and exhalations. Then breathe naturally.

Visualize an infinitely tall ladder made of purest gold. On each rung the words *I AM* are engraved in sparkling letters. In your mind's eye see yourself climbing the ladder.

As you climb the ladder, feel your left hand and right foot reach for the next rung, then your right hand and left foot, and so forth. On each rung, repeat "I am." Keep climbing the ladder until you feel yourself enter an altered state of consciousness—it may take as long as twenty minutes. In this altered state, ask yourself, "What is my purpose in life?" Or, "What is my right livelihood?" Tell yourself that your higher consciousness will answer within thirty seconds, and it will. You may get goose bumps as confirmation that this is your true purpose. Take another few minutes to climb back down to earth.

You may use the golden ladder to ask your higher self any question. You may want to ask how you can accomplish your purpose or who will help you. Write down your answers and act on them immediately when you are finished with your visualization.

M. V. H

Read Your Own Gauges for Good Health

If you have a recurring headache or other seemingly minor symptom, pay attention. It's your "inner knower" trying to get your attention.

Ignoring those little signals is like reaching under the dashboard and pulling out the wiring when you see the gas gauge hit empty or the oil light flash on. That's essentially what we do when we anesthetize ourselves with painkillers instead of listening to our inner wisdom. The little headache may be trying to tell you that you're too tense or have toxicity that needs to be recognized.

Read your inner gauges and respond to your real needs. It's easier to relax for delightful fifteen-minute periods during the day and to take preventive health measures than it is to have a health crisis.

M. V. H.

Award Yourself a Trophy

If you tried and failed, if your dream didn't come true, if your golden moment didn't pan out, take time to mourn—then get over it. Next stop, the trophy shop.

You absolutely deserve a trophy for all of your good thought and effort, all of your planning and commitment, all of your daring, your desire, your initiative, your hopes. You made real progress!

Think of the experience you've gained, the focus you've developed, the learning you've accumulated. That in itself is worth a prize. Plaster your bulletin board with blue ribbons, have a plaque engraved, frame testimonials from friends. And put that trophy in a prominent place where you can see it every day.

Appreciate yourself and be grateful for the experience. And get on with your life.

M. V. H.

Fill Your Home and Workplace with Art

⁂

Once you have experienced the delight of fine art, your life will never be the same. It makes a huge difference in people's lives to be able to turn to something lovely in their surroundings and resonate with its greatness. Art elevates your mind, heart, and spirit. Appreciating art is part of the creative process.

While touring galleries in Europe, I noticed that people from all over the world shared a very special communication. With smiles and radiant eyes, we communicated our joy and appreciation for the loveliness around us without words. It's not something you experience when you go to the grocery store. Being around great art makes us feel alive.

Your bed, tables, lamps, chairs, dinnerware, jewelry, and mirrors can be made by talented artisans. You can have sculpture everywhere, your walls can be covered with paintings. Surround yourself with beauty. Your soul will glow with satisfaction, your guests will smile with pleasure, and your heart will be filled with delight.

Paul Adelson

Inhale a Blissful Fragrance

Since the beginning of time, natural aromas have brought us great delight. Practitioners of aromatherapy prescribe natural scents for lifting moods and dealing with various ailments.

Romancing by enhancing and enchanting with fragrance is an ancient art. Lovers plant night-blooming jasmine along the walkway to stimulate romance; roses are associated with love, lavender is for purity, and lilies of the valley make us feel close to heaven.

Try scented oils and bath products, lotions and scented candles. Notice how you respond to certain scents. If you want the natural results, be sure to use natural scents.

Nympha Cole

Explore the World

Get up and go. There's so much delight in the world just waiting for you, it's a shame to wait another minute. Discovery is delight!

Read about your destination first. Learn all you can. Try new places—why ever go to the same place twice? Cruise, fly, drive, climb, crawl—do whatever it takes to have a trip to a place you've never been. Once you get there keep your eyes, ears, and heart alert for delight. Meet new people, savor new flavors, learn new customs, listen to new music, wear silly hats, dance new dance steps on into the night. Nothing creates more expansion than a new place.

Eugenie West

Pass the Torch for Peace

Every other year, people from eighty countries on all seven continents join together in harmony to run an international relay. A flaming torch of peace is passed from hand to hand by more than a million participants. Runners include every level of athletic prowess, from Olympic champions like Carl Lewis to people in wheelchairs. All boundaries dissolve in delight as these radiant runners make the world's biggest statement for peace. The Peace Run goes everywhere, from Louisville to Liechtenstein, Florida to the Philippines, Manhattan to Mexico, Schenectady to the Isle of Skye . . . from England to Russia to Australia, the flame is passed from one runner to the next. Everyone feels the joy of being united with people from every part of the planet. Their lives and energies merge in a moving prayer of hope and healing for the world.

The Peace Run is the inspiration of peace philosopher Sri Chinmoy, who has led a meditation group at the United Nations for more than twenty years. Join with millions of others to sponsor or participate—and offer your own heart's desire for peace to this world-wide delight of high hopes and high energy.

Contact: Peace Runs International
61-20 Grand Central Parkway
Forest Hills, New York 11375
718-760-0250; fax 718-592-1696
Internet: http://www.peacerun.com

B. N.

Find a Sacred Place

Have a spiritual center—a silent place within yourself where you can come into the stillness and speak with God.

Build a beautiful temple for yourself within your imagination. Put this sacred space of your inner being on top of a snowcapped mountain with a view of forever; at the shore, where the rhythm of waves soothes your mind; or in the hush of a giant redwood forest. Fill it with precious pearls or with simple wooden objects. Make time during the day to go there and breathe in the pure light of creation.

Set aside a space in your home to meditate and pray. An unused bedroom, or just the corner of any room can be designated as your meditation space. Decorate it with candles, flowers, and pictures of anyone or anything that brings you spiritual delight.

Go for a week, or a weekend, to sacred sites such as ashrams or retreat houses. Some of us have places in nature that we deem holy, where we feel at one with all creation. Be sure you have at least one place that evokes a meditative, prayerful state of mind for you, where you can find spiritual nourishment.

M. V. H.

Write Yourself a Million-Dollar Check

Get out your checkbook right now and write yourself a check for a million dollars. Deposit it into your delight account.

Million-dollar checks make great gifts for loved ones, too. Tuck one in a card for someone's birthday and tell them that they mean that much to you.

No one can possibly have a bad day on a day they receive a million dollars.

M. V. H.

Tell One Person a Week That You Love Them

In our busy world of work, family, play, and school activities we sometimes tend to forget one of the most important communications we can give to someone we love—to *tell* them that we love them.

Start with your own family and tell them today that you love them.

Make a list of all the people you can think of throughout your life that you have loved.

Call the easiest ones to reach first, one person a week. Think about that person for the entire week before your call—the times you spent together, what the person has meant in your life. When you tell them that you love them, tell them why they are valuable to you and what you appreciate about them.

Try and find people that have disappeared from your current life. Sometimes they are not as hard to reach as we think they are. On a visit to my childhood home recently, I was able to find one of my third-grade friends after calling several people. I was nervous about talking to him after so many years, but I found him to be as kind and easy to talk to as he was in the third grade. He was surprised at first, and actually had a hard time remembering me, but he was pleased and gratified about the call. It made him happy to know that he had made a difference in someone's life.

If someone important that you love has passed away, write a letter telling them all about the important feelings you have. Put the letter in a safe place. The message may not be able to be received, but it is important for you to communicate it.

P. H.

Rock and Roll It

Old rock and roll songs have a way of getting under our skin and releasing the ham in us. When we were kids we were constantly told to "Turn that noise down!" Turning it *up* is a great way to relieve boredom and stress.

When you are in your car—alone—find an "oldies" station and turn the volume up as loud as you want. Keep the windows rolled up and sing along with your favorite songs from the '50s, '60s, '70s, or '80s. Sing loud and clear. Sing the main vocals and all the background parts. Scream with Tina Turner, growl with Mick Jagger. Imitate the saxophone, the guitar—play all the drum parts on your steering wheel. Don't let it bother you if people in cars around you start to stare. Have fun, and remember to continue to drive safely!

P. H.

Declare a Holiday

❦

When the spirit moves you, wake up in the morning and announce a holiday. Everyone gets an unofficial break from work, from school, from chores.

Declare a holiday for reasons like birthdays and anniversaries, or to commemorate events special only to you. Our family has a holiday every year to celebrate our cat Herb's birthday. We invite friends for a barbecue (which Herb appreciates greatly), ice cream (he once got his head stuck in the Häagen-Dazs carton), and birthday cake (which he ignores). We don't know his exact birthday, but declare it arbitrarily every spring, with great merriment and delight.

Best of all, spontaneously declare a holiday for no reason at all, and do something delightful.

B. N.

Find a Great and Inspiring Teacher

Great teachers in any field charge the atmosphere with their very presence. In this atmosphere of high energy we, as students, learn more easily. Our intellect opens at a new level and knowledge pours in.

I had the good fortune of being a research assistant in graduate school to R. Buckminster Fuller, or Bucky, as he was affectionately called. Every time he came into our building, my six colleagues and I could feel the energy rising to a new level. Bucky told us that he had felt the same phenomenon when he met and studied with Albert Einstein.

When you are ready to look for a teacher, the easiest thing to do is to audit the classes that you are interested in. Sit in the back of the room and watch the students—are they involved, or falling asleep? Feel the atmosphere in the room—is there a buzz of electricity? Is there interaction between the class members and the instructor?

Even if it seems to be a subject that you don't feel is easy for you, when you find the right teacher, you have found the key to unlocking new portals of learning, and your life will expand in sheer delight.

M. V. H.

Try Something New

✥

To break up the patterned behavior that interferes with your creativity and delight, do something new *every week*. Develop your skills and talents in easy increments, concentrating on the things you never thought you'd do.

If you are an extrovert and are usually around people, try some quiet time on your own. Go for walks, plant a garden, learn to meditate. Try to get in touch with your intuition. Read poetry, or a novel. Learn to make friends with yourself, the best friend you will ever have.

If you are an introvert, join Toastmasters and learn to give a speech. Call Toastmasters International at 800-993-7732 and ask for the location of the nearest meeting. Or take an acting class and express yourself on stage. Join a choir and sing out loud.

Make a promise to try new foods that you have never eaten before. Go to an Indian restaurant, or try Thai, Cambodian, or Middle Eastern food.

Learn to square dance, do the salsa or the tango. Try the Irish jig. Buy Rollerblade skates and learn to skate. Go ice skating. Learn to refinish furniture or to cook with a wok.

Break free from your rut—life is a grand adventure waiting for you!

B. N.

Attend a Seminar or Rally

We live in a very exciting time in the world, when we can attend a seminar or rally on almost any subject—presented by some of the best teachers and trainers of our time.

There are many business-related seminars and rallies that will help with your career. Universities bring in top-notch teachers for special focus weekends. A program that offers a professional speaker can inform, entertain, enlighten, motivate, and inspire any group.

Various churches provide outstanding programs and seminars throughout the year. Call the larger churches in your area and ask for a brochure on their coming events.

This is not only a great way to enlarge your mental capacity and become inspired, but also a wonderful way to meet other people who are interested in the same things that you are.

B. N.

Make a Clean Sweep

All of us need to clean up some area of our mind, relationships, or environment.

Perhaps you need to clean up the relationship you have with your sister—or maybe even your relationship with God. What about the mess in your checkbook? Maybe your closet could stand to be organized. Or perhaps the backyard could be pruned back and cleaned up.

Make a list of your messes. Write next to each mess what you are going to do in order to clean it up. For instance, if your relationship is in a mess, you may write down: go to counseling, spend more time together, be more supportive. If your closet could stand to be cleaned: organize clothes by color and season, give away items I haven't worn for over one year, shine all my shoes.

Most of us are loaded down with clothes we haven't worn for years, household goods we haven't used in ages, shelves of canned goods rapidly approaching their expiration date, used computers and sporting goods we just can't bear to part with.

Today is a great day to jettison the lot of it. Take it to your church or synagogue, call Goodwill or the Salvation Army, or find a homeless shelter that can put your excess to good use.

Besides freeing up storage space in your home, you will have the satisfaction of knowing that your unused items are blessings for someone who needs them.

A cleaned-up mess is a burden lifted and a load off your back. Writing your mess-eradicating plan on paper is the start of your soon-to-be-executed experience. Clean up the smallest messes first—it will give you positive feedback and healthy reinforcement so that you can go after the larger messes with vigor. As you accomplish cleaning up your messes, you will feel more freedom, happiness, and productivity.

M. V. H.

Bless Your Insides

❦

How often do we really stop and think about how wonderful our bodies are? It seems the only time we are very thankful is when we have recovered from an illness. This is a good way to thank our bodies, right now, for doing the best job possible for us, every minute of every day.

Close your eyes and go into a meditative state. Pretend that you can see the inside of your body as clearly as we normally see the outside. Look at your heart, see it pumping the life-giving blood through your system. Say out loud, "Thank you, my heart, for working so hard and continuing to beat for me." Acknowledge your lungs, and tell them how much you appreciate the hard work they have to do, cleaning the air for you and circulating the oxygen into carbon dioxide. Tell your brain, "Thanks for the memories!" Go to your spleen, liver, kidneys. Acknowledge your muscle groups, tongue, joints, stomach, colon, sex organs. Think of as many parts of your body as you can—you don't have to get it perfect.

When you are finished, open your eyes. Notice how relaxed and stress-free you feel.

Try to do this meditation at least once every six weeks. You will find, as I have, that you will feel as if your body and you are working in closer harmony toward a common good—your good health.

P. H.

Hug a Tree

❦

Every living thing on the planet has a certain quality of life that we can reach out and touch. Other forms of life can touch us as well, when we are receptive to the idea and the process.

Many studies have been done investigating the vibration level of plants. In *The Secret Life of Plants* we learn that all plants "feel" differently toward different people and events. A plant that fears harm sends out a distress signal that is picked up on a vibration level by other plants in the area. A happy plant will grow stronger and more rapidly. Plants like certain kinds of music.

It is hard for us, as humans, to feel the vibration levels of plants without equipment to do so. There is one major exception. Hugging a tree will get you in touch with one of the deepest and strongest life vibrations known to the plant kingdom.

Pick a tree in the park, or your own backyard, that looks huggable. Notice which side of the tree is warm to the touch, which is cool to the touch. Wrap your arms around the tree, and hold it in a firm embrace. Rest your cheek on the bark. Put your ear to the trunk and listen. What do you hear? Move your awareness to the area of your heart. What connection do you feel, if any? *Take your time!* Move to the other side of the tree and hug it again. Try other trees.

Pick a tree to make friends with and visit your friend often. It will keep you feeling that the plant world and our world are *really* a part of one big whole.

P. H.

Pray

∞

If you haven't prayed lately, it is time to start. Many of us haven't prayed since we were children and recited "Now I Lay Me Down to Sleep." Direct communication with our Maker through prayer can create miracles for ourselves and for others.

If you feel more comfortable on your knees, then go for it, but it isn't necessary—what is necessary is to first be grateful for what we have, and to tell God this in a prayerful form. Just close your eyes, and express to God your thanks—it creates feelings of unity with God.

Join a prayer group with your local church. There are many ways to be in service to our fellow humans, and praying for them is a very important one.

When you have a prayer request, remember that God answers in one of three ways: yes, no, and not right now. As the Reverend Robert Schuller says, "God's delays are not God's denials." Know that the best is in store for you and trust in God.

End each day with prayer. Pray together with your family. Say your own silent prayers. There is always Someone listening to you, and loving you.

M. V. H.

Adopt a Child

There are many organizations that help children around the world have a better life through "adoptions." For a nominal sum of money each month, you are given the name and location of a child somewhere on our planet, usually in a Third World country. This is your adopted child, and the money you give goes toward buying food, clothing, and medical supplies for your child.

The cost usually runs about $20 a month. If you don't feel you can easily afford this, share the cost with two or three friends or co-workers.

Even helping one child on this planet of ours escape starvation and disease is something to be proud of. If you can support more than one child, then please do. The children of our world belong to all of us.

P. H.

Write a Message in the Sand

Every time you go to the beach, take a moment to leave a positive message in the sand. You may touch someone's life in a profound way with a beautiful idea. Write things like:

Love is alive.
A beautiful day for love.
God loves you.
You are a delight.
Joy!
Happy Birthday!
Magic is afoot.
Life is delightful!

God speaks to us in miraculous ways. When you leave messages in the sand, you may be delivering God's message of love and wisdom to someone who needs to see it.

When you go to the beach, keep your questions in mind. Perhaps you'll find your answer waiting for you in the sand. Watch for it!!

Gay Lynn Williamson

Renew Your Vows

As time passes, relationships ebb and flow. There are times when you do things together as if you are joined at the hip, and then times when one or the other partner is in a period of growth or change and you may feel distanced from each other. This does not mean that the love between you dies in those times of change, it only means that the love evolves.

Renewing your vows allows space in the relationship for individual growth. It is an action that says to your partner, "I am aware of you as an individual who is growing and changing just as I am. I accept these changes as part of our healthy relationship, and I have respect for you. I look at you with new eyes, see your growth, and I still like/love you." By choosing and rechoosing love, respect, and caring, you are continually reaffirming your commitment to the relationship and rebonding with your partner.

Make it an annual celebration. Invite all your friends and family members. If you have children, allow them to have a portion of the ceremony, to affirm their part in your lives. Make it a wild and passionate day, complete with flowers and a cake. You will find that this keeps your relationship fresh—and knowing that your partner has the right to choose you again keeps you from taking each other for granted.

P. H. and M. V. H.

Start the Day with Affirmations of Delight

Copy one of these on a 3 x 5 card and tape it to your bathroom mirror. Use a different one each day, or each week. Say them aloud.

This day will be delightful.
I am delighted to be alive, awake, and enthusiastic.
I am delight.
I see myself expressing delight all day in every way.
I live, thrive, and have my being in delight.
I delight to wake up with a smile.
I delight in all my activities, especially my work.
I share my delight with everyone I meet.
I expect delight in every encounter and it happens.
My delight invokes delight in others.
Delight is my birthright.
I cultivate delight in my life.
All that I am delights me.
All that I am becoming delights me.
I go from delight to delight.
I rejoice in delight.

M. V. H.

Go to a Playground and Swing

While I was baby-sitting for my little nieces, I started pushing them on swings. At their urging, I got onto one myself. As I pushed off, I felt silly, but as I pumped my legs and started to go higher and higher I had the most wonderful feeling of elation! I soared through the air. I felt the dizzying rush of the wind as I saw the ground looming up at me, and squealed with delight as I whooshed past it and completed my arc. I swung upside-down. I swung standing up. I swung backward and forward. I discovered the fabulous feeling of flight that I had known only in my dreams since I became "too old" to swing. Now I don't need the company of small children to enjoy the delights of the playground.

Kathryn Kidwell

Contributors

PAUL ADELSON wrote *Fill Your Home and Workplace with Art*. As "The Art Guy," he represents artists of renown and has sold fine art to corporations and collectors worldwide. He owns Select Art in Dallas and in Sedona, Arizona. He may be contacted at 10315 Gooding Drive, Dallas, Texas 75229, or by calling 800-801-3640.

WALLY AMOS founded Famous Amos Cookie Company and has now formed the Uncle Noname Cookie Company. National Spokesman for Literacy Volunteers of America since 1979, he lectures audiences at corporations, industry associations, and universities. Wally received the Horatio Alger Award, the President's Award for Entrepreneurial Excellence, and the National Literacy Honors Award. He is the author of the book *Man with No Name, Turn Lemons into Lemonade* (Ashlan Press, 1994). His latest release, *Watermelon Wisdom*, will be published in the summer of 1996. He may be contacted at 818-261-6075.

The Reverend Dr. LAUREN ARTRESS is canon for special ministries at San Francisco's Grace Cathedral. She founded QUEST: Grace Cathedral Center for Spiritual Wholeness. She has reintroduced the Labyrinth, a walking meditation. Her new book is *Walking a Sacred Path: Rediscovering the Labyrinth as a Spiritual Tool* (Riverhead Books, 1995). You can reach her at Veriditas, 415-749-6358.

MARVA BELL, a member of the twelve-step community, prefers to remain anonymous.

BRIAN BOITANO won the Gold Medal for the United States at the 1988 Winter Olympic Games. He has won six world professional men's figure skating titles and had his own network television special, ABC's *Canvas of Ice*. He received an Emmy for the HBO movie *Carmen on Ice*. He has starred in numerous touring ice shows, has directed and choreographed the television special *Skating Romance*, and is a commentator for ABC Sports. Off the ice Brian is the spokesperson for Starlight Foundation, which helps grant the wishes of seriously ill children.

ROBERTA C. BONDI, D.Phil., is professor of church history at Candler School of Theology, Emory University, in Atlanta. She has previously taught at Notre Dame, Union Theological Seminary, and Oxford University. She is in great demand as a leader of spiritual retreats and as a speaker on prayer and spirituality.

FERN FIELD BROOKS, television producer/writer/director, has received an Emmy and two Peabody Awards and was nominated for an Oscar. Before forming her own production company, she was director of development for Norman Lear. Fern has received a Humanitas Award and a Distinguished Service Award from the President of the United States for her work with the disabled. Her first book is *Letters to My Husband* (Hall/Sloane, 1994).

LEO F. BUSCAGLIA, Ph.D. is an author with more than 11 million copies of his books in circulation. *Love; Living, Loving and Learning;* and *Loving Each Other* have each sold over a million copies. Editions of Dr. Buscaglia's books are available in nineteen languages, in twenty-four editions. His first book, *Love,* has never been out of print since it was originally published in 1972. He is the chairman of the Felice Foundation, which is dedicated to encouraging and teaching the spirit of giving in our society. Dr. Buscaglia is a contributing editor to *Positive Living Magazine,* and his latest book, *Leo Buscaglia's Love Cookbook with Biba Caggiano* was published in the fall of 1994.

ROBERT BUTCH left the corporate world and is completing his MSW at Southern Connecticut State University. He interns at United Community Services as a child and family therapist. He lives with his wife, Christine Adams, in Colchester, Connecticut, and can be reached at 860-537-5272.

JANICE CAPRIANI is a certified body worker and Reiki expert, both of which she practices while volunteering at a hospice program in New Jersey. She works for a large corporation, has two sons, Scott and Mark, and a beagle, Princess.

DEEPAK CHOPRA, M.D., is the executive director of the Institute for Human Potential and Mind/Body Medicine at Sharp HealthCare in San Diego. He is a best-selling author of both fiction and nonfiction, including *Ageless Body, Timeless Mind; The Seven Spiritual Laws of Success;* and *The*

Way of the Wizard. He is an acclaimed motivational speaker. Dr. Chopra can be reached at 800-757-8897.

NYMPHA COLE is a third-generation herbalist. She presents workshops nationally on the uses and meaning of herbs. She can be reached at 800-303-9339.

CATHY LEE CROSBY is an internationally known star who has played the lead role in over fifty feature films, miniseries, and TV movies, as well as ABC's hit TV series *That's Incredible.* She has also been an international tennis champion, Special Ambassador to Children for the United Nations, and a member of the board of directors of the U.S. Congressional Awards. Currently, she is set to star in and produce the film *Cloud's Cradle*, followed by *Blue Moon* and *The First Earth Battalion.* Her first book, *Let the Magic Begin* (copyright © by Cathy Lee Crosby), will be published in December 1996 by Simon & Schuster.

MARTIN CROWE is the publisher of a newsletter, *Lighten Up! America.* He is an inspirational speaker who specializes in using a unique sense of humor and common sense to help people view themselves and others in a positive way. He can be reached at Lighten Up! America, P.O. Box 207, Palisade, Colorado 81526-0207, or by calling 970-464-0340.

ANGELA ROCCO DECARLO wrote for the *Chicago Tribune;* created and wrote "The Business Traveler" (*Las Vegas Review Journal*); has taught writing at College of DuPage in Glen Ellyn, Illinois; and currently writes for *Disney* magazine and other publications covering entertainment, travel, and lifestyle. She is developing her writing course, "Journaling for a Better Life," into a book. Two other book projects are in the works: *Living an Effectively Organized Life* and *Rockne: What You Learn by Loving a Dog.* She resides in Orange, California, with her husband, Dan, a business executive, and Rockne. Their three sons—actor/writer Mark DeCarlo, Dr. Michael DeCarlo, and Daniel DeCarlo, Esq.—also live in Southern California. She can be reached 714-974-9431.

O. FRED DONALDSON, Ph.D., is internationally recognized for his ongoing play research with children and wild animals. He conducts workshops worldwide to teach adults the significance of play. His book, *Playing by Heart* (HCI, 1993), was nominated for a Pulitzer Prize. He can be reached in Hemet, California, at 909-652-5625.

RAYLEEN DOWNES lives in Huntington Beach, California, with her husband and two kids, Breana, fifteen, and Kelsey, six. She teaches high school English, and in her limited spare time she loves to read and write about those she loves most.

VICTORIA DOWNING is an international business consultant based in Dallas, Texas.

Dr. WAYNE DYER is one of the most widely read internationally best-selling authors today in the field of self-development. His best-sellers include *Your Erroneous Zones, You'll See It When You Believe It,* and *Real Magic.* He has produced many audio and video tapes and has appeared on over 5200 television and radio programs, including *Today, The Tonight Show, Donahue,* and *Oprah.*

ALAN EBERT is the author of novels; *Traditions, The Long Way Home,* and *Marriages.* His articles have appeared in such major magazines as *Good Housekeeping, TV Guide, People, US, Essence, Redbook, McCalls,* and *Ladies Home Journal.* He can be contacted at 353 West 56th Street, New York, New York 10019.

CLEVE FRANCIS, M.D., is a practicing cardiologist and a well-known country-western singer. His music video "Love Light" was in the top-10 on Country Music Television. Cleve has appeared on *CBS This Morning, Today,* and *Good Morning America.* He is president and founder of Mount Vernon Cardiology Associates in northern Virginia.

PAULA GENTRY is a senior sales director for Mary Kay Cosmetics Company. Her delight with the opportunity for women led her to become the first "pink Cadillac" winner in the San Francisco area. She can be reached at 415-771-7249.

DONALD W. GEORGE was travel editor for the *San Francisco Examiner* before joining GNN, America Online's Internet service and content provider, as a cyber columnist. His articles have appeared in *Condé Nast Traveler, Travel & Leisure,* and *Travel Holiday.* He teaches and speaks at conferences around the world. Reach him via e-mail at dgeorge@gnn.com; write to GNN, 2855 Telegraph Ave., Berkeley, California 94705; or call 510-883-7240.

JACK HAWLEY is a management consultant who divides his time between Newport Beach, California, and India. He is the author of *Reawakening the Spirit in Work: The Power of Dharmic Management* (Berret-Koehler, 1993).

MARY-PAT HOFFMAN is the president of Public Images, a public relations firm in Dallas, Texas, that promotes authors, actors, and others in the arts and creates fund-raising events for hospitals and national charities. She is also book editor for *Today's Dallas Woman* magazine. You can reach her at 214-520-3547.

Dr. JEAN HOUSTON has served on the faculties of religion, psychology, and philosophy at Columbia, Hunter College, Marymount, the University of California, and other institutions. Author or co-author of fifteen books, including *A Mythic Life, The Possible Human* and *The Hero and the Goddess*, she has also conducted seminars and worked in human and cultural development in over forty countries. Dr. Houston can be reached at P.O. Box 600, Pomona, New York, 19070, or by calling 914-354-4965.

SUZIE HUMPHREYS is a nationally known speaker who touches the emotions of her audiences through very funny stories, which often conceal a deeper message. She lives in the Texas hill country. For more information, contact Catherine Cargile, P.O. Box 121502, Arlington, Texas 76012, or call 817-469-7323.

CHET HUNTLEY was a news commentator on West Coast radio stations before joining NBC in New York in 1955. With David Brinkley, he was anchor of the popular nightly news show *The Huntley-Brinkley Report.*

VICTORIA JACKSON was on the television show *Saturday Night Live* for six years and made twenty-two appearances on *The Tonight Show with Johnny Carson.* She has appeared in several films, incluidng *Baby Boom* with Diane Keaton and *Family Business* with Dustin Hoffman. Her television credits include appearances on *The Jeffersons, General Hospital,* and *The Smothers Brothers Comedy Hour.* Victoria lives in Hollywood, California, and Miami, Florida, with her husband, Paul Wessel, and two daughters.

JANE JAYROE, Miss America 1967, has had a distinguished career as a broadcast journalist, media talent, and producer. She was recently named the first woman president of the Oklahoma Academy, a public policy think tank. She lives in Oklahoma City, where she is working on her first book.

H. DEE JOHNSON of Dallas, Texas, practices law enough to keep the rent paid, and spends the rest of his time traveling, taking pictures, and playing with his grandchildren. Johnson writes occasionally under the theory that it is cheaper than therapy.

Dr. JONI JOHNSTON is a clinical psychologist in Dallas, Texas, and author of *Appearance Obsession: Learning to Love the Way You Look* (HCI, 1994). She is president of the Growth Company, a professional speaking firm, and is host of the television show *Mental Health Matters*. Joni is an active member of the National Speakers Association, the National Association of Radio Talk Show Hosts, and the American Psychological Association Media Referral Service. You can reach her at 214-521-7715.

LARRY JONES is president of Feed the Children, an international, nonprofit Christian organization based in Oklahoma City that provides food, clothing, educational supplies, medical equipment, and other necessities to people in all fifty states, the District of Columbia, and seventy-one foreign countries. He has appeared on *Good Morning America, Larry King LIVE, Today,* and *Nightline* and is frequently invited to testify on hunger issues before the U.S. Senate and House of Representatives. You can reach him at 405-942-0228.

HELEN ADAMS KELLER (1880–1968) became blind and deaf at eighteen months of age and lost her ability to speak. She overcame barriers of darkness and silence and went on to make the world aware of the rights of the afflicted. Her books include *The Story of My Life, Out of the Dark,* and *Teacher,* which told of her relationship with Anne Sullivan, who taught her to read, write, and speak.

KATHRYN KIDWELL left the hustle and bustle of the big city for the peace and beauty of the North Idaho woods. There, she enjoys nature at its best and delights in life every day. She keeps hearth and home together as an editor and artist. She can be reached at P.O. Box 898, Priest River, Idaho 83856.

JOYCE KING is a technical writer for AT&T. She is at an awkward age between grown children and no grandchildren. She lives on, and as much as possible in, warm Florida waters, spending much of her time in the company of dolphins, whales, pelicans, mosquitoes, and other life forms.

PAM LONTOS is a nationally recognized sales trainer and motivational speaker. She has a masters degree in psychology from Southern Methodist University and has sold retail, health club, and media advertising. She was vice president of sales for Disney's Shamrock Broadcasting, where she raised sales 500 percent in one year. Now she is president of Lontos Sales & Motivation, Inc., in Orlando, Florida. She delivers keynote addresses, seminars, and workshops for corporate conferences and association meetings. She can be reached at P.O. Box 617553, Orlando, Florida 32861, or by calling 407-299-6128.

DENISE MCGREGOR is an award winning speaker, a graduate of USC Business school, and the co-founder of McGregor Plant Sales, an international import/export business. She is author of *Mama Drama: Confessions of a Rebellious Daughter*. She lives in La Costa, California, with her daughters Meghan and Allison. Denise may be reached at (619) 942–6772, 6965 El Camino Real, Suite 105–443, La Costa, CA 92009.

ANN-MARIE MCHUGH is a Chicago based writer/musician/teacher who has written for film and directed musical productions for theater. She enjoys singing jazz and blues. Ann-Marie works at Jobs for Youth, a non-profit organization that helps ready young adults for their first jobs. You can reach her at 1829 W. Wellington, Chicago, Illinois 60657, or by calling Jobs for Youth at 312-782-2086.

PETER MARSHALL was a Presbyterian pastor who was appointed chaplain to the United States Senate, where he served until his death in 1949. His life was the subject of the book *A Man Called Peter* by his wife, Catherine Marshall.

JAMES MICHENER's first book, the Pulitzer Prize–winning *Tales of the South Pacific*, was published when he was forty. Over the next forty-five years, Mr. Michener wrote more than thirty books, including the best-sellers *The Bridges at Toko-Ri, Hawaii, The Source, Iberia, Alaska, Centennial, Texas,* and *Space.* Mr. Michener was awarded the Presidential Medal of Freedom and has served on the Advisory Council to NASA. He received an award from the President's Committee on the Arts and Humanities for his continuing commitment to the arts in America.

SHANNON MILLER won the Silver Medal in women's gymnastics in the 1992 Olympics. Shannon won a state championship at age nine and became the youngest member of the senior national team at thirteen. The very next year, she was the first American ever to qualify for all four events at a world championship. In 1992 she made the U.S. Olympic team just three months after surgery to her elbow and won five medals in Barcelona followed by back-to-back gold medals in the 1993 and 1994 world championships. Shannon donates her time to the Children's Miracle Network, the Red Ribbon Campaign, and to children's hospitals across the country.

W MITCHELL has been a Marine, a gripman on San Francisco's cable cars, the mayor of Crested Butte, Colorado and a nominee for Congress. The National Speakers Association has awarded Mitchell the CPAE (Council of Peers Award for Excellence), the highest recognition in professional speaking. He authored the book *The Man Who Would Not Be Defeated* and hosts the PBS series *Finding Common Ground*. He can be reached at 12014 West 54th Drive, Suite 100, Arvada, Colorado 80002, or by calling 800-421-4840.

MARY MANIN MORRISEY was ordained a minister in 1975. As the founder and spiritual leader of the Living Enrichment Center in Portland, Oregon, she counsels and leads seminars. She wrote *Building Your Field of Dreams* (Bantam, 1996). For more information about Mary or Living Enrichment Center, call 800-893-1000.

ROBERT P. O'BRIEN, Ph.D., is a psychologist who specializes in treating people with trauma disorders. He spent a number of years living the fast-paced life of the East Coast but gave it up to live on a lake near Austin, Texas, with his wife and two youngest children. His hobbies are writing, bird watching, and hiking.

MARY OMWAKE has been the senior minister of Unity Church of Overland Park in suburban Kansas City since 1989. Mary is chairman of the Church Growth and Development Committee for the Association of Unity Churches and is often asked to speak at national ministers' conferences, national Youth of Unity, and adult retreats.

GARY PAULSEN is a well-known writer of fiction and adventure novels for children and adults. His work has won the American Library Association Best Book Award, ALA Notable Book award, and a Newberry Medal. *Winterdance: The Fine Madness of Running the Iditarod* chronicles his adventure as a rookie dog-sled driver in the grueling trans-Alaskan race.

MELISSA POE ignited a spark in 1989, campaigning for kids to get involved with environmental issues. Since the age of nine, Poe, of Nashville, Tennessee, has worked to raise the level of environmental consciousness among youth and adults, becoming one of the most effective and influential advocates for a cleaner environment. Over the last seven years, using her slogan "People who care will do something ...," Poe has organized and led one of the world's largest environmental action groups for kids, Kids for a Clean Environment. Contact her at Kids F.A.C.E.,. P.O. Box 158254, Nashville, Tennessee 37215, or by calling 800-952-3223.

J. B. PRIESTLEY (1894–1984) was a twentieth-century English novelist, essayist, dramatist, and journalist whose love for the human spirit was evident in his work.

HOMER T. PYLE is an ex-newspaperman, writer, and editor from Fort Myers, Florida, who should have put his feet up and begun enjoying his retirement, but he's still stuck to the keyboard. His inspirational books include *Turning It Over* (HCI, 1992) and *Stairway to Serenity* (Hazelden, 1989).

MARY LOU RETTON gained international fame by winning the All-Around Gold Medal in women's gymnastics at the 1984 Olympics, becoming the first American woman ever to win a gold medal in gymnastics. Mary Lou is in great demand as a motivational speaker and corporate spokesperson, and she travels the world promoting proper nutrition and regular exercise. She is national chairperson of the Children's Miracle Network. Her children's television series *Mary Lou's Flip Flop Shop* can be seen on PBS.

NAOMI RHODE, RDH, CSP, CPAE, is the past president of the National Speakers Association and is known for her inspirational, dynamic speaking to both health-care and corporate audiences. She is co-owner and vice president of SmartPractice, a marketing and manufacturing company that provides products and services to the health-care industry worldwide. Mrs. Rhode is the author of two inspirational gift books: *The Gift of Family: A Legacy of Love* and *More Beautiful than Diamonds: The Gift of Friendship*. Naomi Rhode can be contacted at 3400 East McDowell, Phoenix, Arizona 85008–7899, or by calling 602-225-9090.

ELIXIS RICE, Ph.D., in private practice in Irving, Texas, has presented programs on mental and physical health for corporations and organizations both nationally and internationally. She is author of *101 Thoughts for Becoming the Real You* and *Spiritual Simplicity: Fast Food for the Soul*. You can reach her at 214-402-9691.

DORIS ROBERTS won an Emmy for her portrayal of a bag lady on *St. Elsewhere*. Her television series included *Remington Steele* and *Angie*, and she has been a guest star on *Murder, She Wrote, John Larroquette, Dream On,*

Walker–Texas Ranger, Empty Nest, Barney Miller, and many other series. On Broadway, Doris began her career in *The Time of Your Life* and went on to lead roles in *The Desk Set* and *Last of the Red Hot Lovers.* She won the Outer Circle Critics Award for *Bad Habits.* She has appeared in leading roles in almost thirty movies, including *The Rose, The Glass Harp,* and *National Lampoon's Christmas Vacation.* She is spokesperson for the Leukemia Society of America and chairman of CAAF, a fund to benefit children affected by AIDS.

FRED ROGERS is the creator, writer, composer, puppeteer, and host of *Mister Rogers' Neighborhood,* the longest-running program on PBS. Besides continuing to produce new *Neighborhood* programs to add into the series each season, Rogers is also author of books for adults and children. His awards and honors include two Peabody Awards, several Emmys, and honorary degrees at more than thirty colleges and universities.

JANICE ROSE is an actress, writer, and poet. She has received several awards for her poetry and has been published in *New Texas, 95,* and *Concho River Review,* as well as in several newspapers. She is currently working on a book collection of her poems and often appears in Dallas area theaters.

CHRISTINE RUSSELL is study abroad advisor for the Coast Community College District and operates a typing and editing business in her spare time. She has four grown sons and lives with her husband, writer David Allen Russell, in Huntington Beach, California. She can be reached care of Allen Publishing, P.O. Box 164, Huntington Beach, California 92648.

ROBERT D. SIMMERMON is a psychologist, playwright, and speaker. He is a fellow of the American Psychological Association, member of the Film Committee of the American Psychological Association, past member of the board of directors of the Division of Media Psychology, and editor of the *Georgia Psychologist.* He is a fellow of the Georgia Psychological Association and a member of its board. He is also a member of the playwright unit of the Academy Theater in Atlanta. In addition to his work as a consultant, writer, and editor, Robert maintains an independent practice. He can be reached at 34 Lenox Pointe, Atlanta, Georgia 30324, or by calling 404-364-0986; fax 404-264-0743.

AL SIZER lectures throughout the United States and Canada to life insurance agents covering positive mental attitude, goal setting, the power of enthusiasm, sales ideas, and the recruiting process. Mr. Sizer has been awarded many distinctions within the life insurance industry for his consistently high performance. He lives in Portland, Oregon, with his wife, Linda, and their two daughters. Al Sizer can be contacted at 9570 S.W. Barbur Boulevard, Suite 212, Portland, Oregon 97219, or by calling 503-293-0221.

MAURICE TAYLOR, M.A., and SEANA MCGEE, M.A., co-directors of Taylor McGee Human Relations (Southeast Asia/U.S.A.), teach the laws of love for the next millennium. They are co-authors of the groundbreaking new book *The New Couple: Ten Principles for Creating a Life You Love with the Love of Your Life*. As speakers and relationship educators they have been featured on MTV Asia and in *Elle* and *Cleo* magazines. For inquiries, contact T.M.H.R.: 140 Holly Road, #3, Carpinteria, California 93013, or call 805-684-1987; or 33 McNair Road, Singapore 328530, where the telephone is (65) 299-0482.

JAMES M. THOMAS, JR., Ph.D., is a clinical psychologist in private practice in Ponca City, Oklahoma. He is an Episcopal lay preacher and a consultant to international corporations. Author of *The Seven Steps to Personal Power* (HCI, 1992), Dr. Thomas presents workshops on spiritual healing at Omega Institute and other conference centers. You can reach him at 405-765-5128.

JIM TURRELL has more than twenty-five years of experience as a teacher, professional musician, businessman, and minister. Minister of the Costa Mesa Church of Religious Science, Jim Turrell is the author of the courses Visionary and Intimacy: Guides to Understanding Change, Productivity, and Happiness. He has spent over four years in the research and development of Heart-Talk, a new approach to the art of speech and communications. You can contact Rev. Turrell in care of Heart-Talk, 2850 Mesa Verde Drive East, Suite 107, Costa Mesa, California 92626, or by calling 714-642-1985.

BARBARA VAN DIEST is a spiritual counselor, public speaker, and Reiki master teacher. She hosts the television show *It's About You*, which airs in Southern California and Arizona. You can contact her in Tucson at 502-299-4696.

GEORG VIHOS was awarded a Fulbright Fellowship to study painting in Italy. His work has been shown in the Metropolitan Museum of Art in New York and is exhibited frequently at the Detroit Institute of Arts.

His paintings hang in private and museum collections all over the United States and he has been commissioned by such major corporations as Peat, Marwick and Mitchell. Vihos is living in a "palatial" studio he saw in a dream, which manifested out of the blue. You can reach him at P.O. Box 218, Birmingham, Michigan 48012.

MARLISE WABUN WIND is co-author of ten books, including *Woman of the Dawn* and *The Medicine Wheel: Earth Astrology,* which sold more than half a million copies. She spent twenty years working with Sun Bear, the well-known Ojibwa visionary with whom she founded the Bear Tribe community, and has organized and orchestrated Medicine Wheel Gatherings throughout the world.

EUGENIE WEST is a travel writer who has circled the globe on assignment for major publications. She teaches and lectures on the inner and outer journeys and conducts tours to sacred places. You can reach her at P.O. Box 762, Spokane, Washington 99210.

JON WILLIAMS is currently in his third year of working toward his degree in history to teach at the high school level. He lives in Mission Viejo, California, with Lisa and their daughter Sabrina. He can be contacted care of M.V.H. and Associates, 800-433-2314.

GAY LYNN WILLIAMSON is a psychotherapist based in Hollywood, Florida, where she and her husband, David, are the ministers of Unity Church. She facilitates Women's Wisdom Weekends and presents rituals and ceremonies at conferences all over the country. She is the co-author of *Transformative Rituals: Celebrations for Personal Growth* (1994) and *Golden Eggs: Spiritual Wisdom for Birthing Our Lives* (HCI, 1996). You can reach her at 305-922-5521.

MARIANNE WILLIAMSON is the author of the runaway best-sellers *A Return to Love* (Random House, 1993) and *A Woman's Worth* (Random House, 1994). She lectures regularly across the country and in Europe and is a frequent guest on television and radio shows. A native of Texas, she lives in New York.

Copyright Acknowledgments

"Mike's Dream" by Robert D. Simmermon, reprinted by permission of Robert D. Simmermon. Copyright © 1995.

"A Little Piece of God" by Robert P. O'Brien, reprinted by permission of Robert P. O'Brien. Copyright © 1995.

"Performance Under the Stars" by Rayleen Downes, reprinted by permission of *Reader's Digest*, in which it originally appeared in August 1995. Copyright © 1995 by Rayleen Downes.

"Lisa" by Jon Williams, reprinted by permission of Jon Williams. Copyright © 1995.

"A Perfect Dinner Together" by Leo Buscaglia, from his book *Love*, published by Fawcett Crest, New York. Copyright © 1972. Reprinted by permission of Leo Buscaglia.

"Looking for Grandma's Swing" by Joni Johnston, reprinted by permission of Joni Johnston. Copyright © 1995.

"Puppy Love" by Angela Rocco DeCarlo, reprinted by permission of Angela Rocco DeCarlo. Copyright © 1996.

"The Joy Is in the Journey" by Martin Crowe, reprinted by permission of Martin Crowe. Copyright © 1996.

"The Angels of San Luis Potosí" by H. Dee Johnson, Jr., reprinted by permission of H. Dee Johnson, Jr. Copyright © 1995.

"The Making of an Organization" by Melissa Poe, reprinted by permission of Melissa Poe. Copyright © 1996.

"The Picture of Success" by Pam Lantos, reprinted by permission of Pam Lantos. Copyright © 1996.

"A Very Special Gift" by Naomi Rhode, reprinted by permission of Naomi Rhode. Copyright © 1996.

"The Knight on a White Charger" by Christine Russell, reprinted by permission of Christine Russell. Copyright © 1996.

"My Vision Took Flight" by Jim Turrell, reprinted by permission of Jim Turrell. Copyright © 1996.

"The Sound of Spring" by Chet Huntley, from his *The Generous Years*. Copyright © 1968 by Chet Huntley. Reprinted by permission of Random House, Inc.

"Springtime" by Robert Butch, reprinted by permission of Robert Butch. Copyright © 1995.

"Avalanche of Love" by Kathryn Kidwell, reprinted by permission of Kathryn Kidwell. Copyright © 1995.

"Buffalo Games" by Gary Paulsen, from *Winterdance: The Fine Madness of Running the Iditarod*. Copyright © 1994 by Gary Paulsen. Reprinted by permission of Harcourt Brace and Company.

"The Dance of the Fishes" and "Walk a Sacred Path" by Lauren Artress, reprinted by permission of Lauren Artress. Copyright © 1996.

"Member of the Pod" by Joyce King, reprinted by permission of Joyce King. Copyright © 1995.

"Two Looks Away" by O. Fred Donaldson, reprinted by permission of O. Fred Donaldson. Copyright © 1995.

"The Night the Stars Reached Down" by Donald W. George, reprinted by permission of the *San Francisco Examiner*. Copyright © 1995 by the *San Francisco Examiner*.

"Little Flames of God" by Roberta Bondi, from *Memories of God* by Roberta Bondi. Reprinted by permission of Abingdon Press. Copyright © 1995 by Abingdon Press.

"Heartstone" by Janice Capriani, reprinted by permission of Janice Capriani. Copyright © 1995.

"Message in the Sand" and "Write a Message in the Sand" by Gay Lynn Williamson, reprinted by permission of Gay Lynn Williamson. Copyright © 1995.

"A Larger Life" by Jean Houston, reprinted by permission of Jean Houston. Copyright © 1995.

"Golden Moment" by H. T. Pyle, reprinted by permission of H. T. Pyle. Copyright © 1996.

"Wedding Bell Blues" by Maurice Taylor and Seana McGee, reprinted by permission of Maurice Taylor and Seana McGee. Copyright © 1995.

"Nikki" by James M. Thomas, Jr., reprinted by permission of James M. Thomas, Jr. Copyright © 1995.

"The Delight of Sight" by Helen Adams Keller, from *The Story of My Life*. Copyright 1902.

"Give Flowers" by Suzanne McCardle, reprinted by permission of Suzanne McCardle. Copyright © 1996.

"Fill Your Home and Workplace with Art" by Paul Adelson, reprinted by permission of Paul Adelson. Copyright © 1996.

"Inhale a Blissful Fragrance" by Nympha Cole, reprinted by permission of Nympha Cole. Copyright © 1996.

MARK VICTOR HANSEN, a professional speaker for twenty-two years, is the coauthor of *Chicken Soup for the Soul, A 2nd Helping of Chicken Soup for the Soul,* and *A 3rd Serving of Chicken Soup for the Soul.* PATTY HANSEN is his wife and business partner, and is also a published author. They live in Southern California with their two children.

BARBARA NICHOLS, a professional writer for more than twenty years, was editorial director at the company that published the Chicken Soup books. She lives in the Pacific Northwest.